Planning in Eastern Europe

T0257424

Edited by
Andrew H. Dawson

Routledge
Taylor & Francis Group

First published in 1987
by Croom Helm Ltd

This edition first published in 2015 by Routledge
2 Park Square, Milton Park, Abingdon, Oxon, OX14 4RN
and by Routledge
711 Third Avenue, New York, NY 10017

Routledge is an imprint of the Taylor & Francis Group, an informa business

Publisher's Note
The publisher has gone to great lengths to ensure the quality of this reprint but
points out that some imperfections in the original copies may be apparent.

Disclaimer
The publisher has made every effort to trace copyright holders and welcomes
correspondence from those they have been unable to contact.

A Library of Congress record exists under LC control number: 86017654

ISBN 13: 978-1-138-85334-8 (hbk)
ISBN 13: 978-1-315-72278-8 (ebk)
ISBN 13: 978-1-138-85339-3 (pbk)

PLANNING IN EASTERN EUROPE

ANDREW H. DAWSON

CROOM HELM
London & Sydney

© 1987 Andrew H. Dawson
Croom Helm Ltd, Provident House, Burrell Row,
Beckenham, Kent, BR3 1AT
Croom Helm Australia Pty Ltd, Suite 4, 6th Floor,
64-76 Kippax Street, Surry Hills, NSW 2010, Australia

British Library Cataloguing in Publication Data

Planning in Eastern Europe.
1. Europe, Eastern — Economic policy
I. Dawson, Andrew H.
338.947   HC244

ISBN 0-7099-0863-6

Printed and bound in Great Britain by Mackays of Chatham Ltd, Kent

CONTENTS

LIST OF CONTRIBUTORS

Dr. F.W.Carter, Department of Geography, University College London

Dr. P.A.Compton, Department of Geography, The Queen's University of Belfast

Dr. A.H.Dawson, Department of Geography, University of St. Andrews

Dr. D.R.Hall, Department of Geography and History, Sunderland Polytechnic

Professor R.E.H.Mellor, Department of Geography, University of Aberdeen

Dr. D.Turnock, Department of Geography, The University, Leicester

LIST OF FIGURES

LIST OF TABLES

PREFACE

Let me begin with two admissions! It was not my intention to produce a book about Planning in Eastern Europe, and the fact that this volume has appeared is due in very large part to the encouragement of Michael Bradford, who was very keen that an important gap in the literature about the area should be filled. Nor would the book have been possible without the assistance of the team of writers whose work this publication is, for it depends in large part upon their personal knowledge and long experience of the wide variety of landscapes, societies and languages which make up Eastern Europe. It is doubtful whether a single author could have done justice to this variety at the level of detail which has been attempted here, and it is certain that the editor could not. I am most grateful for their assistance.

There is no doubt that Eastern Europe is important to the rest of the world. The westward advance of Soviet influence after the Second World War, and the establishment of communist governments in the eight countries of the region, offered an alternative route to economic and social development to that of the mixed economies and parliamentary democracies of Western Europe; and, if the achievements of that alternative had proved to be manifestly superior, it is doubtful whether the Western way of life, as we know it today, would have survived. That that alternative path has not been perceived to be superior is in large measure the consequence of a series of major crises, beginning with the East German riots of 1953 and culminating in martial law in Poland in the early 1980s, which have shaken most of the Eastern European societies to their foundations at some time or other since 1945. However, the achievements and failures of the building of socialism in the eight countries have rarely been examined in detail, and this is particularly true of the planned development of the space economy. Even before the establishment of the communist governments there had been many examples of states intervening in the economy in the pursuit of regional and urban development, and many landscapes still bear witness to that earlier activity. However, since 1945 the countries of the area have been characterised by central-government planning of the distribution of manufacturing, the development of towns, changes in land use, and the protection of areas which are of value on environmental or historic grounds, as never before. Furthermore, this has all occurred during a time of very rapid population and economic growth. Thus, the book takes as its context the insistence of the communists that development should not be left to the workings of the market, but that its path should be explicitly chosen, and that the efforts of society should be fully harnessed to achieve goals which will be of benefit to the whole population of workers and their dependents. In short, it is concerned with the announced aims and the actual achievements of the authorities in Eastern Europe in the field of planning the space economy. However, it is not concerned with either the way in which those aims have been formulated, nor with the manner in which they have been executed, and those who seek information about how decisions are made and implemented in Eastern Europe must look elsewhere.

The topic of the book should be of direct concern to geographers, with their interests in the changing distributions of people and production, the form of the landscape, and the relation between man and his environment, and it is no accident that the contributors are all professionals in that field. But it is hoped that it will also appeal to a much wider audience. Economists may find in its descriptions of the spatial problems of development reasons for the slowing down which has occurred in growth rates over the period. Planners may reflect on the inability of their colleagues in Eastern Europe, who often appear to enjoy much greater power to direct the path of development, to control a wide range of phenomena and prevent the appearance of new problems. Readers of the book in Eastern Europe are offered a British view of their achievements and difficulties, and those elsewhere an opportunity to follow in some detail a period of remarkable and unprecedented change in that region.

Andrew H. Dawson
St. Andrews
May Day 1986

ACKNOWLEDGEMENTS

Andrew Dawson acknowledges with gratitude the generous assistance of the Carnegie Trust for the Universities of Scotland for their support for fieldwork in Eastern Europe in connection with this publication. He also wishes to thank the cartographic and secretarial staff of the Department of Geography in the University of St. Andrews for their assistance in the preparation of the figures and tables. Derek Hall wishes to thank David Orme for drawing the maps in Chapter 3.

Chapter 1

INTRODUCTION

Andrew H. Dawson

To write of planning in Eastern Europe is to
essay a large topic. German lokatoren created much
of the rural settlement pattern of the Silesian
lowlands during the Middle Ages. Powerful
authorities are commemorated by such fortress towns
as Zamość, built in the sixteenth century, and
Terezín, in the eighteenth. Regional economic
development by the government, of the Congress
Kingdom of Poland between 1815 and 1830 laid the
foundations for the Łódź industrial conurbation of
today; and, inter-war strategic planning aimed to
achieve major changes in the pattern and level of
economic development in Poland's Central Industrial
Region. But this book is not about these examples
of planning. Nor is it about any of the others
which occurred during the period which ended in
1945. Rather, it is concerned with that totally
different form, scale and purpose of planning which
has characterised Eastern Europe since the end of
the Second World War. It deals with the central
direction of the economy by the state. It is
concerned with planning in the context of the public
ownership of the means of production; and, it has
regard to the aims of the post-war governments of
the area, which have been, firstly, the building of
socialism and, ultimately, the establishment of a
communist society.
However, even to describe the post-war system
in all its facets would be an ambitious undertaking,
and the aim of this book is much more modest.
Firstly, it seeks to parallel Pallot and Shaw's
study of Planning in the Soviet Union (1981) by
examining the manner in which the problems of the
space economy have been tackled in Eastern Europe
during the period in which that region has been
following a communist road to economic and social

1

development. Secondly, in concentrating upon spatial issues it aims to complement Smith's description of The Planned Economies of Eastern Europe (1983) and writings by Adam (1984), Bornstein (1973), Brus and Matejka (1985), Fallenbuchl (1974), Hohmann et al. (1975) and others which deal with the management of production, trade and wages in an economic and aspatial manner. And thirdly, in concentrating upon the aims and achievements of post-war policies it devotes little attention either to the political process through which those policies have been chosen or to the mechanisms and instruments by which they have been implemented. Pallot and Shaw have drawn attention to the peculiar difficulties which face western students in any attempt to unravel the decision-making processes within centrally-planned economies of the Soviet type (1981, p.32), and no comparable attempt to those by Churchward (1975), Lane (1972, 1976), McAuley (1977) or Skilling and Griffiths (1971) in the case of the Soviet Union, or of Granick (1975) and Selucky (1972) in the case of Eastern Europe, or more generally by Holmes (1986), will be made here.

Any account of spatial planning might be approached in a variety of ways. One might be to consider each of the many subordinate topics within such a broad theme - regional, urban, rural, industrial, agricultural, service, land-use and environmental planning - individually, and to compare the countries of Eastern Europe with regard to the emphasis which they have placed upon each. Alternatively, each country might be discussed separately, thus allowing the examination of the relationships both between the various topics within the theme and between the policies which have been adopted and the physical, economic and political character of each country. It is this second approach which has been adopted as the dominant one for this set of essays for, as we shall see, although the general political and economic systems of all eight countries have been similar during the post-war period, other important influences have not. Thus, contrasts in the resource base, in the inherited settlement systems and levels of economic development, and in post-war geo-political relations amongst the countries have been reflected in wide variations in the priorities which have been accorded to spatial planning by governments since 1945. For instance, Romania has attempted to rationalise its dense network of small, rural settlements; the German Democratic Republic has been

2

fitting its relatively well-developed industrial base to a new set of frontiers and trading links; Albania has adhered closely to Stalinist policies, and Yugoslavia, in contrast, has experimented with its own interpretation of socialist control - the self-management of enterprises by their workers. In short, the context within which post-war planning has taken place has varied so widely, and the emphases which governments have chosen have been so different, that it has been felt more appropriate to present the material through a country-by-country approach. Accordingly, contributors have been free to select those topics within the general theme which, in their view, are either most fundamental or representative of the spatial planning concerns in each country. So, Hall emphasizes the Albanians' concern with Marxist-Leninist purity, Compton discusses in some detail the National Regional Plan and Settlement Development Strategy for Hungary, and Turnock concentrates upon two issues which have been of particular importance in Romania - Planificare and Sistematizare.

But the systematic approach has not been rejected entirely. As has been mentioned above, the resource base and the patterns and levels of development which were inherited from before 1945 varied so widely between the eight countries that some comparison of their condition at the start of the post-war period is necessary by way of introduction. Also, as all the systems of planning in Eastern Europe have been modelled in large part upon that of the Soviet Union, at least at some stage in its history, it is desirable that some of the most important of that system's features should be described at the outset. Both of these tasks will be undertaken in Chapter 2. Moreover, all the countries of the region have been connected at one time or another during the post-war years through the trading organisation COMECON (Council for Mutual Economic Cooperation). Because this body has attempted to integrate their economies with that of the Soviet Union, and thus to influence the economic structure and pattern of development within each, an account of its activities will be given in Chapter 11. Lastly, although the country chapters each contain their own emphases, a general assessment will be made of the achievements in Eastern Europe under socialist planning and of the role which planning may have played in those achievements in Chapter 12.

3

Introduction

REFERENCES

Adam, J. (1984), *Employment and wage policies in Poland, Czechoslovakia and Hungary since 1950*, Macmillan, London.

Bornstein, M. (ed) (1973), *Plan and Market*, Yale University Press, New Haven.

Brus, W. and Matejka, H. (1985), *The Economic History of Eastern Europe 1919-1975*, vol. III *Institutional Change Within a Planned Economy*, Clarendon Press, Oxford.

Churchward, L.G. (1975), *Contemporary Soviet Government*, Routledge and Kegan Paul, London.

Fallenbuchl, Z.M. (ed) (1974), *Economic Development in the Soviet Union and Eastern Europe*, 2 vols., Praeger, New York.

Granick, D. (1975), *Enterprise Guidance in Eastern Europe*, Princeton University Press, Princeton.

Hohmann, H., Kaser, M. and Thalheim, K.C. (eds) (1975), *The New Economic Systems of Eastern Europe*, C. Hurst and Co., London.

Holmes, L. (1986), *Politics in the Communist World*, Oxford University Press, Oxford.

Lane, D. (1972), *Politics and Society in the USSR*, Weidenfeld and Nicolson, London.

Lane, D. (1976), *The Socialist Industrial State. Towards a Political Sociology of State Socialism*, Allen and Unwin, London.

McAuley, M. (1977), *Politics and the Soviet Union*, Penguin, Harmondsworth.

Pallot, J. and Shaw, D.J.B. (1981), *Planning in the Soviet Union*, Croom Helm, London.

Selucky, R. (1972), *Economic Reforms in Eastern Europe*, Praeger, New York.

Skilling, H.G. and Griffiths, F. (eds) (1971), *Interest Groups in Soviet Politics*, Princeton University Press, Princeton.

Smith, A.H. (1983), *The Planned Economies of Eastern Europe*, Croom Helm, London.

Chapter 2

THE ECONOMIC AND POLITICAL BACKGROUND

Andrew H. Dawson

INTRODUCTION

No understanding of the planning of the space economy of Eastern Europe since the Second World War would be complete without a consideration of two fundamental influences - the inheritance of pre-1945 patterns of economic development and war-time destruction, and the influence which the Soviet Union has brought to bear upon the governments of the area since then.

The space economy of Eastern Europe in 1945, and the severe problems which it posed, owed something to the physical environment of the area. But it was also the consequence of a century of slow, patchy and interrupted development. Between the middle of the nineteenth century and 1920, the Austro-Hungarian, Prussian, Russian and Turkish Empires in Europe were decaying or being destroyed by wars, and after that the emergent nations of the area were struggling with the effects of the severance of many of their former economic links, and of the world recession of the 1930s. By 1945, many areas had also suffered extensive physical damage, and some were obliged to adapt to yet another dislocating shift of frontiers. It was upon this basis that post-war reconstruction and development had to build. However, neither the distribution of natural resources, nor the malign effects of history affected all parts of Eastern Europe equally, and wide variations existed in the degree of economic development, and in the problems which faced the newly-established, post-war governments. This variety will be sketched in this chapter in order to provide a reference point against which progress since 1945 in the eight countries can be assessed and compared.

5

However, any description of the background to the systems of planning which have been adopted in the individual countries should not stop there for, during the post-war years, these countries have been linked together, as never before, by the influence of a single great power - the USSR. As a result, their policies and methods of managing the space economy have been very strongly, but by no means entirely, determined by those which had been adopted earlier by that power, and therefore a brief account will also be given in this chapter of the policies and methods which have been employed by the Soviet Union.

EASTERN EUROPE IN 1945

The wide contrasts which existed in the level of development among the various parts of Eastern Europe before the Second World War were the consequence, in large part, of three factors - the differing agricultural potential of the natural environment, the availability or otherwise of mineral resources, and the economic policies which had been pursued by the states which had formerly existed in the area, together with the pattern of their frontiers.

Two contrasting types of region may be recognised in any description of the agricultural potential of Eastern Europe - the mountains and the lowlands (Figure 2.1). Large parts of central and southern Eastern Europe are made up of mountains of alpine origin, some of which are of karst topography. These are ill-suited to agriculture, and are extensively forested to this day. Nevertheless, they proved to be attractive to settlement in past times when Turks and others invaded the intervening lowlands from the east, and much foothill and valley land was cleared by cultivators and settled at high densities. Moreover, animals have been widely pastured at higher altitudes, with disastrous consequences for the natural vegetation, soils and river regimes of some parts of Albania, Bulgaria and Yugoslavia.

The largest of the lowlands are the North European Plain of East Germany and Poland, and the Danubian basin, both up and downstream of the Iron Gates, in Bulgaria, Hungary, Romania and Yugoslavia. In addition, there are many smaller lowlands, such as the Polabí in Bohemia, the Moravian and Croatian Lowlands, the Transylvanian Plain in Romania, the

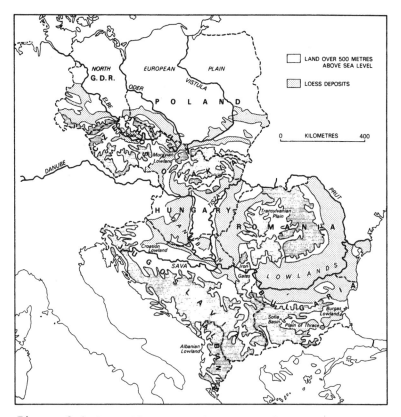

Figure 2.1 Some Elements of the Physical Environment of Eastern Europe

Albanian lowland, and the Plain of Thrace, the Burgas Lowland and the Sofia Basin in Bulgaria. These lowlands vary widely in both climate and soils. South of a line from Magdeburg through Wrocław and Kraków to Lublin, many of them are covered by loess. This gives rise to stoneless, freely-draining soils, which warm up quickly in spring, are of moderate or high natural fertility, and yield heavily when irrigated. However, in the absence of such assistance, the low level of precipitation in the Danube basin and the lowlands of Bulgaria, and the high incidence of summer drought, make for low and irregular yields of crops, especially root crops. To the north of the loess the soils of East Germany and Poland have been

7

developed upon outwash sands and gravels, which are of low base content and are rapidly leached, or upon cold, wet, boulder clays of glacial origin. What is more, the climate to the north of the Carpathian Mountains is both wetter and cooler than in the Danube valley, and spring comes late, in particular, to the north-east of Poland.

Much of the North European Plain, both on the poorer and better soils, and most of the smaller lowlands, have been settled and farmed for many centuries. The interfluvial plateaux of the Danube basin, in contrast, were only brought into cultivation between the early eighteenth and later nineteenth centuries, as the risk of invasion from the east decreased, and as the introduction of tube wells solved the problem of water supply in areas away from the rivers. However, by the early years of the twentieth century all except the higher mountains of Eastern Europe had been settled, and about forty-five percent of the area cleared of its natural vegetation – be it grass or forest – and brought under the plough. A quarter of the land remained under forest, and almost a fifth was in meadows or pasture (Royal Institute of International Affairs 1944, p.89).

The distribution of extractive industries, of manufacturing and of the concentrations of population associated with these types of activity, in contrast, have been very much less widespread. The largest deposits of mineral fuel in Eastern Europe are the bituminous coalfields of Poland and Czechoslovakia, the brown coals and lignites of East Germany and Poland, and the oilfields of Romania. Smaller deposits of fuels also exist in Bulgaria, Hungary and Yugoslavia. There are also substantial reserves of potash in East Germany, and of copper ore and sulphur in southern Poland, and there was considerable working of iron ore in Poland and Czechoslovakia during the nineteenth century. Not all of these minerals had been discovered before the Second World War, let alone exploited, but large industrial conurbations had grown up in Upper Silesia, in neighbouring Moravia, and in Saxony; and there were lesser groupings of industry, based on local mineral deposits, in Bohemia and the Sudeten Mountains. In addition, several cities of national or regional significance, such as Berlin, Budapest, Warsaw and Wrocław, had attracted a wide range of manufacturing industries, in spite of a lack of local mineral resources, and during the nineteenth century the great textile town of Łódź developed in a previously scantily-populated and poor part of central Poland. However, there was little modern industry in the rest of Eastern Europe, and with the exception of the few areas mentioned above, the economy was almost entirely rural.

Thus, there are marked contrasts between one part of Eastern Europe and another in both agricultural potential and mineral resources, and these were reflected, in part, in the patterns of settlement and economic development before 1939. However, those patterns also owed a good deal to the contrasting policies of the various imperial powers to which the area had belonged during the nineteenth century. For instance, those parts which lay within the Prussian Empire benefited from the substantial industrial growth which took place in Germany during the last century, the tariff protection which was afforded to agriculture there, and the development of a dense rail network. During that century the bituminous coalfields became the sites of major concentrations of metallurgical and engineering industries, and agglomerations of chemical and textile production also appeared. Food-processing industries were widely distributed among the towns, and agriculture became an increasingly intensive activity, whose aim was the production of goods for sale, rather than for consumption by the farming community itself. Major regional centres of administration, transport, services and manufacturing developed, and Berlin became a city of world status. Those areas which remained longest under German control - the modern state of East Germany and the Western and Northern Territories of Poland (Figure 2.2) - benefited most, but the Poznań-Bydgoszcz part of central Poland, which lay within Prussia throughout the nineteenth century, also enjoyed a more developed economy and richer infrastructure than the other parts of the re-established state of Poland in 1919. In the Austro-Hungarian Empire, in contrast, development was more patchy. While Bohemia and Moravia were favoured by the Austrians as a matter of policy in the establishment of new industry, and produced most of the coal, chemicals and metal goods of the Empire, other parts enjoyed little industrial development. One exception was Budapest, which became the economic as well as the administrative focus of Hungary after the Ausgleich of 1867, and the site of more than half of all the manufacturing in that country. A similar situation occurred in the Congress Kingdom of Poland within the Russian

Figure 2.2 International Boundaries in Eastern Europe since 1919

Empire. Some factory industry was established in
Warsaw, Łódź and on the small part of the Upper
Silesian coalfield which lay within its frontier,
but much of the country was entirely rural. Lastly,
the Turkish Empire, with its stifling of local
enterprise, was a by-word for backwardness, and
there was little economic development even in its
successor states, save for the exploitation of
petroleum in Romania.

Some attempts were made to redress the uneven
pattern of industrialisation within individual
countries during the twenty years between the wars,
such as the beginnings of the strategic Central
Industrial Region in southern Poland, but the legacy
of the nineteenth century was still very apparent in
the late 1930s. Only three of the countries (in
their present boundaries) - Czechoslovakia, East
Germany and Poland - possessed a substantial
industrial capacity in fuels, cement, electricity
and steel, and Albania and Bulgaria were almost
totally unindustrialised (Germany 1938). Similarly,
whereas two-fifths of the population of what are now
East Germany and Czechoslovakia were engaged in
industry and construction, and about a quarter of
the population of Hungary, the proportion in the
rest of Eastern Europe was less than a sixth.
Conversely, that part of the population which was
dependent upon agriculture exceeded three quarters
of the total in Albania, Bulgaria, Romania and
Yugoslavia, and in much of Poland and Slovakia,
while in Hungary it was more than half (Royal
Institute of International Affairs 1944, p.87).

The effect of these widely differing histories
of economic development may be seen also in the
urban structure of the area (Figure 2.3). Of the
eleven cities which had populations of 300,000 or
more in the late 1930s, five were in East Germany,
three in Poland, and one each in Czechoslovakia,
Hungary and Romania. There were none in Albania,
Bulgaria or Yugoslavia (Germany 1938).

These contrasts in the patterns of industrial
and urban development were reflected in the state of
agriculture. Farms in what are now East Germany and
western Poland, and in Bohemia and Moravia, were
relatively large between the two World Wars,
covering more than ten hectares each on average.
They were well equipped, possessed large numbers of
cattle, followed intensive systems of cultivation
and fertilisation, and sold almost all of their
products. Furthermore, farmers in Czechoslovakia
and Germany were protected from the breakdown of the

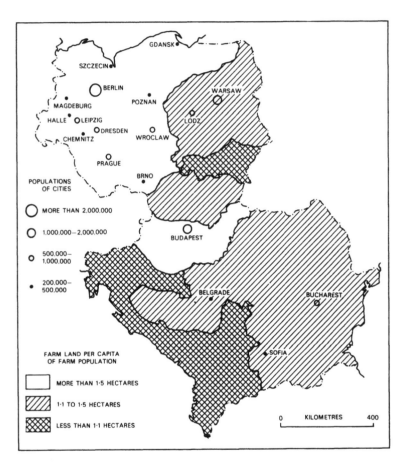

Figure 2.3 Pressure on Land and Urban Development in Eastern Europe before the Second World War

international market in wheat between the wars by tariffs and price supports. In Hungary, in contrast, agriculture was dominated by a few, huge estates. In 1930, a mere 3,000 of these, each of 300 hectares or more, accounted for upwards of a quarter of all farmland, and holdings of thirty hectares or more accounted for fifty-three percent of the land. Most of the agricultural population, in consequence, were either smallholders, operating on a scale which was inadequate to provide both a satisfactory standard of living and a surplus for

12

investment, or landless labourers. Some evidence of the pressure of this population upon the land is given by the fall which occurred between 1911 and the 1930s in the numbers of cattle and pigs, and by the fact that much of the cereal cultivation was proceeding without the assistance of regular manuring. Yields of wheat in the early 1930s were only about two-thirds of those of Bohemia and the Poznan area of Poland (Warriner 1964, pp. 97-147). The closure of the German market to Hungarian cereals depressed the incomes of these people still further, and led to some consumption of their meagre stock of farm capital.

Elsewhere in Eastern Europe agriculture lacked both land and capital, and it suffered from a surplus of population. As a result of the land reforms after the First World War few large estates existed, but the typical holding in Albania, Bulgaria, Romania, Yugoslavia, central and southern Poland and Slovakia, was still small. In none of these areas in 1930-31 did the area of land per capita of the farm population exceed 1.5 hectares, and over much of southern Poland and Yugoslavia it was less than one (Figure 2.3). Livestock densities and crop yields were generally about half of those in Germany, Bohemia and western Poland, and production per capita of the farm population was between a third and a quarter (Warriner 1964, p.84). As in the case of Hungary, that part of the farm product which did reach the market, and upon which these countries depended to a considerable extent for their exports, was subject to depressed prices during the 1930s. In addition, population was growing more rapidly in these areas, in spite of relatively high rates of infant mortality, and all this made for severe pressure upon the land. The consequence was that yields fell, the vast majority of the people suffered from a low standard of living, and there was widespread difficulty, both locally and nationally, in accumulating capital, increasing productivity and achieving economic growth.

The effect of the Second World War on these patterns of development was threefold. Firstly, at least 8,000,000 people in the area, or about seven percent of the pre-war population, were killed. Most of these were Polish Jews and Yugoslavians, and many had lived in the cities. Secondly, changes in the frontiers led to large-scale migrations. Most of the German-speaking people fled from the Western and Northern Territories of Poland, and they were

13

replaced by a much smaller number of Poles from what had formerly been eastern Poland. Similarly, most of the German community in Czechoslovakia left. Lastly, the destruction which occurred on the North European Plain, in Budapest and in Yugoslavia, and especially in the industrialised and urban areas, as the German armies retreated, was of such a scale that much of the infrastructure and capital equipment which had been built up before 1939 was destroyed. Much of that which did survive in what is now East Germany was seized by the Soviet forces, and taken back to the USSR. In short, many of the more developed parts of Eastern Europe were greatly impoverished by the war, and much of the economic progress which had been made since the mid-nineteenth century was lost.

Thus, there were wide discrepancies between the different parts of Eastern Europe in natural resources, the degree of their development before the Second World War, and in war-time destruction. Before that conflict began any league table of the countries, as they presently exist, which might have been drawn up on the basis of their economic development, would have shown that East Germany was the most advanced, with Czechoslovakia not far behind. Hungary and Poland would have occupied an intermediate position, and the poorest countries would have been Romania, Bulgaria, Yugoslavia and Albania, in that order. However, the national aggregates and averages upon which such a table might have been based would have obscured much variety at the sub-national scale. For instance, whereas western Poland was in many respects similar to East Germany, the central and southern provinces were more akin in their economies to Romania, and in Czechoslovakia a similar contrast existed between Bohemia and Moravia at one extreme, and Slovakia at the other. Therefore, although the general condition of each country both before and after the war was unique, there were several cases of different countries facing similar problems in its aftermath. For instance, both Czechoslovakia and Poland might have espoused a policy of economic growth based upon their established industrial regions, and might have sought to attract migrants to them from overpopulated rural areas. Conversely, both might have chosen to spread new developments more widely. Similarly, Hungary and Romania both inherited gravely unbalanced urban structures comprising a large, dominant capital and a plethora of small towns, few of which could boast even a few of the amenities and advantages of the metropolis. Indeed, most of the countries were faced with the problem of the small town. Thus, although the policies which have been adopted in each country will be discussed separately in the following chapters, there will be many common themes, and we shall return to a comparison of the extent to which the countries have been able to deal with some of them in the final chapter.

THE SOVIET INFLUENCE

However, before examining each of the eight countries in turn there is one other theme which has been common to them all and has affected their economic development since the Second World War - the influence of the Soviet Union. Whereas that country played little part in their affairs between the wars, and was on bad terms with Poland after the Russo-Polish War of 1919-1920, the Second World War destroyed the power of Germany and created a vacuum in Central Europe into which the Soviet Union moved. Indeed, so great was the westward and southward advance of Soviet influence, with the subsequent division of Europe into two opposing camps, that it can be argued that the earlier concept of Central Europe has been almost entirely replaced by one of Eastern Europe, where that is taken to mean the area which has been coterminous with the extent of Russian, or at least communist, influence since 1945.

Nevertheless, the extent of Russian control - and of Russian influence over the pattern of economic development - has varied widely among the countries. For instance, East Germany was invaded by Soviet forces at the end of the war, and was only established as a separate state by the Russians in 1949. Similarly, Romania, which had sided with the Germans in 1941 but later joined the allies, was effectively occupied by the Soviet Union; a communist government was helped into power; and the Russians exercised close control over the economy until the mid-1950s. In Bulgaria, which had also supported the Germans, Moscow-trained agents joined with the local communists to set up a government immediately after the war, and other Moscow-based groups, installed in the governments of Czechoslovakia, Hungary and Poland as those countries were liberated from the Germans by Russian troops, ousted the non-communist elements within a few years. Only in Albania and Yugoslavia did indigenous communist groups take control without substantial and overt assistance from the Russians or those trained by them. Few of the immediate post-war governments were made up entirely of communists. However, by 1948 the non-communist elements had been eliminated, and only Yugoslavia retained a significant degree of independence from Moscow. Indeed, it was expelled in that year from the Cominform by Stalin, and unsuccessful attempts were made by him to replace Tito with a more pliant leader. Elsewhere, the Soviet Union retained effective control, though at some cost to itself. In 1953 it suppressed riots in East Germany; in 1956 the Hungarian uprising was savagely crushed; in 1968 Czechoslovakia was invaded; and, following that intervention, the Brezhnev Doctrine - that no country which has come within the socialist group can be allowed to leave it - was enunciated. Apart from Yugoslavia, only Albania has broken away from Soviet domination in the post-war period, but in neither country has the system of one-party government been removed, nor has the aim of building socialism been abandoned. Indeed, Albania claimed in 1961 that in transferring its allegiance to China it was turning away from a degraded and perverted form of socialism to a more correct road to communism. Nevertheless, Russia has enjoyed a greater degree of control over Eastern Europe throughout the post-war period than at any time in that area's history, and thus it has been able to exert a powerful influence, not least in matters of economic, environmental, social and spatial planning.

But the model of development which the Russians have been pressing upon Eastern Europe has not been a constant one. Immediately after 1945 the influence of Stalin was supreme. After his death, however, and Krushchev's denunciation of him in 1956, different emphases and means of implementing policies were adopted in the Soviet Union, and these were quickly communicated to Eastern Europe. Nevertheless, the initial post-war decisions about the system and aims of planning in all the countries of the area were taken during the Stalinist era, and these have continued to exert a major effect upon the pattern of development since then. It follows that we must describe the Russian model of development, both in its Stalinist and later forms, if the background to what has occurred in Eastern Europe since 1945 is to be understood.

16

(1) The Stalinist Model

Before describing the Stalinist model of development it should be noted that in several important respects the country of which he assumed dictatorial control in the mid-1920s was very similar to Eastern Europe at the end of the Second World War. Most of it was rural; more than four-fifths of the population was directly dependent upon agriculture; much farming was of a subsistence, rather than a commercial, character; the growth of rural population since the abolition of serfdom in 1861 had led to a halving of the size of the average holding; and, agricultural productivity was low. Industry had grown rapidly in the late ninteenth and early twentieth centuries, but it was still restricted to a few, widely-scattered centres, such as the Donbass, Moscow and Leningrad. Thus, the socialist revolution did not occur, as Marx had envisaged, in an economically developed country. Nor did it spread to other countries, and so allow the peaceful sharing of development between them and the removal of the antagonisms which had arisen in part as a result of the commercial rivalry of the European powers before 1914. Rather, socialism had to be built upon the foundation of a largely peasant economy in a single and isolated - though enormous and populous - country.

Within the first few years of the Revolution under Lenin it had become apparent that, in taking as its goal the establishment of, first, a socialist, and later, a communist, society in the manner laid down by Marx, the Soviet model of development was to be in stark contrast to any of the existing systems of economic and political management amongst the other great powers of the time. Moreover, Stalin adopted even more unusual and extreme aims and methods from 1928 onwards. However, it would not be of great value to describe the way in which the Soviet government tackled the problems of regional economic development, land-use allocation, urban design and environmental protection in its early years, for, as we shall see, these problems were in large measure the consequence of other policies which were adopted, and were only recognised belatedly and in part. Rather, it would be appropriate to outline the policies which were pursued, if not from the beginning of the Revolution at least under Stalin, with regard to the use and organisation of the country's economic resources, for it was these which were exported to Eastern Europe after the Second World War. We shall do this

17

by looking at the way in which each of the factors of production — land, labour, capital and entrepreneurship, or management — was handled.

In the case of <u>land</u> the Marxist attitude was very clear. As the fundamental means of production it was not to be held in private ownership, and those who used it were not to be allowed to expropriate the unearned rents of fertility and situation — the profits of monopoly — which accrued to landowners under capitalism. Accordingly, the nationalisation of all land was proclaimed by Lenin on the morrow of the Revolution in 1917. However, a socialist system of land-use control did not develop smoothly from this change of ownership. Rather, the large estates and rented lands in rural areas were seized by the peasants, who treated them thereafter as their own, and began to behave as capitalists. Attempts were also made on several occasions between 1917 and 1929 to reduce the prices of farm products in order to bring the value of the agricultural product into line with that of the industrial output of the towns, and thus to supply the towns with food at prices which the urban proletariat could afford. But, on each occasion, the peasantry resisted through the reduction of deliveries to the market. Stalin's response was, first, to drive the owners of middle-sized farms — the kulaks — from their lands, and second, to bring almost all agricultural land into collective farms, from which compulsory deliveries could be extorted at fixed, low prices. In this way peasants were deprived of the opportunity to make profits — or even to make a modest living — at the expense of industrial workers, for the prices which were set for compulsory deliveries were too low to cover even the costs of production. However, collective farmers were allowed to keep small private plots, often in the vicinity of their houses, and to sell the crops grown there in relatively uncontrolled markets. The result was that the private plots were cultivated intensively, while the communal lands were relatively neglected. Nevertheless, firm control had been established over the use of, and the income derived from, agricultural land.

It was also thought that land should be free, for it was believed that any price which was charged, net of improvements, was no better than a capitalisation of the value of the types of rent referred to above. As a result, land in communal ownership — either for agriculture or belonging to the factories which had been seized by the workers

at the time of the Revolution - was made available
for other forms of communal or socialist use without
payment. However, this merely encouraged state
enterprises to hold more land than they required,
for it cost them nothing to do so, while the
exchange of plots between those for whom they
produced little revenue and those who could have
made more efficient use of them was discouraged, to
the detriment of the whole economy. Moreover, the
introduction of cheap, flat-rate fares on city
transport, and the adoption of artificially low
freight rates on the railways had the effect of
obscuring the true rents of situation and the
associated opportunity costs involved in location
decisions.

Attitudes to labour were also marked by a
radical break with the past. The growth of
population in Russia after the abolition of serfdom
had created a huge 'reserve army of labour', and
kept down the level of industrial earnings.
Substantial quantities of British, Belgian and
French capital had been attracted to Imperial Russia
to take advantage of this situation, and factory
employment had grown rapidly during the twenty-five
years before the First World War. However, urban
housing and amenities had remained at a low standard
(Pallot and Shaw 1981, pp.190-191). The Marxist aim
was to replace the bourgeois and conservative
elements in the labour force by the proletarian, and
to develop the 'whole person' of the socialist
worker. But, it was believed that, if this was to
be achieved, the industrial sector of the economy
would have to be enlarged, while the peasant element
would need to decline. Labour would have to be
attracted from the land, and farming reorganised
into more industrial and socialist forms.

In the event, a variety of methods were
employed to ensure that an adequate supply of labour
was made available in the places required. Wage
differentials were used to attract people into those
activities, such as coal and iron mining, and oil,
electricity, steel and machine production, which
were singled out for expansion; and higher wages
were also paid to some of those working on new
infrastructure and in the far north and Siberia.
However, much of the work in the east and north of
the Soviet Union under Stalin was accomplished by
forced labour. Many kulaks and their families were
deported to the north and east under the
collectivisation programme, and some ethnic
minorities and victims of the purges of the 1930s

were also forced to work on such projects as the
White Sea Canal and the construction of the
metallurgical combine at Magnitogorsk. There were
many Gulag Archipelagoes of the type described by
Solzhenitsyn. It is not certain how many people
were obliged to work in these harsh and remote
environments, but the figure was probably between
3,000,000 and 6,000,000 in the late 1930s, or
between five and ten percent of the total labour
force (Munting 1982, pp.172-174). Nor is it certain
that the enforcement of service in this manner made
the cost of building these projects much cheaper
than if wage labour had been employed, for the
workers were poorly motivated and had to be guarded
(Hutchings 1982, pp.104-108). However, it is very
unlikely that equivalent numbers of workers could
have been attracted by incentives, and the whole
system of forced labour provided the authorities
with a means of disciplining the population.

The movement of labour was also controlled in
other ways. Each of the people's commissariats (or
ministries) which ran the various sectors of the
economy, recruited labour. At first, each was given
a particular area of the country within which to
operate, but after 1938 some restriction was imposed
upon the distance over which such recruitment could
take place. Nevertheless, the take-up of labour
from the countryside for the expanding industries
was highly selective; collective farmers were not
allowed to leave the land unless recruited
officially, and the movement of labour in general
was controlled after 1932 by the issue of internal
passports. Between 1940 and 1956 workers could not
change jobs without permission, and those who
received college training were subject to an initial
three-year placement. Thus, labour could be made
available for whatever purpose and almost anywhere
within the Soviet Union. However, just as with
land, much labour was probably employed in the wrong
way and in the wrong place, with the result that
economic growth was retarded.

However, it was to be through the control and
investment of capital that the Soviet Union was to
establish one of the most important elements of the
model of economic and spatial development which it
imposed upon its Eastern European allies after 1945.
Almost all factory production, mining, commerce,
external trade, banking and public services had been
taken into public ownership during the first three
years of Bolshevik rule; and, after the end of the
New Economic Policy in 1928, that which had remained

in private hands had either been nationalised or suppressed. Shortly after, the collectivisation of agriculture brought much of the largest remaining privately-owned sector of the economy under tight control; and, in this way, almost all price-setting and investment decisions were brought within the control of the government. This done, the government was then obliged to decide both the rate of capital accumulation, through its price-setting activities, and the way in which that capital should be invested. During the 1920s there was considerable debate about the way in which economic growth could be achieved, and it was argued by Bukharin that the fastest road to development lay through a balance between investment in the producer and consumer goods industries, not to mention agriculture and the service sector. However, by 1928 the emphasis had swung away from Bukharin's position in favour of rapid industrial growth through the expansion of the output of producer goods. There were at least two reasons for this change in emphasis. Firstly, relations with the major European powers had remained poor since the invasions of Russia immediately after the First World War, and there was a fear that the infant Revolution was threatened by 'capitalist encirclement', and perhaps renewed attacks. Therefore, the defence of the country, and the concomitant growth of the heavy, strategic industries, were perceived to be of paramount importance. Secondly, it enabled Stalin to undermine the position of Bukharin, and thus to rid himself of a serious rival for power.

Whatever the reasons for the policy, the results were startling. Between that year and 1937 the output of coal rose from 35,000,000 tonnes to 128,000,000, that of steel from 4,000,000 to 18,000,000 tonnes, that of electricity from 5,000 to 36,000 million kilowatt hours, and the number of machine tools from 2,000 to 49,000. More generally, while the value of agricultural production increased by about forty percent, and that of consumer goods by 230, the output of producer goods, which had been rather less than half of each of the other sectors in 1928, rose more than ninefold. Thus, whereas these three sectors had contributed forty-four, thirty-eight and eighteen percent respectively of the gross output of agriculture and industry by value in 1928, the proportions had become eighteen, thirty-eight and forty-four percent by 1937. In other words, the roles of agriculture and the producer goods had been reversed. What is more, this emphasis continued under the impact of, first, the war against Germany, and, later, the onset of the Cold War. By 1955, coal production had risen to 390,000,000 tonnes, electricity to 170,000 million kilowatt hours, and steel to 45,000,000 tonnes (Hutchings 1982, pp.308-309).

This emphasis had implications for both the scale and the location of production. The producer-goods industries generally offer substantial economies of scale, and it was policy from the start to build big. Also, because all major industry was in the hands of the state, entry to, and exit of enterprises from, the market ceased to be related to technology, managerial competence and the general level of activity in the economy, as it had in the past. Factories were not closed; new, small-scale, privately-owned producers were strongly discouraged; and, much investment was allocated to the enlargement of existing plants. During the First and Second Five Year Plans (1928-1937) 6,000 large industrial enterprises were constructed (Huzinec 1976, p.165) - a tiny number in comparison with the number of new firms entering production in, say, the United States - but all tended to be large. Moreover, many of the rapidly-growing industries were closely tied to raw materials of localised occurrence, such as coal and iron ore, with the result that the very large growth of factory and mining employment was not only concentrated into a limited number of large establishments, but also in a restricted series of locations. Perhaps the most impressive of these was the Urals-Kuzbass complex, which was established during the 1930s. Both areas had possessed a little industry before 1928, but fears of invasion from the west in the 1930s, and the effect of that invasion in 1941, led to such a growth of output that by 1955 fifteen percent of the USSR's coal came from the Kuznetsk Basin, fifteen percent from the Urals, and seven from Karaganda. These areas also produced about thirty percent of the iron ore and forty-three of the pig iron (Lydolph 1964, p.219). However, the consequence of such a concentration of industry was that large areas of the country received relatively little industrial investment.

Furthermore, this pattern of industrialisation, together with the system of economic management, placed increasing burdens upon the transport system. The establishment of far-flung new industries led to an increase in the average length of freight hauls

on the railways; and cross hauls became common as
individual commissariats found it easier to acquire
materials and accessories in many cases by providing
them themselves, rather than relying on the
ministries whose prime responsibility they were. As
a result, some attempt was made after 1938 to
increase the degree of regional self-sufficiency in
industry, and the Urals-Kuzbass complex ceased to be
organised as a single economic unit.

Looking back on the period before the Second
World War, Koropeckyi (1967, pp.23-24) felt able to
identify six 'principles of the location of
production forces' which, in his view, had served to
guide the choice of sites for investment under
Stalin. These were
   (1) Location as near to raw material sources
   and centres of consumption as possible
   (2) An even distribution of economic activity
   throughout the country
   (3) A rational division of labour between
   economic regions, with an integrated
   development of the economy of each
   (4) A raising of the economic and cultural
   levels of backward areas
   (5) The elimination of the contrasts between
   town and country
   (6) The strengthening of the defence of the
   country.
Not all of these were relevant to every location
decision, but each was involved in at least some of
them. However, in so far as they are not all
compatible it should be no surprise that emphasis
was placed on some, such as 'location close to raw
materials', in preference to others, such as the
'even distribution of activity'.

The growth of industry had important
consequences for the pattern of employment and of
urban settlement. Between 1926 and 1940 the number
of those engaged in industry and construction in the
Soviet Union doubled, and a further doubling
occurred by 1955, when it reached 14,300,000
(Hutchings 1982, p.198). Towns and cities, both old
and new, grew rapidly. However, the progress of
both infrastructural provision and urban design was
less marked. In particular, the supply of housing
was seriously inadequate, and in 1931 a prohibition
was placed upon the establishment of further new
industry in Moscow and Leningrad in view of their
housing shortages. Other cities were also closed to
new settlers during the late 1930s. In spite of
some construction of accommodation by the industrial

ministries for their employees, the per capita
floorspace in Soviet cities fell throughout the
Stalin period from 6.45 square metres in 1923 to
3.98 in 1950 (Di Maio 1974, p.15); and that which
was built was in strict accord with the space
limitations laid down by the building norms, and
often in the form of large blocks of flats.
Similarly, little attention was paid to physical
planning either at the regional or the urban scale.
It is true that infrastructural plans were drawn up
for a number of rapidly-developing industrial areas
during the 1930s and 1940s, including the Crimea,
Donbass, Kuzbass and Mineral'nye Vody in the
Caucasus, but these were concerned with the needs of
industry rather than of the residents, and at the
urban scale little was achieved apart from the plan
for Moscow in 1935. Most towns and cities did not
have plans to guide their growth, and the views of
local soviets on developments by republican or
all-Union ministries were of little consequence
despite the theoretical power of such local bodies
to control what occurred on their territory.
Physical planning was very weakly connected to
economic planning, which, in any case, received much
greater emphasis. Conversely, substantial progress
was made in the provision of educational and health
facilities for the urban population, at least in
comparison with what had existed under the Tsars.
For example, creche and nursery provision was made
in order to allow mothers to return to work, and
thus alleviate a growing shortage of labour during
the Stalin period, and the decline of illiteracy
helped to provide a more skilled labour force, as
well as giving rise to a substantial growth in the
educational sector of the economy.

However, nowhere did the Stalinist model of
development depart more radically from the economic
systems which existed in the rest of Europe and the
United States at that time than in the matter of the
management of the economy. Early in the Revolution,
a Supreme Council of the National Economy had been
established, and within four years the scheme for
the electrification of the country (GOELRO) had been
launched, and a State Planning Commission (Gosplan)
set up. However, it was Stalin who made full use of
the idea of comprehensive, centralised planning
through the introduction of the first of the Five
Year Plans in 1929, thus establishing a vehicle for
development which has been used, except for a few
brief periods, ever since. He also replaced the
Supreme Economic Council with a series of central

government commissariats, or ministries, each of which was responsible for a single industry. By 1957 their number had grown to fifty. The Five Year Plans were drawn up by Gosplan in conjunction with the commissariats and the republican and lower-level planning authorities. Production targets were laid down for each industry, and flows of materials between them were balanced. Targets were then disaggregated by the commissariats among the groups of plants for which they had responsibility. Prices and foreign trade were also fixed and incorporated in the Plan. Plans had the status of law, and great significance was attached to the achievement of the targets. However, because the overall targets and the most important decisions about new investments - which were taken at the highest political level - were, as a matter of policy, ambitious, plans tended to be very taut. The consequence was that failure in one sector to fulfil the Plan usually prevented its fulfillment in others. Moreover, the high degree of centralisation in the planning process, allied to the predominantly sectoral organisation of the economy through the commissariats, meant that Plans were often inadequately coordinated at the regional and local levels. Complaints were made that sectoral targets did not accord with those of city soviets, and that they could not be reconciled locally in a way which would create balanced regional economies. It was also claimed that advantage could not be taken of the external economies which were available through the use of by-products by factories belonging to other commissariats, or even by those of another branch of the same commissariat, within a local area (Dyker 1976, pp.90-91); and the increasing incidence of cross hauls was taken as a further indication of the aspatial and autarkic approach which this type of planning engendered. Nevertheless, the scale of the planning operation far exceeded any previous example of government intervention in the working of an economy, requiring as it did the coordination of the output of thousands of products within a vast country. Furthermore, Soviet planning did achieve by these means what Britain, France and the United States failed to do during the 1930s, namely, the employment of its workforce to the full and output greatly in excess of its previous record levels.

Thus, the Stalinist model of economic development was exceptional in many regards. Of course, it was not a Marxist model. Although private ownership of the means of production had almost disappeared, and spectacular increases achieved in industrial output, the state had been enlarged to the point where, through central planning, it determined even the smallest details of life. However, it is hardly surprising that this growth of planning should have occurred, for the abandonment of market forces inevitably required compensating innovations in the organisation and regulation of the economy, if that economy was not to collapse. Nor is it surprising that the system of government, in its secrecy, should have had more in common with the revolutionary cells which opposed the Tsarist governments before 1917, and in its use of terror emulated the cruel and despotic behaviour of some of those governments, than the concept of democratic decision-making by the people as a whole, for the new forms of economy could only be preserved if counter-revolutionaries could be restrained. Moreover, although substantial economic growth was achieved, little attention appears to have been given directly to the redressing of regional disparities in the levels of development or the standards of living, or to those between town and country which had developed under capitalism, and which Marx had so much deplored. Land use was marked by a contrast between great intensity on the private plots and overcrowding in residential areas, at one extreme, and low productivity on the collectivised and state-owned farms, at the other. Labour was not always used in the places in which it was likely to produce to the full; transport costs were probably higher than necessary as a result of the choice of locations for industry and the autarkic tendencies of the commissariats; little time was spent on the planning of either the settlement network as a whole or on individual towns and cities; and, the environmental issue was not recognised during Stalin's lifetime in spite of a rapacious exploitation of the Soviet Union's natural resources on a scale far greater than before the Revolution, and of the known criticisms by Marx of the wasteful and damaging treatment of nature by large-scale industry, albeit in capitalist ownership. However, because the Soviet Union defeated its enemies in the Second World War, as Russia had failed to do during the First, it was the Stalinist model of socialist development which was imposed upon the countries of Eastern Europe after 1945.

(2) Modifications of the Stalinist Model

However, the model was subject to much criticism after Stalin's death, and considerable amendment by Khrushchev and, later, Brezhnev. Firstly, more attention has been paid to the costs which are involved in the use of the factors of production, and to the way in which these vary over the country. A charge has been made since 1965 for the use of capital by industry, though it has been at a level which is probably too low to reflect its real scarcity (Dyker 1976, p.16), and since 1967 extractive industries have also been obliged to pay a rent for the use of land, which varies with the level of output. The range of wages between one part of the country and another has been increased in order to attract labour to harsh environments, and housing privileges have been offered since 1964 to those willing to work for a period in such environments. Forced labour disappeared almost entirely after 1956; internal passports have been made available to collective farmers; and a supply of cheap labour has been maintained for high priority and prestige projects in remote and harsh regions through the use of 'moral incentives' to students and members of the Young Communist League. Many students helped to open up the Virgin Lands of Kazakhstan and western Siberia, to bring in the first harvests there in the late 1950s, and to build the Baikal-Amur railway during the 1970s and 80s. It should also be noted that uniform official prices for agricultural products have been replaced by a range which is supposed to reflect the different costs of production in various parts of the country. Thus, something has been done to reintroduce the price mechanism as a signal to those making investment and production decisions, but prices are still determined centrally, are rarely changed, and extend over a much narrower range than in market economies. In other words, the true costs and opportunities involved in location and investment decisions are probably but weakly revealed by the Soviet price system.

Secondly, there has been a change in the balance of investment. This is illustrated in Table 2.1 which shows that, although the percentage share of each of a variety of sectors in the total capital investment fluctuated widely between one Five Year Plan and another, even under Stalin, in general the shares of Group A industries (producer goods) have been somewhat lower in the four plans since the death of Stalin. Conversely, the shares of

Table 2.1: Range of Shares of Total Capital Investment of Various Sectors in the Soviet Economy
during Five Year Plans

	Shares (in percent)	
	Under Stalin	Since Stalin
Group A industries	30.5 to 36.5	29.9 to 31.7
Group B industries	4.5 to 6.8	4.8 to 5.3
Agriculture	11.8 to 15.6	14.3 to 20.1
Housing	12.8 to 19.8	15.3 to 23.5
Science, culture, arts and education	2.6 to 4.8	4.9 to 6.2

Definitions:
"Range" refers to the highest and lowest proportion
of total capital investment in each sector recorded
during the Five Year Plans covered by each period.
"Under Stalin" refers to the First, Second, Fourth
and Fifth Five Year Plans, i.e. the period from
1938 to 1945 is omitted.
"Since Stalin" refers to the Sixth, Seventh, Eighth
and Ninth Plans.

Source: Hutchings (1982), p. 198.

agriculture, housing and 'non-productive' services
have been larger. One consequence of this has been
that the amount of houseroom available per capita,
which fell throughout the Stalin period, has doubled
since then (Pallot and Shaw 1981, p.191).
Nevertheless, industry as a whole continues to
receive the lion's share of investment, and its
number of workers has risen much faster than that of
the economy as a whole - doubling between the
mid-1950s and 1980. Coal output rose to 716,000,000
tonnes in that year, electric power to 1,295,000
kilowatt hours, steel to 148,000,000 tonnes, and
machine tools to 230,000. Moreover, the production
of mineral fertilisers, synthetic fibres,
refrigerators and televisions, which was small in
the early 1950s, has grown substantially (Hutchings
1982, pp.308-9). All this has required the
extension of the exploitation of mineral and energy
resources into formerly untapped areas. For
example, the output of natural gas has increased
dramatically since 1955, especially from the far

north of the country, and a large copper mine has been opened at Noril'sk, within the Arctic Circle. It has also required the expansion of existing plants, as well as the establishment of new ones, in urban areas, thus drawing more of the population into towns. Whereas 73,000,000 people lived in towns in 1951, the figure in 1980 was 167,000,000, and the number of those in the countryside had, at last, begun to fall (Munting 1982, p.168).

At the same time more careful attention has been paid to regional development. Early, simplistic ideas of an even distribution of industry have been replaced since 1956 by an acceptance that, in view of the shortage of both labour and capital, greater efficiency in the use of the factors of production is essential if output is to be increased, and that one way in which such increases can occur is through the development of regional specialisation in production. So, labour-intensive industries have been sited in relatively labour-rich areas, while automation has been introduced in places with labour deficits (Pallot and Shaw 1981, p.109). There has also been an attempt to increase the degree of regional specialisation in agriculture since 1961, and the composition of the farm output which each region is expected to produce, which showed little variation in previous plans between one region and another, has been altered to reflect the differing opportunities which are offered by the natural environment among the various parts of the country. Specialisation has also been encouraged at the level of the individual state and collective farm. More generally, charges were imposed in 1966 on enterprises which, because of favourable locations, should be able to make larger profits than others (Horowitz and Whitehouse 1973). Since the mid-1950s, all Five Year Plans have included a territorial component for each of the fifteen constituent republics of the USSR, while ten and fifteen-year perspective plans, which were introduced in 1965, have also been concerned with the regional distribution of production. However, it must be noted that regional disparities have persisted. For instance, industrial investment was surprisingly low between 1959 and 1975 in much of Soviet Central Asia, in view of its generally rural and backward character, but high in the northwest of the USSR, in Estonia and Latvia, which were relatively well-developed (Pallot and Shaw 1981, p.158). Fuchs and Demko (1979) have shown that much geographical inequality persists within the Soviet

29

Union with respect to standards of living. Thus,
Brezhnev's 1974 claim that "the task of equalising
the level of development...is in all essentials
solved" (Pallot and Shaw 1981, p.71) cannot be
accepted.

Regional and town planning of a physical,
rather than an economic, nature has also been
emphasised to a greater extent since the mid-1960s.
Indeed, a hierarchy of plans has been developed for
much of the country under the aegis of the State
Construction Committee (Gosstroi). These plans,
like those for the regional distribution of
production, are long term, covering up to thirty
years. They are drawn up at many scales, from that
of the General Scheme for the System of Settlement,
which covers the whole country, through those for
regions (oblast) and districts (rajon), down to
those for individual towns; and, in the case of
these last, a detailed pattern of future land use,
green belts, forest-park zones and infrastructural
needs are shown. Much of the impetus for this
development has come from the increased construction
of housing, begun under Khrushchev, and from the
growing concern over the way in which farmland is
being built over on the urban fringe or affected by
opencast mining. Almost all cities and about half
of the other urban settlements possessed such a
general urban plan by the mid-1970s (Shaw 1983,
p.394). Many of the plans which refer only to small
areas are drawn up locally, whereas those for
regions of national importance are usually the work
of central government (Nekrasov 1978, p.88). These
physical plans are related to the economic plans for
the same areas. However, because they are drawn up
by a different body, coordination between the two
may be lacking, and rivalry can even occur. At the
local level the power of the soviets, at least on
paper, has always been very great, especially with
respect to the refusal of permission for
developments which, in their view, would not conform
with the physical plan for their area.
Nevertheless, the great power of central government,
the lack of resources for local soviets, the system
whereby local budgets are a part of the central
budget and must therefore be approved by Moscow, and
the ability of industrial enterprises to extend and
to build housing and social facilities for their
employees out of their own funds, have all meant
that local authorities have often been dependent
upon enterprises to supply basic urban
infrastructure, exercised little real control over

the pattern of development in the days of Stalin,
and have only enjoyed slightly more power since the
early 1960s. What is more, the emphasis of central
government has continued to be on economic growth,
and the physical planning of development appears to
have remained of secondary importance. As a result,
the largest cities have continued to grow rapidly
(Pallot and Shaw 1981, pp.222-226); many plans have
had to be scrapped within a few years of their
adoption, long before their terminal dates; and
there have been renewed attempts during the 1970s
and early 1980s to improve the coordination of
economic and physical planning at local levels (Shaw
1983, pp.394-400).

Concern for the environment has also only
developed since the death of Stalin. The earlier
belief that pollution and other forms of
exploitation of the 'commons' by individual
factories and mines to the detriment of society at
large was the consequence of a capitalist
organisation of society, and therefore would not be
a problem under socialism, has given way since the
early 1960s to a more realistic assessment of the
effects of the huge increases in industrial output
which have occurred since the 1920s upon air and
water quality, to a recognition of the soil erosion
problems of the Virgin Lands, and of the need to
protect some areas of special interest, such as Lake
Baikal, from pollution, to the establishment of
several conservation agencies, the passage of
anti-pollution legislation, and to the incorporation
of some environmental-protection measures in the
most recent Five Year Plans.

Another marked change has taken place in the
matter of trade with other countries. Not only has
it been possible to establish links with all the
other communist governments which have been
established since the Second World War, but there
has also been a substantial growth in trade with
other countries. Much advanced equipment and
machinery has been bought from the West, especially
during the 1970s, and links with developing
countries have been extended wherever possible since
the 1950s. To some extent the motive behind this
has been political, rather than a desire on the part
of the Soviet Union to develop the production of
those goods in which it enjoys a comparative
advantage, but, whatever the reason, it has given
rise to a slightly more specialist profile of
production and associated locational pattern of
economic activity within the country.

Lastly, since the fall of Khrushchev the Soviet Union has toyed with 'economic reform', by which is meant the devolution of power over production, purchasing and investment decisions from the central planners to managers of factories. However, all major investment decisions - those which determine the structure of the space economy - have remained the prerogative of central government or of the ministries. Nevertheless, the Russians appear to have allowed their allies in Eastern Europe somewhat greater latitude to experiment with and adapt the model of development to their own conditions. As we noted earlier, radical departures from the approved Russian pattern have led to direct, and in some cases brutal, intervention by the USSR, but much local variation has occurred. We shall be able to assess the extent to which this has been the case, and the effects which it has produced, more fully after the problems and planning systems of each of the countries of Eastern Europe have been described in the following chapters.

REFERENCES

Di Maio, A.J. (1974), Soviet Urban Housing: Problems and Policies, Praeger, New York.
Dyker, D.A. (1976), The Soviet Economy, Crosby Lockwood, Staples, London.
Fuchs, R.J. and Demko, G.J. (1979), Geographic inequality under Socialism, Annals, Association of American Geographers, 69, 304-318.
Germany (1938), Statistiches Jahrbuch für das Deutsche Reich, Berlin.
Horowitz, B. and Whitehouse, F.D. (1973), Soviet Land Value and Enterprise Location, Land Economics, 49, 233-237.
Hutchings, R. (1982), Soviet Economic Development (2nd ed), Blackwell, Oxford.
Huzinec, G.R. (1973), Some initial comparisons of Soviet and Western regional development models, Soviet Geography, 17, 552-566.
Koropeckyi, I.S. (1967), The development of socialist location theory before the Second World War, Soviet Studies, 19, 1-28.
Lydolph, P.E. (1964), Geography of the USSR, Wiley, New York.
Munting, R. (1982), The Economic Development of the USSR, Croom Helm, London.
Nekrasov, N.N. (1978), Regional'naya ekonomika, teoriya, problemy, metody (2nd ed),

Ekonomika, Moskva.

Pallot, J. and Shaw, D.J.B. (1981), _Planning in the Soviet Union_, Croom Helm, London.

Royal Institute of International Affairs (1944), _Agrarian Problems from the Baltic to the Aegean_, London.

Shaw, D.J.B. (1983), The Soviet Urban General Plan and recent advances in Soviet Urban Planning, _Urban Studies_, 20, 393-403.

Warriner, D. (1964), _Economics of Peasant Farming_ (2nd ed), Cass, London.

Chapter 3

ALBANIA

Derek R. Hall

THE CONTEXT OF PLANNING

Of all the countries of Eastern Europe, Albania
was not only the least developed before the Second
World War, but since then it has come under a wider
range of influences than any of the others. The
effects of the sequence of Yugoslav, Russian and
Chinese allegiances upon the country's development
are outlined below, together with those of the
country's recent, more independent stance, and
consideration is then given to the associated plans
for the spatial development of each of the major
sectors of the economy and of the settlement
pattern.

The Communist partisans of Albania, who fought
the Germans and Italians during the war and seized
power in 1944, had close links with those in
Yugoslavia, and within a short period of the end of
hostilities no less than twenty-seven treaties had
been signed between the two countries, governing
many aspects of their economies. In particular,
links of the type which were being forged by the
Soviet Union through joint companies with several of
its Eastern European satellites, including
Yugoslavia, were established. Joint companies were
set up for the exploitation of Albania's oil and
metallic ores, and for railway construction,
electrification and foreign trade; and a joint bank
was created, whose credits amounted to half of
Albania's revenue in 1947 and 1948. It now appears
that the pro-Yugoslav faction in the Albanian
Communist Party was preparing for the eventual
incorporation of the country into Yugoslavia, but
this process was cut short by Yugoslavia's expulsion
from the Cominform in 1948, and within a few weeks
the Albanian government had unilaterally terminated

all its economic agreements with Yugoslavia.
Albania also refused to accept that it owed
Yugoslavia the 2,500,000,000 dinars' worth of
credits which it had previously received.
The break with Yugoslavia necessitated a twenty
percent reduction in the investment plan for 1949,
and was partly responsible for the underfulfillment
of the 1949-1950 economic plan. The Soviet Union
stepped in to cover forty percent of Albania's state
revenues, and advisers from other Eastern European
states, particularly Czechoslovakia and East
Germany, supplanted Yugoslavs. Between 1948 and
1951 Albania traded exclusively with members of the
CMEA - an economic constraint which none of its
other members imposed upon themselves - and, during
the 1950s, the Soviet Union alone accounted for more
than half of the country's foreign trade. By the
end of that decade it was receiving ninety-five
percent of Albania's oil exports, seventy-six
percent of its tobacco, and thirty-eight percent of
its bitumen. During Stalin's lifetime CMEA members
encouraged Albania's attempts to establish heavy
industry.
The formulation of the country's First Five
Year Plan for 1951 to 1955 represented the most
tangible crystallisation of Soviet inspiration in
Albanian planning procedures. Forty-three percent
of funds was earmarked for industry and mining,
fourteen percent each for agriculture and transport,
and sixteen for social welfare. The plan was not
fulfilled, and a steel mill, paper factory, and a
plant for briquetting coal were cancelled. However,
by 1953 the ratio of industrial to agricultural
output was 60:40 compared to 18:82 in 1938; and by
1955 the Albanians considered that they had
established sufficient of a light industrial base to
ascribe to themselves the term 'agrarian-industrial
society'. Industrial production increased threefold
over the plan period, and was eleven times greater
than in 1938 (Klosi 1969, p.15). Nevertheless,
seventy percent of the population was still employed
in agriculture. However, it was during the Second
Five Year Plan, from 1956 to 1960 that
Albanian-Soviet cooperation reached its zenith.
During this period a long-range plan, similar to
that which had been adopted in the USSR, was
promulgated, and the collectivisation programme was
speeded up. Soviet economic assistance was
increased in 1958 in response to the Chinese 'Great
Leap Forward', and Soviet, East German and
Czechoslovak technicians assisted in new mineral

developments and HEP schemes.

Nevertheless, a wind of change was blowing through Eastern Europe during the late 1950s. Khrushchev's denunciation of Stalin filled the Albanian leadership with foreboding, which was increased by the events in Hungary and Poland in 1956. Secondly, China's 'Great Leap Forward', which emphasised local self-sufficiency in contradiction to the Soviet model, appealled to the Albanian authorities, who were, like the Chinese, faced with severe problems of underdevelopment. Thirdly, Khrushchev outraged the Albanian leaders during a visit in 1959 by suggesting that they should improve their relations with Yugoslavia and abandon their heavy industrialisation plans, which, he argued, were 'unfeasible and disadvantageous' since Albania could receive all the machinery it needed from Eastern Europe through CMEA (Prifti 1978, p.79). As a result, the Albanians increasingly voiced support for China in the ideological struggle with Moscow, and, during a severe drought and serious food shortages in the summer of 1960, when the Albanians only had fifteen days' supply of wheat, a Soviet shipment of 50,000 tonnes failed to arrive (Freedman 1970). Within one month of the 1961 Soviet Party Congress, when the Sino-Soviet dispute was finally brought into the open, diplomatic relations between Albania and the USSR were broken off, Soviet, Czechoslovak and East German credits for the 1961-1965 Five Year Plan were cancelled, and experts were withdrawn. Albania was again faced with a major political and economic reorientation, and one which was even greater than that of 1948 (Griffiths 1962, Hamm 1963, Logoreci 1961, Skendi 1962).

Albanian planners subsequently claimed that these events delayed the completion of 250 of the projects in the country's Third Five Year Plan (1961-1965) by three years, with a 'knock-on' effect for subsequent plan periods (Klosi 1969, p.17). Although China stepped in to provide ninety percent of the financial and technical aid which had been promised by CMEA members, the industrialisation programme had to be substantially modified. (The claim that the country was about to enter a new historical stage - the complete construction of a socialist society (Pano 1982, p.200) - conveniently imposed no time limit.) However, two significant trends emerged from the dislocation. In the first place, increasing emphasis was placed upon self-sufficiency, which was pragmatically necessary in view of the uncertain character of Albania's

external assistance, and dogmatically convenient as
a reason for calling for unstinting effort in
domestic production; and secondly, greater attention
was paid to rural development - a move which was
interpreted by some observers as representing the
influence of the Chinese advisors.

The Chinese contribution to Albania's
development was very considerable. Western
estimates put the value of Chinese loans to Albania
between 1954 and 1975 at almost 500,000,000 dollars
(Marmullaku 1975, p.96; Prifti 1978, p.81; Prybyla
1976, pp.9-14); and, with Chinese aid, the
technology employed within Albania gradually
increased in sophistication (Hall 1975). In 1970
the Chinese Academy of Sciences presented Tiranë
University with a nuclear radiation research
laboratory; in 1971 the country's first electronic
computer centre and television station were
established; and a national telephone system was
completed in 1973 (Prifti 1979, p.197). However,
Chinese influence on Albania has tended to be
overemphasised, particularly by western observers.
For instance, although trade with the Soviet Union
ceased completely in 1963, Eastern Europe still
accounted for about a quarter of Albania's foreign
trade. Furthermore, although Albania's own
'cultural revolution' of 1966 to 1969 (Pano 1974;
Prifti 1968) saw the abolition of direct taxation, a
reduction in wage differentials and an emphasis on
rural projects through Chinese inspired 'open
schooling' for students, bureaucrats and other urban
dwellers, it was far more tightly controlled than
the Chinese prototype, and hardly penetrated the
upper echelons of party and governmental activity.

Eventually, despite the inauguration of a
regular air service between Tiranë and Peking in
1974, and the signing of a pact to cover the Sixth
Five Year Plan from 1976 to 1980, disagreements
grew. As early as 1971 the Albanian leader, Hoxha,
was openly declaring, and thus warning Peking, that
the struggle against imperialism was 'indivisible'.
He suggested that it was wrong to make compromises,
as China had begun to do with the USA, with either
of the two super-powers or their allies; and by 1975
the Sino-Albanian special relationship was
effectively at an end. After Mao's death in 1976
and the adoption of 'revisionist' policies by his
successors, the Albanians declared that they were
the only true socialists, and the Chinese advisors
were removed (Kaser 1979).

None of the three major projects undertaken with Chinese guidance - the Ballsh oil refinery, Elbasan metallurgical complex and Fierzë HEP scheme - were completed on time. Agricultural and industrial production goals were significantly reduced from 1976 onwards, and an all-round financial tightening, clothed in ideological rhetoric, was imposed. The people were exhorted to save electricity; a thirty to forty percent reduction was made in the imports of spare parts, a further mass movement of 14,000 students and 'working youth' to the countryside was arranged in order to help agricultural production, and another narrowing of wage differentials was imposed. A series of vicious purges and a wave of xenophobic paranoia in the mid-1970s seemed to indicate that calls were being made within the higher echelons of the Communist Party and government for some degree of economic reform; and the break with China, with its inevitable requirement to turn to other, more diverse, trade and aid partners, might well have been an appropriate point for such a change. However, rather than question the structure and organisation of the economic system, the Party leadership blamed the malfunctioning of the system and the failures of the plan on the managers of the economy and the technocratic intelligentsia (Prifti 1978, p.87). The rhetoric of self-sufficiency, with its emphasis on higher productivity, import substitution, export growth, and the expansion of existing facilities rather than the establishment of new developments and techniques, continued into the 1981-1985 Plan. As a result, the economy's rate of growth has slowed down, and the introduction of new technologies from abroad, such as electronics, has been reduced to a minimum. Moreover, foreign trade has been further constrained by Article 28 of the 1976 Constitution, which forbids the granting of concessions to, forming of joint companies with, or obtaining of credits from, any foreign country or institution (Anon 1977, pp.15-16).

Thus, the planning of Albania's economic development has been severely disrupted on three occasions since 1945. However, it should not be assumed that this has prevented major changes in the structure and output of the economy. For example, at the time of the Chinese withdrawal Albania was claiming to be self-sufficient in grain production, eighty-five percent so in other food, eighty percent in consumer goods and ninety percent in spare parts, with an industrial output in 1978 which was 4.6

times greater than in 1960 (Anon 1979), and a net
export of oil and electricity; and all this had been
achieved despite a very large increase in the
country's population. Nor should the background of
disruption be allowed to obscure the fact that clear
and consistent trends have appeared in the policies
for the various sectors of the economy.

INDUSTRY, ENERGY AND TRANSPORT

In the case of industry and the strategic
services the Albanians had embarked upon a socialist
reorganisation of their economy even before the end
of the Second World War. In December 1944 all
factories were nationalised, and this was followed
by the seizure of the banks, mineral resources,
motorised transport and trade. No compensation was
given, and by 1948 all private ownership of
industrial production had been eliminated. The
nationalisation of Albania's meagre industrial base
was intended to achieve three objectives (Prifti
1978, p.53) - to draw the country out of its
traditional backwardness, to destroy the economic
power of the bourgeoisie and foreign capital, and to
consolidate the power of the Communist Party by
giving the state control over the economy. A
centralised planning system of the 'command economy'
type was established, and through it resources were
concentrated in a few areas of production.
Proponents within the Party of a mixed, rather than
a socialist, economy were gradually removed from
decision-making positions, and no significant
relaxation or reform of this system has taken place
since.
Industrial policy has also been consistent in
its emphasis upon the importance of large-scale
production - in administrative, structural and
spatial terms. During the 1940s small enterprises
were grouped together into larger units, and in 1954
and 1955 transfers of activities were made between
enterprises in order to enhance the degree of
structural concentration and administrative control
of production. Pressure for further concentration
in the 1960s came from improvements in technology,
labour organisation and infrastructure, and the
output of larger quantities of goods. In contrast,
emphasis upon the heavy industries, in preference to
a broad development of both heavy and light forms of
production, has only occurred since 1961, when it
was decided that that road to development was

essential if an adequate socialist economic base was to be created, and if the defence of the country was to be ensured in view of the hostility of both the capitalist world and the Soviet Union. Official statements about the location of industry have emphasised three desiderata. Firstly, that the 'rational utilisation of natural resources' requires that raw materials should be processed close to their sources, even in a small country, in order to reduce transport costs. Secondly, that the "harmonious and proportional distribution of industry to all the districts of the country" (Anon 1982, p.256) is necessary for tne well-being of the people; and thirdly, that the distinctions between town and country should be narrowed through, amongst other measures, the growth of the urban population, the founding of new towns in association with new industrial centres, and the 'industrialisation' of rural production through the development of auxiliary activities such as the production of construction materials and food processing.

The ambitious plans for increased output, together with the realisation of the structural and spatial goals of Albanian industrial policy have also required the expansion of the energy and transport systems (Figure 3.1). The growth of electricity output has been notable, together with the concentration of generating capacity into relatively large units and the elimination of uneconomic small-scale units, the regrouping of power stations to supply the national grid more effectively, and the harmonisation of hydro-electric and thermal stations to compensate for seasonal fluctuations in water flow and thus ensure uninterrupted power supplies. An early post-war long-term plan aimed to complete the electrification of the country by 1985, but in 1967 it was decided to complete this process by 1971 - a move which
"impelled the masses to mobilise their forces in a self-sacrificing project of gigantic proportions"
(Anon 1982, p.275) - and which was officially completed thirteen months ahead of schedule. Moreover, sinee then a 'cascade' of HEP stations has been constructed on the Drin river in the north of the country (Cuedari 1983; Paloka 1981), which has permitted the export of electricity to Czechoslovakia and Yugoslavia (BBC 1982; Gurney 1978), and provided a spatial complement to the exploitation of lignite in the centre of the country and of petroleum and gas in the south. The

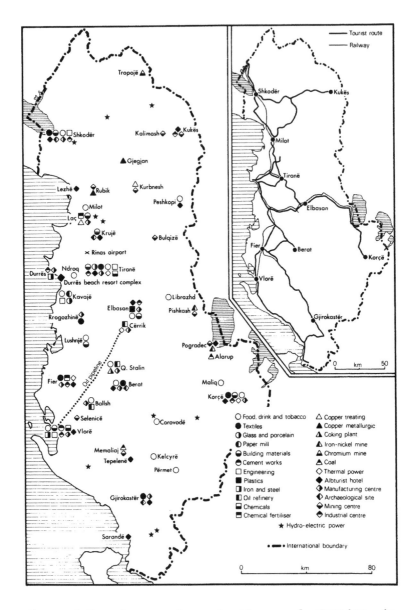

Figure 3.1 Industry, Communications and Tourism in Albania

development of a petrochemical industry is promised for 'the near future' in association with the oil refinery at Ballsh.

As for transport, the length of roads in the country has been more than doubled since 1938, and numerous new roads have been built to villages in the mountains. Passenger transport movements in 1979 were claimed to be 2863 times, and goods transport 163 times, greater than in 1938; transport by coastal shipping increased seventeenfold between 1960 and 1979, and that by long distance shipping ninefold, while the tonnage of the merchant fleet increased nearly twenty times, albeit from very small or almost non-existent bases before the war (Hall 1981, pp.317-318). One of the major projects pursued since the 1960s has been the construction of a railway network extending out from the central Tiranë-Durrës-Kavajë area (Figure 3.1). This has linked the iron and steel plant at Elbasan with its ore sources to the west of Lake Ohrid, the chemical fertiliser centre at Laç, and the northern city of Shkodër, and has now joined up with the Yugoslav rail system (Hall 1984a, 1985). During the 1981-1985 Plan the capacity of the rail network is to be doubled, including its extension to the Yugoslav border in the north and to the city of Vlorë in the south (Kromidha and Konduri 1984).

AGRICULTURE

Prior to the Second World War Albanian agriculture - though dominating the economy - had been backward. Furthermore, it had been characterised by an imbalanced structure of land tenure. Much of the cultivatable area had long been in freehold ownership, though a quarter of the agricultural area was owned by only three percent of farm households. Forests and pastures were usually in communal ownership. This structure has been radically altered in three stages. The first, undertaken in 1945, saw the expropriation of lands formerly held by 'foreigners', private institutions, banks, religious bodies and other large landowners. All holdings of more than twenty hectares were confiscated unless the owners were deemed to be employing 'advanced methods' of cultivation, in which case forty hectares could be kept; and by 1946 the Albanian leaders declared that the landlord class had been destroyed for all time. In the second stage, 30,000 hectares were redistributed, with existing tenant farmers having priority of allocation. However, the size of new holdings was restricted to about five hectares, and the effect was to substitute numerous dwarf farms for large estates. Finally, in the third stage, the land was collectivised.

However, the process was not as simple as the three stages above might suggest, especially in the case of the state farms. Many of the former church and foreign-owned lands, large estates, flocks, olive plantations, forests and water bodies were immediately transformed into, or simply retitled as, state property. Initially, thirteen state farms were established, including much of the newly reclaimed and irrigated land of the coastal plains and Korcë Basin; but since then state farms have also been planned for the hilly and mountainous regions of the country as part of the long term process or transforming rural property relations. By 1979 state farms accounted for a quarter of agricultural production, and 20.5 percent of the sown area.

As for the collectivisation of peasant holdings, the declared ideal was for a gradual and voluntary process which would ultimately result in a totally collectivised and mechanised rural sector, but because of food shortages in the early post-war period top priority was initially given to increasing both the cultivated area and the yields from it. Some cooperatives were established in 1946, but in spite of increased pressure for collectivisation after 1950 cooperatives only accounted for 12.8 percent of total agricultural output in 1954. However, by 1960 86.9 percent of the agricultural sector had been collectivised, incorporating the lowland plains and upland basins, and a Party decision to extend fully collectivisation to the highlands was eventually fulfilled in 1967, despite the unsuitability of much of the terrain for large-scale agriculture.

In the meantime, under the influence of the apparent success of China's people's communes, a rationalisation of Albania's socialised agriculture was pursued after 1959. Small cooperatives were merged, and their numbers fell from 1,915 to 423 by 1978, whilst the total number of cooperative families rose from 114,000 to 235,000 (Anon 1980, p.16; Drejtoria e Pergjitheshme e Statistikes 1974, p.104). As in the earlier concentration of industry, the regrouping of agricultural cooperatives was justified on grounds of greater specialisation and improved cooperation in production, and cooperatives in adjacent plains and upland areas were united with the aim of diminishing the differences in socio-cultural development, incomes and standards of living between the inhabitants of the two areas (Baci 1981).

In 1971, however, a new form of agricultural cooperative was established as a means of facilitating the transformation of all cooperatives into state farms, in what Schnytzer (1983) views as an ingenious solution to the ideological problem of agricultural machinery. The first 'higher-type agricultural cooperative' (HTC) was inaugurated in that year, and was given exclusive access to one MTS, thereby creating an agricultural unit which was intermediate between the typical cooperative farm, which shares an MTS's equipment with other cooperatives, and the state farm, which owns its own machinery. Moreover, methods of payment to the members of HTCs were made to resemble those of state farms more closely than those of other cooperatives in that ninety percent of the planned salary is paid during the year, with the remaining ten percent being paid at the end, if the plan is fulfilled. If the plan is overfulfilled, members receive an extra ten percent. Furthermore, each member of the cooperative is guaranteed a minimum wage. However, its level is determined by the economic capacity of the HTC, and so variations occur across the country, and particularly between the plains and upland areas. By 1981, forty-one of the country's agricultural cooperatives had been transformed into HTCs, encompassing twenty-three percent of the country's arable land and twenty percent of the labour in the cooperative sector.

In addition to the HTCs it has been claimed that Albanian agriculture has also made two other unique contributions to Marxist-Leninist theory (Anon 1984; Xhuveli 1984). Firstly, previously scattered, privately-owned livestock has been brought together into joint herds, and, secondly, the extinguishing of the personal plot, in the wake of the transition to complete state farming, has been explicitly adopted as an aim of policy. Already, in contrast to other Eastern European countries which Albania regards as 'revisionist', personal plots have been progressively reduced in size (Madhi 1982), though increases in agricultural procurement prices, reductions in the prices of goods bought by farmers from the state, and state pensions for the members of cooperatives have been introduced by way of compensation. Nevertheless, it is argued that personal plots are incompatible with social ownership, and that in any case the farmer can now buy products at prices in the cooperative shop which are lower than the cost of growing them on his plot.

The consequences of these changes for the landscape have been considerable. Much larger units of production have been created with a higher mechanical input, which has led, in turn, to the regularising of field shapes and the removal of hedgerows and other field divisions. Effective access roads and extra buildings have been constructed. Moreover, the former monocultural tradition has been eliminated. In 1938 bread grains occupied 83.5 percent of the country's sown area, but by 1979 they accounted for only fifty-three percent, and the area under industrial crops has grown significantly. Thirdly, there has been an increase in the regional specialisation of production with a view to exploiting the wide range of physical conditions within the country. An important step along this path was the completion in 1973 of a national agricultural land survey, which included comprehensive pedological and agrochemical analyses of all state farms and cooperatives, and permitted the compilation of a land register for the country's entire arable area. The pattern of regional specialisation now includes cotton in the central coastal districts of Durrës, Fier and Lushnjë, sugar beet in the Korcë Basin and the reclaimed Lake Maliq area, and vegetables in districts surrounding the main urban centres of Tiranë, Durrës, Shkodër and Vlorë. Lastly, irrigation and land reclamation has allowed the range of crops to be extended over large areas of the cultivated land. Between 1969 and 1973 the Institute for the Study and Design of Land Improvement undertook a national enquiry into potential irrigation schemes as a blueprint for future developments, and by 1980 366,000 hectares were under irrigation, representing fifty-three percent of the cultivated land, and ninety percent of the plains. Sprinkler irrigation had also been applied to a further 70,000 hectares. Furthermore, 48,530 hectares of new land were brought into agricultural use, and 186,376 hectares were improved between 1946 and 1978 (Nuri 1982). Some of this was in the former marshes of the coastal lowlands, but after they were drained the greatest reserves of reclaimable land were in the uplands. With this in

mind, the Fourth Five Year Plan was marked by the slogan
> 'Let us take to the mountains and the hills and make them as beautiful and as fertile as the plains',

and young people and farm workers were mobilised to terrace slopes and plant fruit trees on them. However, since the mid-1970s the potential for further expansion of the cultivable land has diminished, despite the fact that the area under crops in the early 1980s only accounted for forty-two percent of the country, and emphasis has been placed increasingly upon more intensive land use and higher yields.

SETTLEMENT AND ENVIRONMENTAL PLANNING

Just as Albania has had to struggle with the effects of centuries of neglect of its economy under Turkish rule, so it has also been faced by a settlement system characterised by few facilities, poor construction, and inadequate sanitation and hygiene. Indeed, because there had been very little economic development before 1939 little urban development had occurred either. Three decades of independence before 1944 led to some suburban development along European lines to serve a small administrative and middle class, and central Tiranë had been laid out under Italian influence as a modern capital, but wartime devastation and impoverishment had checked these improvements. Even today Albania has by far the least urbanised population in Eastern Europe, and is distinctive in having a rural population which is still increasing in absolute, if not in relative, terms (Table 3.1). This is due in part to high birth rates, but it is also the result of a deliberate emphasis upon rural development, and reflects the high degree of control over migration and the direction of labour to rural areas in the 1960s and 1970s by the government. Nevertheless, during the industrialisation of 1951 to 1955, the country's urban population increased by fifty-two percent, and eighty percent of that increase was attributable to in-migration (Geco 1970), although since then it has been a less important contributor to urban growth than natural increase (Geco 1973).

Four, not necessarily compatible, goals appear to have motivated Albanian settlement policy since the war. There has been an attempt to reduce

Table 3.1: Urban Population Growth in Albania

Town	Urban Population (thousands)			Urban Population Growth (percent)	
	1938	1960	1979	1938-1960	1960-1979
Tiranë	25.1	136.3	190.2	443	40
Durrës	10.5	39.9	65.9	281	65
Shkodër	25.3	43.3	64.7	71	49
Elbasan	12.7	29.8	61.1	135	105
Vlorë	9.9	41.4	46.4	418	36
Korcë	21.2	39.4	52.6	86	34
Berat	9.6	18.7	33.3	95	78
Fier	1.4	14.4	32.4	929	125
Lushnjë	4	12.5	22	213	76
Kavaje	7.3	14.2	20.9	95	47
Gjirokastër	8.8	14.1	19.4	60	33
Qytet Stalin	-	10.3	17.2	-	67
Total Urban	160	502.5	881.8[1]	214	76
Total Rural	880.4	1123.9	1681.6[1]	28	50
Total	1040.4	1626.3	2563.4[1]	56	58

1 1978

Sources: Anon (1980), pp. 3-5; Drejtoria e Përgjitheshme e Statistikës (1974), pp. 22, 30; Mason et al. (1945), pp. 265-303.

socio-economic differentials, and especially those between urban and rural areas, agricultural and industrial workers, manual and non-manual labour, the north and the south of the country, and between the Albanian majority and the ethnic minorities; and this has been achieved in large part by the creation of new industrial towns in formerly rural areas. Secondly, the provision of guaranteed living standards and facilities has been seen to be an important socialist ideal. Thirdly, there has been a concern to preserve the country's agricultural land; and lastly, a desire to protect its architectural and archaeological monuments.

Although official sources vary as to the number of new towns which have been established since the war (Anon 1982, p.497 says thirty-two, Vejziu 1982, p.20 suggests 'about forty', and the author has only been able to locate the twenty-four which are shown in Figure 3.2 from Anon 1971, 1974 and 1981a, Mosko 1984, p.26, and Ostreni 1974, p.102), and some are very small, a large number have been set up, providing planned residential and service facilities for workers and their families in association with a variety of types of economic development. Some, such as Bulqizë (chromite), Prrenjas (haematite), Memaliaj and Valias (lignite), are mineral extraction centres, often located in remote areas. Others, such as Kurbnesh, Kukës and Rubik (copper), and Ballsh, Cërrik and Patos (petroleum), are mineral processing centres. New, heavy manufacturing plants in previously sparsely populated locations, such as Fushë-Krujë (cement), and Laç (chemical fertilisers), have given rise to new urban settlements. New food processing industries at Maliq (two sugar beet refineries) and Corovodë (food and drink) have led to the growth of others; and, 'pioneer' state farms, carved from virgin land, at Ksamil and Lukovë (both characterised by terraced citrus groves), relocated settlements adjacent to areas drowned by the HEP schemes at Kukës and Bajram Curri, administrative centres for remote districts, such as Bajram Curri, Burrel, Ersekë, Pukë and Rreshen, and the agricultural college for the wheat producing area at Kamzë, have been other examples. The growth of the largest new towns is shown in Table 3.1. Ballsh, for example, was planned to increase its population tenfold between 1970 and 1985 as a result of the construction and operation of the country's most advanced oil refinery there, and over the same period, Bajram Curri was to have trebled its

Albania

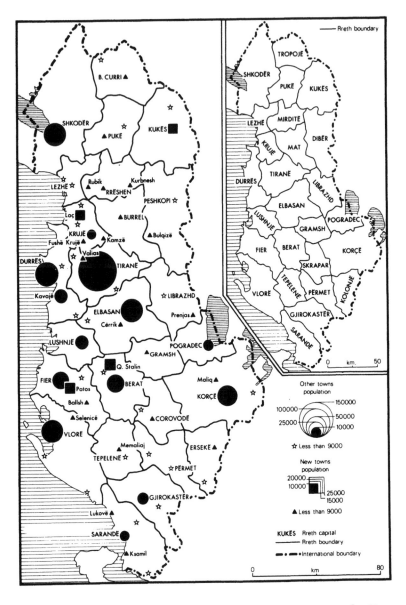

Figure 3.2 Administrative Districts, Towns and New Towns in Albania

population (Anon 1972a). Thus, the urban network has become increasingly dense, and urban facilities have been brought closer to the rural population.

What is more, each town, both new and old, now has its own structure plan. For example, the plan for Vlorë city, published in 1972, covered a period of up to twenty-five years and envisaged a doubling of the city's population to 120,000 by the end of the century. Both a major expansion of the urban area and a comprehensive redevelopment of the city's central area were planned, the latter encompassing a new city hall, palace of culture, theatre, tourist hotel and market place, interspersed with pools, fountains and greenery. New residential districts were to incorporate public gardens, schools, kindergartens and creches, shops and playgrounds (Anon 1972a).

However, urban expansion has often been at the expense of agriculture. In the early 1970s the then Prime Minister, Shehu, pointed to the country's limited arable area and extremely rugged relief in an uncharacteristically critical public assessment of land use management and declared that the Party, state and economic organs had been very "negligent and careless". At a time when great efforts were being put into opening up new agricultural land, often under very difficult conditions, he stated that the misuse of the existing land was impermissible, and noted with particular concern the loss of 5,000 hectares of the most fertile arable land to various construction projects. Shehu emphasised that land-use planning controls had not been sufficient, either in their theoretical basis or in their implementation, and in one of the most explicit urban physical planning directives ever to be voiced by an Albanian leader he argued that all new urban buildings should be of several storeys, and implied that existing single or two-storey dwellings and institutions should be replaced (Shehu 1976).

There have also been implicit contradictions between economic and urban growth, on the one hand, and the desire to preserve the country's architectural and archaeological heritage, on the other. For example, mediaeval castles dominate the skyline at Berat, Gjirokastër, Krujë and a dozen other places (Figure 3.1), two of which are highly important symbols of Albanian identity. Krujë is the fortress city of the national hero, Skënderbeg, who kept the invading Turks at bay there for twenty-five years (Adhami and Zheku 1981; Riza

1975), while Gjirokastër is the birthplace of the Albanian leader, Enver Hoxha, whose personality cult was tailored in many respects to fit the Skënderbeg image, and thus to imply a direct line between one 'great patriotic leader' and another. Berat, Durrës, Gjirokastër and Krujë have been designated as 'museum cities' on account of their rich architectural and archaeolgical heritage (Karaiskaj and Bace 1975; Toci 1971), and are focal points on the prescribed itineraries of foreign tourists (Hall 1984b, 1984c; Hall and Howlett 1976). In Gjirokastër, which gained 'museum city' status in 1961 by 'special decision' of Albania's Council of Ministers, all buildings and activities within a prescribed area were put under the protection of the state. Furthermore, the conservation of existing buildings and controls over new development were strengthened in 1965 when the Institute of Monuments of Culture was established specifically to preserve and restore buildings in such areas, and these powers were extended in 1972 when specific spatial guidelines were established (Anon 1972b, 1972c, 1973b, 1977b, Papa 1972). Following this, three zones were recognised in Gjirokastër – a 'museum zone' of the highest merit within the historic centre, which was to be restored and enhanced, a second 'protected zone' of less merit, though still important, which was to be protected from new development, and, outside these, the remaining built-up area, made up largely of post-war residential and industrial growth below the historic city on its hill, which was declared a 'free zone' for new, but planned development (Anon 1973a, Riza 1971, 1978, 1981).

In addition to these conservation measures there has also been much debate about the wider issues of environmental protection in a developing economy. Article 20 of the 1976 Constitution blandly states that

"Protection of the land, natural riches, waters and the atmosphere from damage and pollution is a duty of the state, of the economic and social organisations, and of all citizens" (Anon 1977a, p.14),

and a number of the Party's policies, derived from Albania's particular circumstances, will indeed probably enhance the country's environmental quality. For instance, attractive terraces of orchards and olive groves and reclamation works have noticeably improved many of the previously eroded or waterlogged and malarial marginal environments.

However, extensive collectivised agriculture, increasing inputs of chemical fertilisers – currently at about 145 kilogrammes per hectare (BBC 1984b) – and pollution from the new industries have doubtless destroyed many native habitats and ecosystems. Secondly, because it perceives itself to be set apart ideologically and to lack hard currency, the Albanian leadership has exhorted the populace to wage war against waste and to reuse and recycle materials. This is made easier by low consumer spending and the absence of such waste as disposable packaging, and particularly by the absence of private car ownership. Photographs suggest that even in Tiranë there are fewer motor cars now than in the 1930s (von Luckwald 1942, p.49; Matthews 1937, p.24); it is possible to stand in the middle of Skenderbeg Square untroubled by traffic; and, on leaving Albania by road, the sight of Yugoslavian scrap yards full of rotting cars provides early culture shock.

Official interest in the need for environmental protection is reflected in a Central Commission for the Protection of the Environment which exists at the level of the Council of Ministers. Such commissions have been set up in every ministry and central institution and in the executive committees of the people's councils in the twenty-six districts or rrethi, and groups have been established at every enterprise, agricultural cooperative and institution in the country for the protection of the environment. No industrial project or major construction is supposed to be built without a prior environmental impact study, which is supposed to consider the distance of industrial projects from residential areas, the methods of transporting and disposing of industrial wastes, steam and dust, the protection of water and vegetation, the nature of the raw materials to be used and the technological processes to be applied (BBC 1983a). However, there are almost no data as yet to assess the effectiveness of these initiatives, and so one can only ponder such statements as

"...the development of industry in general, and in particular of the heavy extracting and processing industry...have not affected the cleanness of the environment, of the water, air and soil. This was possible because the industry was correctly distributed geographically...and especially because the necessary measures for the protection of environment and the health of the working

people were always taken in time" (Banja and
Toci 1979, p.157),

and

"If an enterprise or institution does not carry
out carefully the measures for the protection
of the environment, but allows its pollution,
then besides the special organism (sic) charged
with the control of this problem, the
collective of the enterprise itself or of the
institution, public opinion and the workers'
and peasants' control groups act immediately:
they demand the reestablishment of the normal
situation and put under moral and legal
responsibility those responsible for neglect or
carelessness" (Banja and Toci 1979, p.160).

SOCIAL PLANNING

In addition to concern over the spatial and
environmental effects of industrial, agricultural
and urban development, attention has also been given
since the war to the contrasts in the standard of
living between different parts of the country –
attention which has manifested itself in adjustments
in the levels of pay, and perhaps in the provision
of housing, but has not yet eradicated demographic
contrasts. In particular, concern has been
expressed about the relatively low standards of
living of those in the rural and upland areas, and a
wide variety of measures has been adopted in the
attempt to redress this imbalance with considerable
success (Tables 3.2 and 3.3).

Some of the most important measures have
concerned variations in earnings. Up to the
mid-1960s Albanian pay scales were similar to those
in the rest of socialist Eastern Europe, but a
shortage of suitably qualified experts led to the
emergence of income differentials aimed at
encouraging the attainment of better qualifications,
and physically difficult jobs were also rewarded
with higher pay. As a result, income differentials
of up to 4:1 were thought to have occurred within
individual sectors (Schnytzer 1983, p.113), and
significant differences between sectors saw workers
in the highest paid sector, transport, receive an
average of seventy-one percent more than those in
the lowest paid sector – food (Lika 1964). Attempts
at income equalisation began in 1967 and, at a time
when the minimum salary was about 500 leks per
month, all salaries above 1200 were reduced, though

Table 3.2: Spatial Equalisation Policies in Albania

'Pro-rural'	'Pro-upland'
1. 'Socialising' household work to ease the burden of women and raise living standards: establishment and extension of bakeries, creches, kindergarten, dining halls, public baths, launderies, clinics and maternity homes.	1. Each cooperative is allotted blocks of orchards, olive groves or vineyards with fifty percent state coverage of development costs.
2. Compulsory eight-year school.	2. Encouragement of auxilliary activities: production of building materials, food processing, handicrafts.
3. Extension of part-time education.	3. Rustication of urban workers and youths.
4. Electrification, enabling increased mechanisation of farmwork and higher productivity.	4. Mutual help between upland and lowland cooperatives.
5. Rustication of urban workers and youth in mass campaigns for harvesting and construction projects	5. State support for irrigation projects.
6. Raising cooperativists' pensions.	6. Reduction of between nine and fifteen percent in the price of nitrogenous fertilisers.
7. Improved housing: more than half the peasants live in housing built since the start of collectivisation.	7. Defraying of storage and transport costs of MTSs for cooperatives.
8. Cooperativists' voluntary contributions to construction and the securing of materials.	8. Exemption from paying interest on state loans.

this was 'compensated' for by the abolition of all forms of income tax. However, 'supplementary' payments were still significant in making up wage packets, and all the official claims that the ratio

Albania

Table 3.3: The Changing Distribution of Health and Education Facilities in Albania

	1938 Total	1938 Rural (percent)	1969–70 Total	1969–70 Rural (percent)	1983 Total	1983 Rural (percent)
All Medical Institutions	10	0	238	55	3,500[1]	85
Medical Beds	820	0	13,750	9	17,000[1]	–
Beds per 1000 Population	1	0	7	–		
Population per Doctor	8,527	–	1,181	51	583[1]	
Kindergarten	23	0	748	86	2,541[1]	
Primary Schools	643	82	1,374	80	1,539[1]	
Eight-grade Schools	0	0	1,115	7		
Secondary/Technical Schools	11	0	115		265[1]	

1 1978/9

Note: While all the above data come from Albanian sources, significant discrepancies appeared during their compilation.

Sources: Anon. (1979), pp. 23–24; BBC (1984e); Drejtoria e Përgjitheshme e Statistikës (1974), pp. 205, 223; Klosi (1969), pp. 53–55; Selala (1982), p. 24.

between the highest and the lowest pay scales ranged from 1:2.5 to 1:3 seem to be more than a little unrealistic.

Income equalisation was pursued further during the 1970s with particular regard to the inequalities which existed between rural and urban and lowland and upland areas. Firstly, between 1971 and 1975, while national average per capita real income increased by 14.5 percent, that for rural workers rose by 20.5; and this was followed in 1976 by further changes in favour of rural areas and to the disadvantage of the towns. All salaries above 900 leks were reduced by between four and twenty-five percent, those of teachers and scientists by fourteen to twenty-two percent, bonuses for scientific titles, degrees and publications by up to a half, and other bonuses and payments were abolished. On the other hand, wages of state farm workers were raised, though they were linked to plan fulfillment; all specialists were to be paid according to their field of specialisation and not in relation to the district or institution in which they worked; and certain unspecified 'disproportions' in wages in fishing and maritime transport were to be adjusted. The consequences of these measures were a reduction in the ratio between the average pay of urban and state farm employees, on the one hand, and that of a ministry director, on the other, from 1:2.5 to 1:2 (a figure often subsequently wrongly quoted as representing the whole range of Albanian incomes - see Bollano 1984), and there has also been a faster rise in rural incomes than urban. Between 1960 and 1970 rural incomes rose by 140 percent in relation to those of the urban population, and during the 1970s the rate of increase was three times greater.

There has also been very considerable intervention in the Albanian housing market by the state. Upto 1979 about 300,000 urban and rural flats, comprising two rooms and a kitchen, had been built (Anon 1982, p.312), and new dwellings constructed between 1944 and 1984 accommodate about three quarters of the population (Mosko 1984). The state builds flats in urban areas both through its own organisations and through voluntary labour - the latter method having developed since 1968 when a pioneer programme was inaugurated in Tiranë during the country's 'cultural revolution' - and the state owns all flats in urban areas and those associated with state farms. Under the 1981-1985 Plan 50,000 new dwellings were to be provided within this sector

of the housing market, and 10,500 were said to have
been constructed during 1983 (Mihali 1984). On the
other hand, the cooperative peasantry appear to be
responsible for the bulk of rural housing, which is
not collectivised, and 31,000 dwellings were to be
built in this sector between 1981 and 1985 (BBC
1983b). Biber (1980, p.551) reports a shortage of
flats, particularly for newly-married couples; and,
if this is so, the rising marriage rate of 6.8 per
thousand in 1970, 8.1 in 1980 and 8.9 in 1982
(Skenderi and Vejsiu 1984, pp.34-5) threatens to
create a major problem in the future, though it is
not clear whether this will affect the rural or the
urban areas more acutely.

These rates reflect the very rapid population
increase in Albania of 2.2 percent each year, which
suggests that the population will reach 4,000,000 by
the year 2000. In the early 1980s the rural
population was increasing by 32,000 each year, and
that in the towns by 22,000 (Skenderi and Vejsiu
1984, pp.33-35). The relatively high level of
natural increase reflects in part the Islamic and
Roman Catholic backgrounds of the Albanian people,
but it is also a consequence of the almost total
absence of availability and discussion of birth
control, at least in public, which in turn reflects
the state's requirement for military strength and
for a population which is filled with youthful
revolutionary fervour. Some thirty-seven percent of
the population is under fifteen years of age, the
current average age is only twenty-five, and sixty
percent of those alive in the early 1980s had been
born into and educated within the framework of
Albanian socialism (BBC 1984a). Furthermore, it
should be noted that birth and death rates take on a
greater demographic significance because
international migration is almost totally absent.
However, there are regional variations in the level
of natural increase which, in such a small country,
reflect a picture of diversity which the authorities
would prefer not to be quite so marked (Figure 3.3).
Although detailed demographic data are only
available up to 1973 Figure 3.3 reveals that between
1960 and that year there were significant
differences in the population growth rates between
the northern and southern upland areas. Borchert
(1975, p.179) suggests that the high birth rates in
the northern alps between 1965 and 1971, compared to
the relative low rates in the poorer southern
mountains, are partly the result of religious
differences, for the north has traditionally been

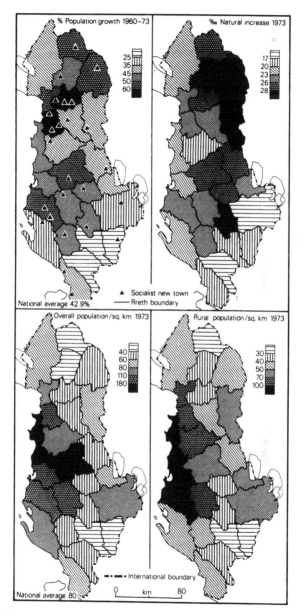

Figure 3.3 Demographic Patterns in Albania

strongly Roman Catholic, whereas the south was Orthodox. (It is assumed that the official abolition of religion in 1967 would have had little effect on relative birth rates in the short term.) However, the map of population growth between 1960 and 1973 also shows that the two districts which had by far the highest growth rates - Krujë and Mirditë - were the only two to contain three major new towns each, the development of which would have contributed significantly to population growth through in-migration and later by natural increase. Only one or two new towns were established, in contrast, in the southern districts before the mid-1970s.

CONCLUSION

Looking back over the post-war period at the development of the Albanian economy it would appear that, having set their hands to the plough of Marxist development - at least as they have perceived it - Albania's leaders have not looked back in spite of the interruptions which have occurred as a consequence of their changing foreign alliances. In this connection, it should be noted that, almost throughout this period, one leader - Enver Hoxha - has enjoyed as tight a control as any in Eastern Europe, and every effort was made after his death in 1985 to emphasise that his policies would continue. However, internal disagreements at the highest level may not have been unknown even during the Hoxha era, and there is some evidence that they may have played a part in the strange circumstances of premier Shehu's death in 1981. (He was officially announced to have committed suicide - one of the worst indignities which can befall an Albanian - was subsequently villified as a 'multi-agent' and traitor, despite having been Hoxha's closest friend for almost forty years, had his name removed from the 'Mehmet Shehu' iron works and other institutions and, as the author noted on a visit in 1982, even from Tiranë's man-hole covers.) Thus, the future path of Albania's economic and political development remains in some doubt. As in the Soviet Union after Stalin, and in China after Mao, the removal of a resolute leader may also precede major changes in Tiranë's corridors of power.

REFERENCES

Adhami, S. and Zheku, K. (1981), Kruja dhe Monumentet e Saj, 8 Nëntori, Tiranë.

Anon (1971), Atlas Gjeografik i Shqiperise, Hamid Shijaku, Tiranë.

Anon (1972a), City Planning and Civic Beauty, New Albania 26, 12-13.

Anon (1972b), Ligji i Ri : Mbi Mbrojtjen e Monumenteve Kulturale e Historike dhe Pasurive Natyrale të Rralla, Monumentet, 3, 223-224.

Anon (1972c), Rregullore për Mbrojtjen e Monumenteve Kultural dhe Historike, Monumentet, 3, 225-228.

Anon (1973a), Rregullore mbi Mbrojtjen, Restaurimin dhe Administrimin e Qytetitmuze të Gjirokastrës, Monumentet, 5-6, 211-217.

Anon (1973b), Rregullore per Mbrojtjen dhe Restaurimin e Ansambleve dhe Ndërtimeve të Tjeva me Vlerë Historike to Qytetit to Korcës, Monumentet, 5-6, 219-222.

Anon (1974), Atlas për Shkollat Fillore, Hamid Shijaku, Tiranë.

Anon (1977a), Constitution of the People's Socialist Republic of Albania, 8 Nentori, Tiranë.

Anon (1977b), Rregullore 'mbi Mbrojtjen dhe Restaurimin e Qendrës Historike të Qytetit Elbasanit, Monumentet, 13, 160-162.

Anon (1979), 35 Years of Socialist Albania, 8 Nëntori, Tiranë.

Anon(1980), Albanian Statistics : a Translation of Statistics Given in 35 Vjet Shqipëri Socialiste, Albanian Society, Ilford.

Anon (1981a), Republika Popullore Socialiste e Shqiperise: Harta Fiziko Politike, 1:800,000, Hamid Shijaku, Tirane.

Anon (1981b), Sesoni i IV Shkencor i Institutit të Monumenteve të Kulturës, Monumentet, 22, 142-146, 150-155.

Anon (1982), Portrait of Albania, 8 Nëntori, Tiranë. (1984), The Radical Transformation of the Albanian Countryside, New Albania, 4, 2-7.

Baci, I. (1981), Agriculture in the PSR of Albania, 8 Nëntori, Tiranë.

Banja, H. and Toci, V. (1979), Socialist Albania on the Road to Industrialization, 8 Nëntori, Tiranë.

BBC, (1982), Summary of World Broadcasts, 12 July.

BBC (1983a), Summary of World Broadcasts, 18 August.

Albania

BBC (1983b), Summary of World Broadcasts, 1 December.

BBC (1984a), Summary of World Broadcasts, 25 October.

BBC (1984b), Summary of World Broadcasts, 1 November.

BBC (1984c), Summary of World Broadcasts, 22 November.

Besemeres, J. (1980), Socialist Population Politics, M.E.Sharpe, White Plains.

Biber, M. (1980), Albania, Alone Against the World, National Geographic Magazine, 158, 530-557.

Bollano, P. (1984), The Limitation of Wage Differentials, Albanian Life, 29, 21.

Borchert, J.G. (1975), Economic Development and the Population of Albania, Geoforum, 6, 177-186.

Cuedari, A. (1983), The Development of the Power Industry in the PSR of Albania, Albania Today, 68, 6-10.

Dede, S. (ed.) (1983), The Earthquake of April 15, 1979 and the Elimination of its Consequences, 8 Nëntori, Tiranë.

Drejtoria e Përgjitheshme e Statistikës (1974), 30 Viet Shqiperi Socialiste, DPS, Tiranë.

Freedman, R.O. (1970), Economic Warfare in the Communist Bloc, Praeger, New York.

Geco, P. (1970), L'accroisement de la Population Urbaine de la R.P. d'Albanie et sa Repartition Géographique, Studia Albanica, 2, 161-182.

Geco, P. (1973), Rendesia e Qyteteve të Mëdha në Popullsinë Qytetare të R.P. Shqipërisë, Studime Historike, 1, 53-71.

Griffiths, W.E. (1962), Albania and the Sino-Soviet Rift, M.I.T. Press, Cambridge, Mass.

Gurney, J. (1978), Energy needs in the Balkans: a source of conflict or co-operation?, The World Today, 34, 44-51.

Hall, D.R. (1975), Some Developmental Aspects of Albania's Fifth 5-Year Plan 1971-5, Geography, 60, 129-132.

Hall, D.R. (1981), A geographical Approach to Propaganda, in Political Studies from Spatial Perspectives, ed. A.D.Burnett and P.J.Taylor, Wiley, Chichester, pp.313-330.

Hall, D.R. (1984a), Albania's Growing Railway Network, Geography, 69, 263-265.

Hall, D.R. (1984b), Foreign Tourism Under Socialism : the Albanian 'Stalinist' Model, Annals of Tourism Res., 11, 539-551.

Hall, D.R. (1984c), Tourism and Social Change: the Relevance of the Albanian Experience, Annals of Tourism Res., 11, 610-612.

Hall, D.R. (1985), Problems and Possibilities of an Albanian-Yugoslav Rail Link, in Soviet and East European Transport Problems, ed. L.Symons et al, Croom Helm, London.

Hall, D.R. and Howlett, A. (1976), Neither East Nor West, Geographical Magazine, 48, 194-196.

Hamm, H. (1963), Albania = China's Beachhead in Europe, Weidenfeld and Nicolson, London.

Karaiskaj, G. and Bace, A. (1975), Kalaja e Durrësit dhe Sistemi i Fortifikimit Përreth në Kohën e Vonë Antike, Monumentet, 9, 5-33.

Kaser, M. (1979), Albania's Self-chosen Predicament, The World Today, 35, 259-268.

Klosi, M. (1969), 25 years of Construction Work in Socialist Albania, Naim Frashëri, Tiranë.

Kosinski, L.A. (ed.) (1977), Demographic Development: in Eastern Europe, Praeger, New York.

Kostanick, H.L. (1977), Characteristics and Trends in Southeastern Europe, in Population and Migration Trends in Eastern Europe, ed. H.L.Kostanick, Westview, Boulder, Colorado, pp. 11-22.

Kromidha, T. and Konduri, P. (1984), Achievements and Development of Transport, Albania Today, 78, 33-35.

Lika, Z (1964), Disa Cështje mbi Përmirësimin e Mëtejshëm të Planifikimit...., Naim Frashëri, Tiranë.

Logoreci, A. (1961), Albania : a Chinese Satellite in the Making, The World Today, 17, 197-205.

Luckwald, G.E. Von (1942), Albanien : Land Zwischen Gestern und Morgan, F. Bruckmann Verlag, Munich.

Madhi, R. (1982), The Process of Strengthening the Socialist Psychology of Property and Work, Albania Today, 63, 25-33.

Marmullaku, R. (1975), Albania and the Albanians, C. Hurst, London.

Mason, K. et al. (1945), Albania, Naval Intelligence Division, London.

Matthews, R. (1937), Sons of the Eagle, Methuen, London.

McIntyre, R.J. (1975), Pronatalist Programmes in Eastern Europe, Soviet Studies, 27, 366-380.

Mihali, Q. (1984), The Albanian Economy 1983-84, Albanian Life, 29, 34-37.

Mosko, S. (1984), Town-planning in the Service of the People, Albania Today, 77, 24-26.

Nuri, F. (1982), Achievements in Land Reclamation and Irrigation, Albania Today, 66, 43-45.

Ostreni, A. (1974), Geografia e Shqiperise, Shtepia Botuese e Librit Shkollor, Tirane, 4th. ed.

Paloka, A. (1981), Development of the Power Industry in PSR of Albania, Albania Today, 56, 32-36.

Pano, N.C. (1974), The Albanian Cultural Revolution, Problems of Communism, 23, 44-57,

Pano, N.C. (1982), Albania : the Last Bastion of Stalinism, in East Central Europe, ed. M.M.Drachkovitch, Hoover Institution Press, Stanford, California, pp.187-218.

Papa, M. (1972), Mbrojtja Ligjore e Pasurive Kulturale të Vendit Tonë, Monumentet, 3, 139-145.

Popovic, V. and Milic, B. (1981), Montenegro After the Catastrophic Earthquake, Yugoslav Survey, 22, 27-48.

Prifti, P.R. (1968), Albania's Cultural Revolution, M.I.T. Centre for International Studies, Cambridge, Mass.

Prifti, P.R. (1975), Albania - Towards an Atheist Society, in Religion and Atheism in the USSR and Eastern Europe, ed. B.R.Bociurkiw and J.W.Strong, Macmillan, London, pp.388-404.

Prifti, P.R. (1978), Socialist Albania Since 1944: Domestic and Foreign Developments, M.I.T. Press, Cambridge, Mass.

Prifti, P.R. (1979), Albania, in The Communist States in the Era of Detente 1971-1977, ed. A. Bromke and D. Novak, Mosaic Press, Ontario, pp 189-210.

Prybyla, J.S. (1967), Albania's Economic Vassalage, East Europe, 1, 9-14.

Qerimi, V. (1981), Chronicle of Another Battle Won, 8 Nëntori, Tiranë.

Riza, E. (1971), Banesa e Fortifikuar Gjirokastrite, Monumentet, 1, 127-148.

Riza, E. (1975), Studim për Restaurimin e Një Banese me Cardak në Qytetin e Kruja, Monumentet, 9, 107-125

Riza, E. (1978), Gjirokastra : Museum City, 8 Nëntori, Tiranë.

Riza, E. (1981), Banesa Popullore në Qytetin-Muze të Beratit, Monumentet, 21, 5-35.

Schnytzer, A. (1983), Stalinist Economic Strategy in Practice : the Case of Albania, Oxford University Press, London.

Selala, P. (1982), Well-being and its Continuous Uplift in the PRSA, *Albania Today*, 63, 24.

Shehu, M. (1976), *Report on the Directives of the 7th Congress of the Party of Labour of Albania for the 6th Five-Year Plan (1976-1980) of Economic and Cultural Development of the People's Republic of Albania*, 8 Nëntori, Tiranë.

Skenderi, K. and Vejsiu, Y. (1984), The Demographic Processes are Inseparable from the Socio-Economic Development, *Albania Today*, 77, 32-35.

Skendi, S. (1962), Albania and tne Sino-Soviet Conflict, *Foreign Affairs*, 40, 471-479.

Smith, M. (1979), The Earthquake in Albania, *Albanian Life*, 15.

Toci, V. (1971), Amfiteatri i Dyrrahit, *Monumentet*, 2, 37-42.

Vejziu, Y. (1982), What Does the Shift in Population Show, *New Albania*, 6, 20-21.

Xhuveli, L. (1984), Albanian Agriculture on the Road of Its Ceaseless Development and Intensification, *Albania Today*, 77, 19-23.

Chapter 4

BULGARIA

Frank W. Carter

> "I love you, O my beloved homeland! I
> love your mountains, forests, and dunes, cliffs
> and crystal cool springs." (Karavelov 1860,
> p.49).
> "The Bulgarian people have been building
> socialism for a little over twenty years, but
> in this historically short period of time your
> country has changed beyond recognition"
> (Brezhnev 1966).

THE CONTEXT OF PLANNING

These two statements, written roughly a hundred
years apart, reflect but two of the many facets of
this east Balkan country. Physically, Bulgaria's
transitional location between the European and
Asiatic land masses has led to great variety in its
climate, hydrology, soils, vegetation and fauna.
Furthermore, it is a land with a turbulent history
and ancient cultures, where Thracians, Illyrians,
proto-Bulgarians and Slavs have all left their mark
upon the landscape, in addition to five hundred
years of Ottoman rule; and where, in more recent
times, new political, economic and social measures,
based on Soviet principles of management, have been
introduced (Rochlin 1957), and the course set which
Brezhnev was to applaud so warmly. Indeed, among
the post-war socialist states of Eastern Europe
Bulgaria has been one of the least affected by the
winds of change and national self-assertiveness
which have touched her neighbours, and has
maintained, and even intensified, her economic and
political ties with the USSR.

In 1945 Bulgaria was a backward country with
limited natural resources, very largely dependent on

67

peasant agriculture for its livelihood, and possessing a weakly developed transport and communication system. But that was to change very rapidly thereafter. During the four years following the Second World War the country underwent profound institutional changes. Political groups other than the communists were excluded from power; Georgi Dimitrov returned from exile in Russia to take control; and a People's Republic was declared in 1946. In 1947 privately-owned industrial companies and the banks were nationalised, a Two Year Preparatory Plan was adopted, and the Soviet Union became Bulgaria's chief trading partner. By the end of 1946 twenty-seven percent of the arable land had been collectivised (Barev 1958, p.21), and the figure rose rapidly thereafter. Heavy industry began to receive most of the available investment, in preference to both agriculture and light manufacturing, and economic development began to proceed very rapidly within a system of central planning.

Central planning has passed through three major stages - from 1945 until the mid-1960's, from then until the late 1970's, and since then upto the present. The earliest was characterised by the Stalinist system, which allowed the economy to operate at a high level of activity for prolonged periods, and resulted in rapid growth, especially in industry, thus increasing demand for industrial labour and triggering a large-scale migration from country to town. Increases in gross industrial output remained consistently above ten percent per annum during the first four Five Year Plans, ending in 1965, and seemed to prove that the Soviet planning model was working well. However, the Ninth Congress of the Bulgarian Communist Party in 1966, at which Brezhnev lauded Bulgaria's success, should be seen as a watershed in the country's planned economic development. Prior to that year the growth of the economy suggested that central planning in a one-party state was at least as effective an engine of development as the market, and perhaps more so (Zwass 1984, p.65). But that success was not maintained; annual plans became less ambitious; and it is now evident that all the major targets in the Seventh Five Year Plan (1976-1980) proved to be unattainable, with the exception of investment.

This slowdown was the result of several factors. Firstly, it became apparent in the late 1960s that the scope for 'extensive' economic growth was declining and that more 'intensive' alternatives

- the need for improved quality, rather than increased quantity - would have to be pursued. Secondly, a failure to carry out effective economic reform meant that increasing reliance had to be placed on imported Western technology. Thirdly, economic recession in the West affected Bulgaria's economic performance; and fourthly, revised pricing formulas led to a slowdown in the growth of her trade with the Soviet Union. Finally, these problems were exacerbated by the reluctance of the Soviet Union to increase its supplies of fuels and certain raw materials, and by Bulgaria's need to look elsewhere for alternatives. Thus, Bulgarian planners were forced to accept lower growth rates for industrial production, investment and domestic consumption (Spetter 1982, Vanous 1982). Nevertheless, the emphasis in investment continued to be on chemicals, machinery and metallurgy (Miloshev 1974); industry absorbed a large part of the investment of the 1981-1985 Five Year Plan; and Bulgaria has sustained one of the highest growth rates of industrial output in Eastern Europe (Smith 1983, p.42). Foremost amongst its industries are machine engineering and metal working (Donchev 1970, Guev 1981), which together account for nearly thirty percent of the total volume of industrial production; and in 1980 industry as a whole contributed more than half of the gross national product, while agriculture and forestry only produced eleven percent of the total.

Nevertheless, the disappointments of the 1970s gave rise to economic reforms in 1979 which included more sophisticated forecasting methods for long-term planning, a more collective form of ownership and increased initiative at the level of the individual enterprise in industry, agriculture and the tertiary sector. Of course, this greater involvement in planning and decision-making by the lower levels of management was aimed at improving, not weakening, central planning, but it is not yet clear to what extent these changes have affected the long-term rate of economic growth.

This chapter will describe the aims, and assess the achievements, of planning in Bulgaria within the economic context which has been sketched above, with particular reference to three matters - regional development, the protection of the environment and settlement planning.

REGIONAL ECONOMIC DEVELOPMENT

Bulgaria's problems after the Second World War were not only those of marked underdevelopment, but also of regional contrasts in the availability of resources and the degree to which they had already been exploited. The agricultural lowlands, some of which are underlain with coal and other minerals, the Black Sea coast and the mountains all offered possibilities for economic development, only a few of which had been taken up before 1939 (Figure 4.1). Moreover, regional specialisation in production was hampered by a weakly developed transport system, and much of the output of the dominant activity in the economy - agriculture - never entered into trade, but was consumed by the peasants.

The problem of underdevelopment was tackled principally through industrialisation. The Bulgarian Communist Party Congress of 1948 resolved that

> "the main economic and political task of the First Five Year Plan is to lay the foundations of socialism in Bulgaria by means of industrialisation and electrification, as well as the establishment of a cooperative farm system and mechanisation of agriculture"

(Bulgaria 1949, p.30). It was also acknowledged that a territorial plan was necessary if the opportunities for development were to be fully exploited, and that, in particular, any plan should meet several regional development criteria. These were that productive forces should be distributed according to the availability of raw materials and the regional pattern of consumption; that plans should create extensive opportunities for the specialisation and integration of industrial growth in each region of the country; that developments should be within easy access of the population and that the labour resources of each region should be fully exploited; that socio-economic inequalities between regions should be erradicated; and that population growth should be promoted in the most suitable locations. In the event, many large industrial projects were begun during the late 1940s and early 1950s, most of which were in the producer-good sector of the economy, in various parts of the country; the country's energy and mineral resources were exploited on a rapidly increasing scale; and a new industrial town was started in the Maritsa valley. However, not only did these early plans prove to be too ambitious, but

70

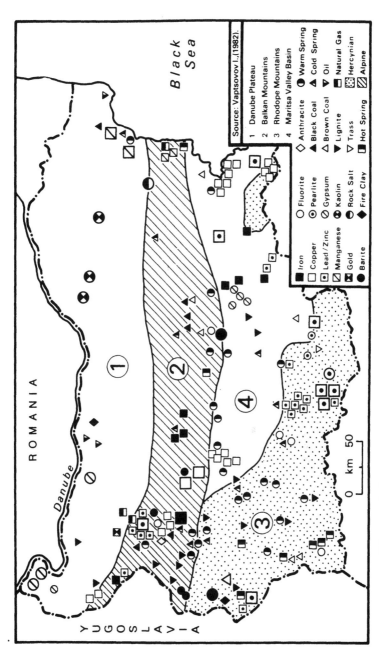

Figure 4.1 Bulgaria's Physical Regions and Mineral Resources

also they were not placed within a regional framework, and, as a result, large parts of the country were still relatively underdeveloped in the late 1950s.

Effective official interest in regional planning probably dates from the territorial reform which was undertaken in 1959, when the country was divided into Economic Regions (Figure 4.2) (Maleshkov 1964). It is not clear what criteria were used to delimit these Regions, but it is of passing interest to note that the new structure bore almost no relation to the many alternatives which Bulgarian economic geographers had been advocating during the 1950s. At first, Regions enjoyed a high degree of autonomy, and People's Councils controlled nearly all industrial plants, farms, construction units and transport facilities within them, as well as the educational, health and social services (Rusinova 1966, p.108). Regional capitals became major administrative centres, the range of services within them was increased, investment was channelled to them, employment grew, and they experienced an influx of population. However, such was the degree of autonomy of the Councils that many invested in similar projects, such as meat packing and dairy product plants, regardless of facilities in neighbouring areas, and so the powers of local government were reduced somewhat during the mid and late 1960s.

Nevertheless, regional clusters of related industries were developed during the 1960s (Khristov 1962 and 1963). For example, three groupings of electricity generating and associated industries were established in the Sofia-Pernik and Plovdiv-Pazardzhik groups of Regions and in Haskovo, while a fourth, which was to be based on imported coal, was planned around Varna (Grull 1961). Most important among the developments were the establishment of coalmining in the Haskovo and Pernik Regions, the building of the Kremikovtsi metallurgical combine, near Sofia, which used local ore and Pernik coal (Buchvarov 1962, Gabensky 1963, p.20; Khristov 1959), and the setting up of non-ferrous metal industries in the Kurdzhali-Plovdiv-Smolyan group of Regions in the south, using lead and zinc ores from the Rhodope Mountains, and in the west around Sofia and Vratsa, producing copper and rare metal derivatives (Krŭstev 1968). Engineering and metal processing, though widely dispersed throughout the country, were also important in the economies of Sofia, Burgas,

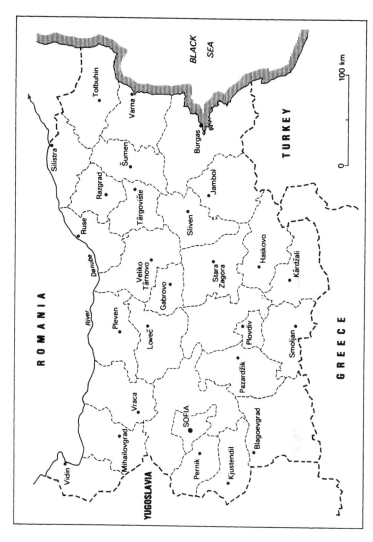

Figure 4.2 The
New Economic
Regions in
Bulgaria, 1959

Plovdiv, Ruse and Varna, and the chemical and rubber
industries were mainly in the Sofia, Haskovo,
Plovdiv, Reka Devnya and Varna Regions.
  Moreover, during the 1960's agriculture and the
food and drink, textile and tourist industries also
showed marked regional patterns of development. For
instance, while the overall scheme for the
distribution of production between Economic Regions
determined the general level of demand for farm
products in each part of the country (Kyurkchiev
1962; Petrov et al.1971), closer attention was paid
to the possibilities for specialisation, and by the
late 1960s specialised agricultural regions had
begun to appear (Cousens 1967). Similarly, while
food and drink production existed throughout the
country, three main groupings could be defined.
That in the south included the towns of Assenovgrad,
Krichim, Pazardzhik, Plovdiv and Purvomai, and
specialized in canning and tobacco manufacture.
That in northern Bulgaria, in Gorna Oryakhovitsa,
Lyaskovets and Turnovo, concentrated on canning,
meat production and sugar refining; and the third,
in the northwest, in Cherven Bryag, Dolna
Mitropoliya and Pleven, became a significant
producer of canned goods, flour, paste products,
poultry, sugar and vegetable oils (Khristov 1964).
Fishing became an important coastal industry (Nowak
1968), while timber production was concentrated in
the Balkan and Rhodope Mountains in the south of the
country. Textile production developed in certain
regions partly as a result of historical accident,
as at Gabrovo, or the presence of local markets, as
at Sofia, Plovdiv and Varna, or in response to local
raw material supplies, as at Sliven and Vratsa
(Straszewicz 1961). Finally, the 1960's saw the
take-off of Bulgarian tourism, not only in the Black
Sea resorts, but also in such historical inland
centres as Sofia and Plovdiv, with their Roman and
later remains, around the Rila Monastery and at the
Borovets winter sports centre in the Rhodope
Mountains (Eperon 1969; Geogiev 1969); and that
growth has continued. The number of foreign
visitors to Bulgaria rose from 8,500 in 1956 to
5,000,000 by 1980, when over a third of them came
from hard currency countries (Anon 1974). Most of
these visitors go only to the Black Sea coast
(Atanasova 1982), but more recently attempts have
been made to extend tourism to some stretches of the
Danube, and the formation of a Danube tourist river
fleet has been suggested (Dakov 1977). Holiday
resorts have also been established recently in the

more mountainous areas of the Stara Planina, Middle and Rhodope Mountains, Vitosha-Osogov and Rila-Pirin, and plans are under discussion for the development of several spas (Dinev 1978a and 1978b).

Thus, many of the country's Regions have experienced significant economic growth since the Second World War in accordance with the policy of promoting the 'balanced' and 'even' development of all parts, but there have also been setbacks, and new problems have emerged. Firstly, it has proved to be difficult to steer development to the more minor settlements. While regional capitals have experienced considerable growth, other towns and the rural areas have been relatively neglected. During the 1960s, when 677 new manufacturing enterprises were established, all Economic Regions benefited, but many of the new enterprises were placed in the regional capitals, while smaller towns received few new jobs (Devedzhiev 1979; Taafe 1974, p.58). Similarly, most health and welfare, equipment maintenance and repair, and cultural activities, and many educational services were only provided in the capitals; and these towns were also often the main reception and dispersal points for agricultural produce.

Secondly, although it was recognised that there was a need to alleviate the overconcentration of industry which had occurred during the 1950s in the largest towns of Sofia, Burgas, Ruse and Varna, it has proved difficult to achieve this. All these towns were identified in 1955 as 'congested cities', as was Pleven in 1956, and restrictions were placed on immigration to them and new industrial development within them (Hoffman and Hatchett 1977). However, their industrial growth was not halted, and they have continued to dominate the map of production (Carter 1973).

Taafe's study of migration in Bulgaria between 1966 and 1970 indicates the extent to which development was concentrated in the chief towns. Eighty-five percent of those who moved in that period either resettled in the same Region (sixty-two percent) - usually in its chief town - or a neighbouring one (twenty-three percent). Only the remaining fifteen percent ventured further, which suggests that each Region was able to offer sufficient alternative employment to that in agriculture to be able to absorb the majority of those wishing to migrate (Dinev 1968). However, the growth rates of the regional centres were significantly greater than those of the next largest town in each Region, and by 1970 all regional centres except Smolyan in the Rhodope Mountains had reached a population of 30,000 (Bulgaria 1973; Taafe 1977). Moreover, it was the Regions containing the largest towns - Sofia, Burgas, Pernik, Pleven, Plovdiv, Ruse, Stara Zagora and Varna - which experienced both the greatest absolute and relative population increases over the decade, despite the government's aim of reducing migration to them. By 1970, these urban centres contained a quarter of the country's total population and nearly half its urban dwellers, and a tenth of the population was living in Sofia alone (Dinev 1965, 1968 and 1969).

Thirdly, regional problems have been threatened by the failure of some sectors of the economy to maintain their progress of the 1960s. For instance, the output of coal reached its peak in the early 1970s, but since then there has been an increasing and substantial need for imports of coal, anthracite and coke from the Soviet Union, and for smaller quantities from Czechoslovakia and Poland, at a time when it was still envisaged that coal would be fundamental to the integrated development of some of the country's Economic Regions. For example, a model of the southeast region (Figure 4.3) shows that the development of the East Maritsa coalfield was to be based upon the linkage of electricity production with the chemical, oil refining and agricultural industries (Popov 1970). However, such a dependence upon a localised raw material source may not be as serious as it might appear for, according to Donchev, technological progress is weakening the links between industries within individual Regions, and in future greater notice will have to be taken of the need for links between industries in all parts of Bulgaria and in other COMECON countries (Donchev 1980; Donchev and Dobrinova 1981; Khristov 1975). For example, the Kremikovtsi Metallurgical Combine near Sofia is dependent on raw material and labour resources from all over the country and abroad (Figures 4.4 and 4.5) (Panayotov 1969).

Fourthly, a more even pattern of economic development among the Regions and a greater degree of linkage between different activities and parts of the country have depended to a considerable degree upon the extension and improvement of the transport system; but, here too, achievements have been limited, perhaps because Bulgarian planners have faced no less than six major tasks since the 1970s. These have been the need for a suitable motorway

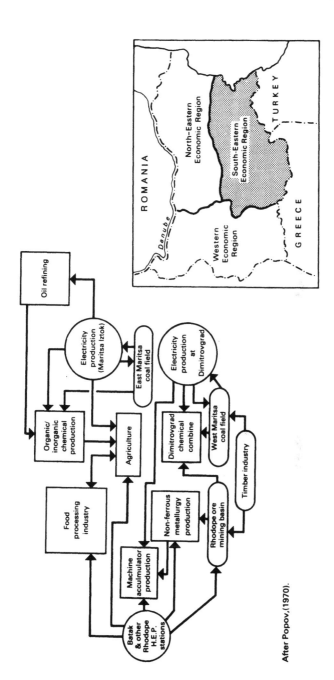

After Popov, (1970).

Figure 4.3 A Planning Model of Bulgaria's South-Eastern Economic Region

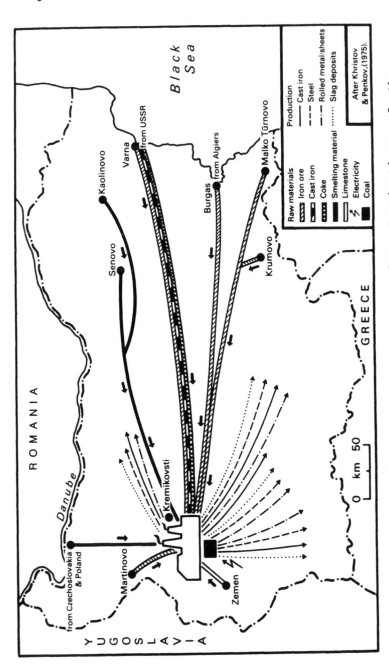

Figure 4.4 Raw Material Sources and Product Destinations of the Kremikovsti Metalurgical Plant in Bulgaria

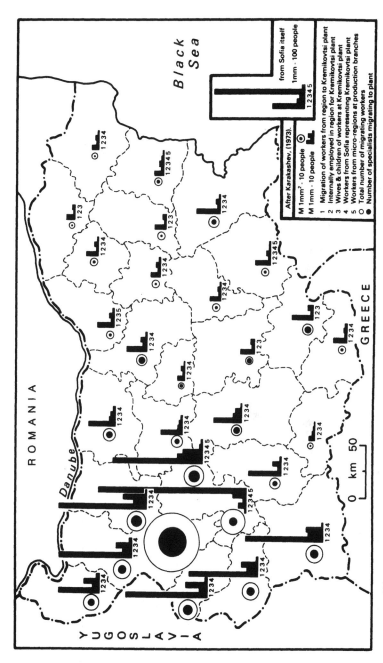

Figure 4.5 Labour Supplies for the Kremikovsti Metalurgical Plant in Bulgaria

system for the whole country, for the intensification of the road network, for new and improved rail links, for improved coordination within the transport system, for better international linkages, for more satisfactory intra-urban and urban-periphery connections, and for improvements in rural services (Mikhaylov 1982).

By the early 1970's the motorway ring linking Sofia with Plovdiv, Burgas, Varna and Pleven was under construction, and the Kalotina-Kapitan Andreevo section of the E-5 European International Highway, which crosses the country from Belgrade to Istanbul, had been thoroughly reconstructed (Figure 4.6) (Anon 1973). Improvements were also made to roads of lesser categories; and relatively high densities of roads now exist in the Regions in the northeast adjacent to the Danube and in the more important industrial areas, such as Gabrovo, Haskovo, Kurdzhali, Smolyan and Turgovishte. Nevertheless, large areas of the country have less than 350 kilometres of roads per thousand square kilometres; Yambol in the southeast has less than 250 kilometres; and in the west only the Pernik and Sofia Regions have more than 350 kilometres. Furthermore, by 1980 only 108 kilometres of the total road network was motorway and 2,352 kilometres highway, while 19,605 kilometres, or sixty percent, still consisted of low quality, third-class routes (Anon 1980; Barbov 1982).

Railway development in the 1970's concentrated upon electrification and on the improvement of links with Sofia and the Black Sea coast resorts. By 1980 1,500 kilometres, or just over a third of all lines, had been electrified (Barbov 1981), and this figure was to be raised to seventy percent by 1985 (Figure 4.7) (Devedzhiev 1981). Much of this electrification has been in the central part of the country, and there has been relatively little in the more southerly, northwestern and northeastern areas. As for improved links, two new main routes were planned for completion by 1985 - a smaller ring linking Sofia, Mezda, Gorno Oryakhovitsa, Dubovo, Karlovo, and so back to Sofia, and a larger ring from Sofia through Gorno Oryakhovitsa, Ruse, Burgas, Stara Zagora, Plovdiv, and so back to Sofia. Even so, much of the network consists of single track lines, and only 535 kilometres, or twelve percent, was double-tracked in 1980 (Barbov 1981).

River and marine transport have also been modernised, and particular attention has been given to the Danube as an international waterway. The

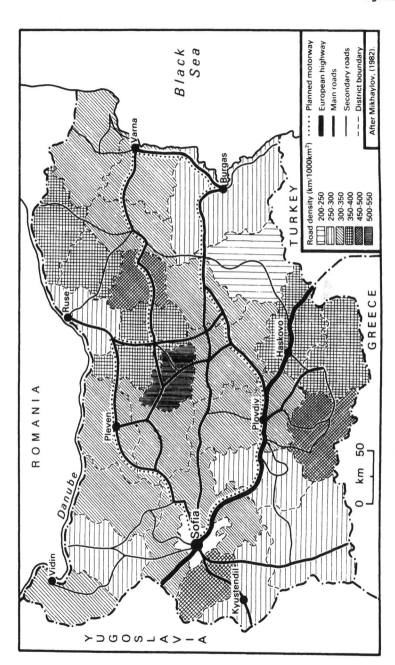

Figure 4.6 Roads in Bulgaria in 1980

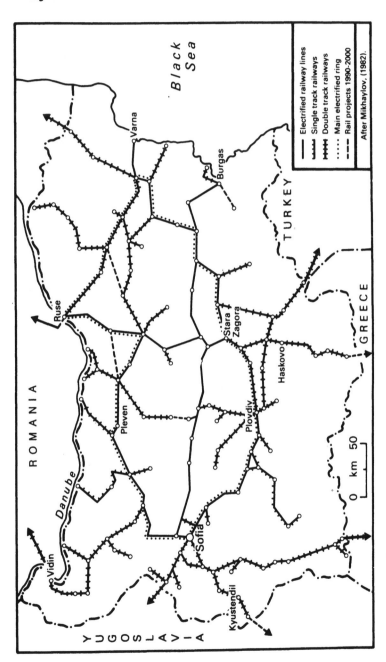

Figure 4.7 Railway Development in Bulgaria between 1955 and 2000

chief ports are Lom, Ruse and Svistov, and tonnages there are expected to increase if there is greater integration of trade between the Soviet Union and its COMECON partners (Carter 1970; Dojkov and Botev 1980). Furthermore, a trunk canal is under construction connecting southern Bulgaria with the Black Sea in order to ease the transportation of agricultural products (Zyapkov and Braykov 1981).

Thus, much has been achieved in the provision of the necessary transport infrastructure to support the ambitious plans for the less developed areas of the country, but there were still many rural areas and towns in the early 1980s with unsatisfactory transport connections.

Fifthly, it should be noted that the full impact of the industrialisation of the 1950s and 60s did not become clear until the period of most rapid economic growth had ended (Kiradzhiev 1975), and that regional problems have emerged which may now not be easy to solve. In particular, by the early 1970s a large part of the urban population was in the early working-age group (Venedikov 1971), and this led to rising birth rates and rapid natural increase in the towns (Kiradzhiev 1983). Conversely, older people had tended to stay in the villages, which since the early 1970s have been showing higher mortality and lower birth rates (Borisov 1983; Dinev 1977). The greatest post-war population decrease has been in the more mountainous areas of west central Bulgaria, the central Stara Planina, and the Strandzha-Sakar region of the southeast; and heavy decreases have also been recorded in the villages of northwest Bulgaria, the central part of the Danube plain and eastern part of the Thracian plain. Increases in village populations have only occurred in the mining region of the eastern Rhodope and in the eastern Stara Planina, which is within commuting distance of the larger towns and industrial centres (Kiradzhiev 1977).

Regional development policies since the early 1970s have tried to remedy these imbalances (Dimitrov 1977); and new industrial investment has been diverted to smaller urban centres, important villages and the less-developed regions of the country in an attempt to utilise local labour supplies more effectively and reduce the demand for new housing. In particular, towns which were not regional capitals received industrial investment during the Sixth Five Year Plan (1971-1975) which was equal to that allocated to the capitals

(Rabotnichesko 1972, Taafe 1973); and the Seventh Plan (1976-1980) assisted the more backward areas by giving high industrial investment to regional capitals ·in the southwest (Blagoevgrad-Kurdzhali) and northeast (Danube-Stara Planina), which both contain areas with substantial Turkish minorities, in an attempt to increase incomes and enable villagers to find employment more easily in local towns (Carter and Žagar 1977; Taafe 1977).

The government's continuing concern about emigration from areas of isolated settlements, limited economic potential and inadequate water and electricity supplies was also demonstrated by a decree in 1982 which aimed to attract younger, skilled people to them. The decree promised improved living conditions and ample employment in agriculture, small business enterprises and forestry. Tertiary services were to be strengthened, the road network improved, and opportunities created for tourism. Moreover, rent-free housing and improved education facilities, free travel to previous areas of residence and free holidays in other Eastern bloc countries were to be provided as incentives to move to these areas (Rabotnichesko 1982; Radio Free Europe 1983). The main emphasis was placed on the Strandzha-Sakar region in the southeast, and some success has been recorded (Rabotnichesko 1983). However, problems remain. A lack of employment opportunities in such areas, a failure to attract skilled people into two of their most important industries - building and agriculture - a shortage of housing, and the psychological barrier between local people and new arrivals are all impeding the efforts of Bulgaria's regional planners to reverse those flows of people from country to town, and from isolated to central areas, which rapid economic development has engendered since the Second World War, and which have led to a fall in the number of young people employed in rural areas from 500,000 in 1972 to half that figure ten years later.

ENVIRONMENTAL PROBLEMS

Problems have also been created by Bulgaria's rapid economic growth in some of the more populous and industrial Regions. Ever since tne beginning of the twentieth century it has been recognised tnat there is a need to protect the natural environment; and some measures were taken between the wars, and some areas preserved. However, this early impetus was lost in the upheavals of the Second World War, and environmental concerns were neglected for much of the post-war period (Carter 1978). Nevertheless, it has become increasingly apparent that large-scale industrial development in many parts of the country has exposed that natural environment which was so celebrated by Karavelov last century to grave dangers.

The government responded to the problem in 1973 by designating seven national parks, eighty-one nature reserves, thirty-nine places of special interest, 885 sightseeing or beauty spots, 712 historic settlements, and several hundred species of protected wild plants and animals; and additions have been made to these lists each year since then (Popov 1976). In 1974 it formed the Council on Environmental Protection and Reproduction, which was charged with the responsibility for combating the country's environmental problems; more than fifty environmental themes, affecting the activities of eighteen ministries and government departments, were included in the Seventh Five Year Plan; People's Councils were given elaborate programmes for environmental protection within each administrative district; the Council of Ministers approved purification schemes for areas containing cement works, thermal generating stations and metallurgical industries; and the budget for purification plants, erosion control, reafforestation and the recultivation of land left derelict by mining and other activities was tripled. In 1976 the government approved plans for the protection of the environmental complexes of the Black Sea coast and the Danube; and in 1977 guidelines were issued which gave specific instructions about the way in which environmental protection was to be achieved. The guidelines required all new industrial and mining projects to take account of the need to protect and improve the environment. They also required the preservation of all areas of outstanding ecological and scientific value, the identification of the best regions for therapeutic purposes, study of the impact of tourism on the Black Sea coast; and they initiated a regular survey of the effects of erosion and dam building on the Danube. The guidelines made obligatory the installation of pollution control machinery and the use of scientifically proven norms and regulations for ensuring a balance between recreational use and the preservation of nature in all future tourist complexes (State Council 1977).

Nor did official interest in the environment cease at the end of the 1970s. During the Eighth Five Year Plan (1981-1985) attention was paid to the possible effects of the growing nuclear power industry (Khristov 1983; Khristov and Dancheva 1983); and there has been discussion about the creation of natural-territorial complexes (P.T.K.), based upon a new delimitation of landscape regions (Figure 4.8) in an attempt to identify the types of risk posed by further economic development to the environment in each part of the country (Daneva 1984; Petrov 1980 and 1981). In that delimitation the country was divided into four landscape regions and twenty-four provinces, sixteen sub-provinces and 127 landscape districts. New nature protection territories (Z.P.T.) have also been designated, and a further four-fold regionalisation of the country has been drawn up in relation to the need for the protection of such areas (Figure 4.9) (Stoilov 1980; Tishkov 1980).

Thus, much has been done by government to protect the Bulgarian environment, but serious problems remain, especially that of pollution. Thermal power stations, metallurgy works and chemical factories – the main polluters – continue as before, and many other industries are also noted for releasing large quantities of hydrocarbons and dust into the atmosphere. Many parts of the country suffer periodically from air pollution (Khristov and Dancheva 1983; Khristov and Stankov 1982). It has been suggested recently that cement, chemical, electricity and metallurgical industries should be placed at least fifteen kilometres away from the Black Sea coast and the Danube River; that no further polluting industries should be located in the Maritsa, Mesta, Struma and Tundzha valleys before the problems which they would create have been fully investigated; and that no large industrial plants should be located at all in narrow valleys such as those in the Stara Planina and Rhodope Mountains. However, experience does not suggest that attempts to keep noxious industries away from areas which would be at risk will necessarily be successful. The chemical works in Dimitrovgrad and Vratsa were initially sited some distance from the built-up area, but by the early 1980's housing had been built to within a thousand metres of them.

The five most polluted areas coincide with the industrial agglomerations of Sofia-Pernik, Plovdiv, Maritsa-Istok, Gabrovo, and the Black Sea coast, of which the Sofia-Pernik agglomeration poses the greatest problem. This is due in part to its valley location and to the frequent temperature inversions in that valley, which prevent pollutants from rising to higher altitudes and escaping (Tishkov 1974). Moreover, prevailing westerly winds carry polluted air from the industrial zone of Sofia-North towards the recently developed residential districts of Hadezhda and Momkova Mahala, whilst easterly and north-easterly winds blow noxious gases and dust from the Kremikovtsi Metallurgical works towards the city centre and its eastern residential areas (Carter 1984). This pollution, and also that of the small Iskar river, resulted in a marked decrease of animal life and vegetation in the Sofia valley upto 1970, but intensive water purification efforts, sanctions against polluters and the establishment of 228 observation sites have reduced pollution levels. Similarly, during the 1970's dust, lead aerosols, and hydrogen sulphide were well above admissible limits around the Kremikovtsi Metallurgical Plant, but stricter pollution control and the installation of filters in most workshops should reduce these dangers to Sofia's one million inhabitants. Lastly, the redistribution of some of the city's industries to the surrounding towns of Elin Pelin, Radomir and Slivnitsa has helped to contain the problem.

The pollution in Pernik, which is another of Bulgaria's major industrial centres, comes chiefly from the large power station there, which uses low calorific but highly polluting lignite, and the cement and metallurgical industries. In 1970 it was the most polluted town in Bulgaria, with the prevailing wind carrying polluted air towards its chief residential areas. However, the allocation of additional capital since then for the purchase of purifying equipment, and especially electronic filters, has reduced emissions to more acceptable levels.

The Plovdiv industrial region, which provided a seventh of Bulgaria's industrial output in 1980, appears to suffer less from air and water pollution than the Sofia-Pernik region, perhaps because of its more open site on the Upper Thracian Plain (Ziapkov 1974). Nevertheless, dangerous emissions have occurred from the non-ferrous metallurgical plant near Plovdiv, the storage battery combine at Pazardzhik and the cellulose and paper factory at Stamboliiski into one of the country's main agricultural regions, but diligent control and modern purification methods have done much to reduce

Bulgaria

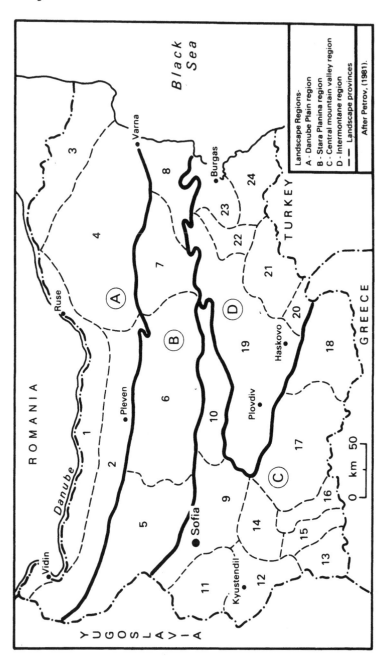

Figure 4.8 The Landscape Regions and Provinces of Bulgaria

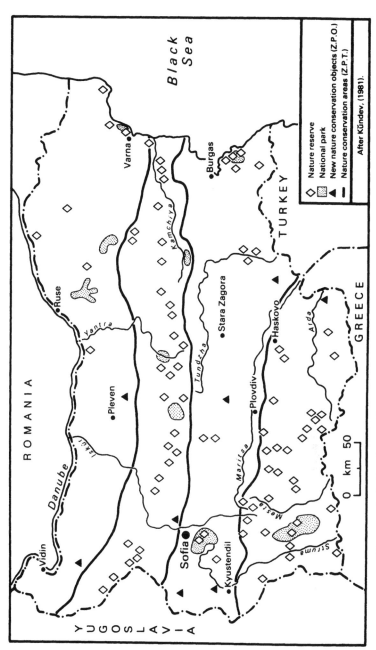

Figure 4.9 Protected Areas of Bulgaria's Natural Environment

the problem.

Less satisfactory conditions exist in the third and most recently established of Bulgaria's industrial agglomerations, Maritsa-Iztok (Khristov and Popov 1976). The agglomeration is based upon large deposits of brown coal, and open-cast mining supplies three power stations. The coal is high in ash, moisture and sulphur, and in spite of tall chimneys and electric filters both air and water pollution in the region are excessive. The agglomeration is sited on fertile chernozem soils, which are rich in humus and are noted for their high quality cereal and industrial crops, but pollution has led to decreases in the output of both crops and livestock products. Moreover, open-cast mining has led to a reduction in groundwater in an area which is dependent on irrigation for much of the year (Markov 1978). Thus, planners face a dilemma over whether to increase industrial output still further in the area, or to give higher priority to farming.

The fourth industrial agglomeration is centred on the towns of Gabrovo, Gorna Oryakhovitsa, Lyaskovets and Veliko Turnovo in the Yantra valley. It is Bulgaria's oldest industrial region, dating back to mid-nineteenth century textile production, but during the post-war period it has also become important for machinery, food, wine and tobacco. Strong winds in the valley quickly disperse any air pollution, but contamination of the river by industrial waste is serious. It is hoped that the construction of biological and chemical purification plants will alleviate this in the near future.

Finally, and perhaps most serious, is the pollution along the Black Sea coast, especially around Burgas and Varna. The coastal zone is an attractive location for industry, with its access to both land and sea transport, and local supplies of coal, copper and manganese ores, natural gas, marble, quartz sand and rock salt (Figure 4.1); and in 1980 it produced a sixth of Bulgaria's industrial output. At present, chemical and engineering industries, oil refining, building-material and furniture production, food-processing and tobacco manufacture occur in and around the main ports of Burgas and Varna, but elsewhere the coast contains important tourist centres; and the juxtaposition of the two poses a severe dilemma over the direction of further development. In general, any new industrial zones should be located at considerable distances from tourist complexes, but this may limit the usefulness of the Varna-Devnya Canal for future economic development. Moreover, stricter protection is required for some of the nature reserves which are close to hotel complexes and which have been subject to trespass and damage by tourists (Carter 1978, p.72).

In short, the desire for economic growth and higher living standards must be restrained if the country's natural environment is to be preserved. Greater thought must be given to the location of industries; protective legislation must be enforced (Mishev 1982; Tishkov 1984); more factories could be moved from city centres to peripheral sites; anti-pollution equipment must be provided in all major industrial enterprises; and all sewage and industrial waste should pass through purification plants. If this is done, some of the more recently created industrial agglomerations, such as those at Burgas and Maritsa Iztok, may yet be saved from greater environmental disasters.

SETTLEMENT PLANNING

Industrial development and the movement of people from country to town have also required the planning of urban expansion on a large scale since the Second World War. New settlements have been established throughout the country as the urban population has grown; the average town population increased from 16,000 in 1946 to 25,000 in 1979; and in 1969 the urban population exceeded the rural for the first time. Seven cities now have more than 100,000 residents (Penkov and Dimitrov 1981). Three stages of urban development may be distinguished since World War Two. The first, from 1944 to the late 1950s, was characterised by rapid population growth, largely within the existing urban network. The second, from the early 1960s to 1975, witnessed continued growth and the creation of new towns; and in the third, from the late 1970s onwards, attempts have been made to integrate town with country and to minimise the differences between urban and village life by bringing all settlements into a more unified system.

The urban planners' greatest challenge has been provided by the exodus from rural areas, resulting from the government's industrialisation policy. During the decade 1965-1975, for instance, the urban population rose by 1,300,000, 700,000 of whom came from rural areas, while the total population of the country increased by only 500,000 (Volle 1979). The

large cities of Sofia, Burgas, Pleven, Ruse, Stara
Zagora and Varna, with more than 100,000 inhabitants
each, have all experienced rapid population growth
as a consequence of both immigration to them and
natural increase, while rural depopulation and
retarded development have been the lot of many
smaller towns (Ganev and Cukova 1980). Yet
everywhere there has been pressure for housing and
new public utilities, and commuting times for the
journey to work have gradually increased (Apostolov
1980 and 1981; Kiradzhiev 1982).

The response of the government was the Country
Planning Act of 1973. This Act laid down the likely
pattern of development until 1990, when the
population was expected to reach 9,400,000. It
divided the country into five regions, each centred
upon a major town. A western region, which would
have 3,000,000 inhabitants, was delimited around
Sofia and two subsidiary centres of Blagoevgrad in
the south and Vratsa in the north. A northern
region, for 1,850,000, was to be formed around
Pleven, Ruse and Velika Turnovo; a central-southern
region, for 2,300,000, was to be created along the
Plovdiv-Stara Zagora axis; the southern littoral of
the Black Sea was to contain 930,000 people around
Burgas; and its northern counterpart was to be
focussed on Varna and have a population of 1,200,000
(Naidenova 1977; Volle 1979, p.118). In 1970 there
were great differences between the levels of
urbanisation in these regions, and the Act called
for a more careful choice of investment projects, in
order to reduce them. It is the intention that this
should be achieved by 1990, when it is planned that
forty percent of the working population in each
region should be employed in industry and
twenty-five in the tertiary sector.

A successful housing programme is critical to
the achievement of the aims of the 1973 Planning
Act, but this may be difficult if Bulgaria's earlier
post-war experience is repeated. Severe housing
shortages occurred as a result of the rapid
industrialisation of the predominantly rural country
after the war, and of population growth; and blocks
of flats were built on the edges of most towns, and
especially where new industries were being
established (Geshev 1981; Volle 1979, p.123), but
not at a rate which could ensure that every urban
household had its own dwelling. In 1972 the
Bulgarian leader Zhivkov stated that the housing
problem was to be "radically solved", and he claimed
that within the next ten to fifteen years each

family would have a separate dwelling with a room
for every member (Guardian 1973, p.3). One of the
main tasks of the Seventh Five Year Plan was the
acceleration of housing construction, and by 1981
Bulgarian sources were claiming that
> "Almost all houses in the villages were
> replaced by new ones, new housing estates have
> mushroomed in the towns and cities on areas
> twice and even three times those of tne former
> towns"

(Droumeshki and Karapetkov 1981, p.321).
Nevertheless, housing is still recognised to be an
economic, political and social problem in Bulgaria;
and construction targets are rarely achieved. Only
352,000 of the planned 420,000 dwellings in the
Seventh Five Year Plan were built, and ofricial
sources recorded that production during the Eighth
Plan was already about 4,000 dwellings below target
by 1981-2 (Rabotnichesko 1983, p.1; Radio Free
Europe 1983, p.1). Furthermore, a 1983 decree
stated that in future workers' collectives and state
enterprises would be responsible for solving
accommodation problems for their employees, using
"their own forces and means in tne construction,
distribution and management of housing"
(Rabotnichesko 1983, pp.1-2). However, over the
last few years state enterprises have already been
made responsible for developing auxiliary farms,
supplying their own premises with trade and service
facilities, and supporting schools and
kindergartens, and so this new burden may reduce the
chances of meeting the housing targets even further.
If that should occur, long-distance commuting is
likely to increase, and further delays may result in
industrial development as shortages of labour build
up in the main industrial areas.

Housing problems, though of a very different
type, are also afflicting many rural areas. For
instance, there is a growing problem of second homes
for summer and weekend residence in some of tne .
country's more desirable mountain and coastal areas
(Ikonomicheski 1983, pp.4-5). Many have been
constructed illegally, and often on arable land,
private plots or auxiliary farms attached to
non-agricultural enterprises (Rabotnichesko 1978;
Zemedelsko 1978). Moreover, many are much larger
than is strictly necessary for holiday
accommodation. In an economy which is striving for
the maximum possible growth the construction of such
housing amounts to an unjustified diversion of
resources, and this is particularly tne case when

there are large numbers of deserted houses in such rural areas as Strandzha-Sakar and the mountains. Indeed, whole villages lie abandoned in parts of the Stara Planina - where there are 187 in Gabrovo Region and a hundred in Veliko Turnovo Region alone (Radio Free Europe 1983, p.10), and also ninety-six in the Sofia Region - and it has been estimated that by the end of this century a total of about a thousand villages will disappear (Nova 1983,p.3). Some of these places would be ideal for second homes, and in many cases restoration would be cheaper than the building of new houses. Thus, there would seem to be a role in this matter for the Bulgarian planners. In particular, a state-run, second-home organisation could be established with responsibility for locating, purchasing, reconditioning, furnishing and selling abandoned village dwellings, with a view to preserving some of the earlier rural architectural styles and repopulating, if only intermittently, some of the deserted parts of the country in a planned manner.

Thus, settlement planning in Bulgaria reflects many problems associated with a country which is still undergoing the transition from a predominantly agricultural to an industrial society. Concern for the urban future may be seen in modern well-planned towns, industrial estates and imaginative recreation and resort complexes, while awareness of the urban past is manifest in the careful preservation of historical monuments. Nevertheless, problems abound, not least with regard to the continuing shortage of housing in the towns and the inferior quality of house finishing, while the problems which have been created for rural settlements by urban growth also await solution.

CONCLUSION

Between 1945 and the mid-1980s the population of Bulgaria grew from about 6,900,000 to almost 9,000,000. At the same time the proportion in the countryside was halved - from three-quarters to thirty-eight percent - and that dependent upon agriculture by even more. Less than a quarter of the working population is now attached to farming, and more than thirty-five percent are employed in mining and manufacture. Brown coal, electricity and a wide variety of manufactured goods are now produced. The health of the people has been improved, standards of education have risen markedly, and the rate of natural increase of the population has fallen sharply. In short, the country has experienced an economic revolution, which has brought great social change, and this has been achieved within the framework of central planning and Soviet-style investment priorities. However, economic success has not been without problems, and this chapter has outlined some of the difficulties which have beset regional, environmental and settlement management. The appearance of these problems indicates in part a failure to foresee the long-term effects of policies, in part an unwillingness to recognise just how serious some problems have become, and in part an inability, even under a most orthodox Soviet-style regime, to influence citizens to act in socially-beneficial, as distinct from privately-satisfactory, ways. In other words, central planning has been less than adequate in relation to the aims of the policies which have been pursued. Nor has it succeeded in protecting the Bulgarian economy from the problems of the world at large. If further spectacular economic growth is to be achieved, not only may the mechanisms of planning require to be altered, but the whole range of new industries and services which have been developed in the Western World since 1945 may have to supplant those which have provided the engines of post-war growth in Bulgaria, with major consequences for the location of employment and the form of the settlement system. Before the end of tne century a new economic revolution may be necessary in Bulgaria, but, if this is to be achieved, new systems of government may be required both to engender and direct it.

REFERENCES

Anon (1973), Previsioni di sviluppo delia rete stradale in Bulgaria, Est-Ovest, 2, 151-154.

Anon (1974), Die Problematik des Fremdenverkehrs in Bulgarien Wirtschaftliche Vorteile und ideologische Nebenaspekte, Wissenschaftlicher Dienst Südosteuropa, 4, 70-72.

Anon (1980), Inferiore al previsto la realizzazione delle infrastutture di transporto in Bulgaria, Est-Ovest, 2, 43-44.

Apostolov, N. (1980), Tipologiya na gradovete v Búlgariya spored ezhednevnite trudovi pútovaniya, Problemi na Geografiyata, 2, 53-62.

Bulgaria

Apostolov, N. (1981), Terminologichni i tertitorialni osebnosti na trudovite putovaniya v N.R.Bŭlgariya, **Trudove na Visshiya Institut za Narodno Stopanstvo "D. Blagoev"**, 53, 100-142.

Atanasova, E. (1982), Faktori opredelyashi ikonomicheskata efektivnost na hotelierstvoto Bŭlgarskite Chernomorski kompleksi, **Trudove na Visshiya Institut za Narodno Stopanstvo "D. Blagoev"**, 54, 94-138.

Barbov, T.S. (1981), Usŭvŭrshenstvŭvane strukurata na transportnata sistema v N.R.Bŭlgariya, **Geografiya**, 36, 1-4.

Barbov, T.S. (1982), Edinaya transportnaya sistema v Narodny Respublike Bolgarii, ee modernizatsiya i rekonstruktsiya, **Izvestia Akademii Nauk S.S.S.R. (Seriya Geograficheskaya)**, 6, 122.

Barev, I. (1958), Bulgarian Agriculture under the Communist System, **International Peasant Union Monthly Bulletin**, 9, 21.

Borisov, Z. (1983), Vŭzrastovata struktura na naselenieto v N.R.Bŭlgariya po selishtni sistemi, **Izvestiya na Bŭlgaeskoto Geografsko Druzhestvo**, 21, 83-93.

Brezhnev, L. (1966), **Soviet News** (18/11/1966).

Bŭchvarov, M. (1962), Hutnictwo żelaza i metali nieżelaznych w Bułgarii, **Przegląd Geograficzny**, 34, 333-349.

Bulgaria (1949), **Resolution of the Fifth Congress of the Bulgarian Communist Party**, Sofia.

Bulgaria (1973), **Spisuk na Naselenite Mesta v N.R.Bŭlgariya**, M.I.S., Sofia.

Carter, F.W. (1970), Bulgaria's economic ties with her immediate neighbours and prospects for future development, **East European Quarterly**, 4, 209-224.

Carter, F.W. (1973), Changements fonctionnels de l'après-guerre dans la conurbation de Sofia, **Géographie et recherche**, 8, 25-39.

Carter, F.W. (1978), Nature reserves and national parks in Bulgaria, **L'Espace Géographique**, 1, 69.

Carter, F.W. (1984), Balkan Historic Cities : Pollution versus Conservation, **Proceedings of the Anglo-Bulgarian Modern Humanities Symposium, London, 1982**, vol. II, 20.

Carter, F.W. and Žagar, M. (1971), Postwar internal migration in southeastern Europe, in **Demographic Developments in Eastern Europe**, ed. L.A.Kosinski, Praeger, London, 209-225.

Cousens, S.H. (1967), Changes in Bulgarian Agriculture, **Geography**, 52, 18.

Dakov, V. (1977), Dunav kakto ikonomiski i turisticki resurs za Bŭlgariya, Godishnik na Sofiyskiya Universitet, 69, 177-187.

Daneva, M. (1984), Nyakoi lanashaftno-ekologichni problemi na ratsionalnoto izpolzuvane na pozemlenite resursi v N.R.Bŭlgariya, Problemi na Geografiyata, 1, 34-44.

Devedzhiev, M. (1979), Mekhanichniyat prirast na gradskoto naselenie, Planovo stopanstvo, 27, 62-71.

Devedzhiev, M. (1981), Neobkhodimi novı zhelezopŭtni linii v N.R.B., Informatsionen buletin, 3-4, 211.

Dimitrov, P.P. (1977), Dinamika na migratsiyata i vuzrastovo-polovata struktura na gradskoto i selskoto naselenie v N.R.Bŭlgariya za perioda ot 1965 to 1975 g., Trudove na Visshiya Institut za Narodno Stopanstvo "D. Blagoev", 49, 78-123.

Dinev, L. (1965), Sustoyanie i zadachı na geografiyata na naselenieto i selishtata v Bŭlgariya, Izvestiya na Bulgarskoto Geografsko Druzhestvo, 5, 43-56.

Dinev, L. (1968), Vŭrkhu nyakoı problemi na trudovıte migratsii na naselenneto v Bulgariya, Godishnik na Sofiyskiya Universitet, 61, 251-270.

Dinev, L. (1969), Kharakterni osobenosti v teritorialnoto razpredelenie i gŭstotata na naselenieto v Bŭlgariya, Izvestiya na Bŭlgarsktoto Geogratsko Druzhestvo, 9, 77-87.

Dinev, L. (1977), Development and Estimation ot tne migrational processes in Bulgaria, Geographıa Polonica, 36, 43-47.

Dinev, L. (1978a), Die Entwıcklung und Besonderheiten des Tourismus in Bulgarien, Wirtschaftsgeographische Studien, 4, 83-91.

Dinev, L. (1978b), Regionalizace cestovıho ruchu v Bulharské lidové republice, Sborník Československé Společnosti Zeměpisné, 87, 132-139.

Dojkov, V. and Botev, L. (1980), Dunav i Dunavskiyat voden pŭt, Sofia.

Donchev, D. (1970), Razvitie na mashınostroeneto i metalobrabotnaneto v N.R.Bŭlgariya, Geografiya, 20, 1-5.

Donchev, D. (1980), Vliyanie na naucho-tekhnicheskata revoltuttsiya vŭrkhy razvietieto i teritorialnoto razpolozhenie na promıshıenastta, Problemi na Geografiyata, 4, 3-16.

Donchev, D. and Dobrinova, P. (1981), Vliyanıeto na modernizatsiya i rekonstruktsiyata v promıshıenostta vŭrkhy razvietieto na narodnoto

Bulgaria

stopanstvo v N.R.B., Izvestiya na Bŭlgarskoto Geografsko Druzhestvo, 19, 13-20.

Droumeshki, S. and Karapetkov, N. (1981), A Social Policy in the Interest of the People, in Modern Bulgaria: History, Policy, Economy, Culture, ed. G.Bokov.

Eperon, A. (1969), Tourism opens frontiers in Bulgaria, The New York Times (Supplement), (2/3/1969).

Ganev, K. and Cukova, S. (1980), Geografsko-demografski osobenosti i struktura na zaetost v gradovete s nisŭk estestven prirast, Godishnik na Sofijskiya Universitet, 71, 209-224.

Geshev, G. (1981), Vzaimodeystvi mezhdu protsesite na industrializatsiya i urbanizatsiiya v Narodna republika Bŭlgariya, Problemi na Geografiyata, 1, 36-44.

Grüll, J. (1961), Bulgariens Kraftwerkbau und Elektizitätswirtschaft nach dem Zweiten Weltkrieg, Mitteilungen der Österreichischen Geographischen Gesellschaft, 103, 209-215.

Guardian (2/4/1973).

Guev, B. (1981), Mashınostroeneto i metaloobrabotvaneto v Zapadniya Gorno-trakiyski podrayon i reshavaneto na nyakoi ikonomgeografski problemi, Problemi na Geografiyata, 1, 56-68.

Hoffman, G.W. and Hatchett, R.L. (1971), The Impact of Regional Development Policy on Population Distribution in Yugoslavia and Bulgaria, in Population and Migration Trends in Eastern Europe, ed. H.L.Kostanick, Westview, Colorado, 99-124.

Ikonomicheski Zhivot (19/1/1983).

Karakashev, K. (1973), Geodemografska kharakteristika na trudovite migratsii kŭm rayon na metalurgichniya kombinat "Kremikovtsi", Izvestiya na Bŭlgarskoto Geografsko Druzhestvo, 13, 121.

Karavelov, L. (1860), Bolgarii starego vremeni, Moskva.

Khristov, T. (1962), Geografiya na Promishlenostta v Bŭlgariya, Sofia.

Khristov, T. (1963), Razvitieto na promislenost proizvodstvo v N.R.Bŭlgariya prez godinite na Generalnata Perspektiva, Geografiya, 13, 1-4.

Khristov, T. (1964), Pivoproizvodstvoto v Bŭlgariya, Godishnik na Sofiyskiya Universitet, 57, 99-154.

Khristov, T. (1975), Geografiya na promisnıenostta v Bŭlgariya v usloviyata na sotsialisticheskata ikonomicheska integratsiya, Problemi na Geografiyata, 1, 18-28.

Khristov, T. (1983), Geografski problemi na yadrenata energetika, Problemi na Geografiyata, 2, 3-17.

Khristov, T. and Dancheva, N. (1983), Topoenergetikata, metalurgiyata, i khimicheskata promishlenost i deystvieto na ekologichniya faktor, Problemi na Geografiyata, 4, 29-38.

Khristov, T. and Popov, P. (1976), Sesiya po problema "Teritorialno razpredelenie na promishlenostta i vuprosite po opazvane na prirodata", Problemi na Geografiyata, 2, 91-94.

Khristov, T. and Stankov, G. (1982), Territorial'noe razmeshtenie khimicheskoi promishlenosti v Bolgarii i okhrana prirodni sredi, Acta Facultatis Rerum Naturalium Universitatis Comeniane, (Geographica), 20, 15-22.

Kiradzhiev, S. (1975), Osnovni tendentsii v dinamikata na suotnoshenisto medzhu gradskoto i selskoto naselenie v Bulgariya, Problemi na Geografiyata, 1, 64-72.

Kiradzhiev, S. (1977), Vutreshna migratsiya na naselenieto v Bulgariya, Problemi na Geografiyata, 3, 30-39.

Kiradzhiev, S. (1983), Vliyanie na migratsite na naselenieto vurkhu demografskite protsesi v Bulgariya, Problemi na Geografiyata, 2, 25-35.

Krustev, K. (1968), Ikonomgeografski problemi na promishlenastta vuv Vrachanski mikrorayon, Dodishnik na Sofiyskiya Universitet, 57, 99-154.

Kyurkchiev, M. (1962), A new road for Bulgarian agriculture, Sofia.

Maleshkov, N.N. (1964), Administrativno-teritorialno Ustrystvo na Narodna Republika Bulgariya, Godisnik na Sofiyskiya Universitet, 4, 353-413.

Markov, G. (1978), Dulgosrochno prognozirane na vodopotreblenieto pri polivnoto zemedelie v N.R.Bulgariya, Problemi na Geografiyata, 3, 14-23.

Mikhaylov, M. (1982), Osnovni tendentsii v razvitieto na transportnata sistema v N.R.B. i zadachite na geografiyata na transporta, Izvestiya na Bulgarskoto Geografsko Druzhestvo, 20, 107.

Miloshov, G. (1974), Heavy Industry in Bulgaria, Sofia.

Mishev, K. (1982), Ekologizatsiya na obshtestvenoto proizvodstvo v N.R.B. i suvremennata geografiya, Problemi na Geografiyata, 1, 12.

Naidenova, R. (1977), Methodologische Probleme der Erarbeitung des Generalschemas für die Standortverteilung der Produktivkräfte in der Volksrepublik Bulgarien, Petermanns Geographische

Bulgaria

Mitteilungen, 121, 233-239.
Nova Makedonija (29/1/1983)
Nowak, W.S.W. (1968), The economic geography of the Bulgarian fishing industry, Koninklijk Aardrijkskundig Genootschaf van Antwerpen, 79, 21-52.
Panayotov, V. (1969), Kremikovskoto zheleznorudno nachodishte, Sofia.
Penkov, I. and Dimitrov, S. (1981), Urbanizatsionniyat protses u nas i formiraneto na gradski aglomeratsii, Izvestiya na Bŭlgarskoto Geografsko Druzhestvo, 19, 49.
Penkov, I. and Khristov, T. (1978), Ikonomicheska geografiya na Bŭlgariya (4th. ed.), Sofia.
Petrov, P. (1980), Landschaftno rayonirane na Bŭlgariya, Godishnik na Sofiyskiya Universitet, 71, 121-136.
Petrov, P. (1981), Opit za landschaftno rayonirane na Bŭlgariya, Geografiya, 31, 2.
Petrov, E., Stahilov, Z. and Trashliev, K. (1971), Ikonomicheska otsenka na zemyata v Bŭlgariya, B.A.N., Sofia.
Popov, P. (1970), Suvremenni prakticheski napravleniya i problemi na geografiyata na promishlenostta v Bŭlgariya, Izvestiya na Bŭlgarskoto Geografsko Druzhestvo, 10, 149-159.
Popov, V. (1976), Geografsko razprestranie na rezervatite i narodnite parkove v N.R.Bŭlgariya, Geografiya, 25, 1-4.
Rabotnichesko Delo, (2/3/1972, 25/1/1978, 13/2/1981, 17/8/1981, 18/5/1982, 30/3/1983, 23/6/1983).
Radio Free Europe (1983), New Settlers in the Underdeveloped Regions - Problems, Bulgarian Survey Report, No.14, p.13.
Radio Free Europe, Bulgarian Situation Report, (4/3/1983, 12/9/1983).
Rochlin, R.P. (1957), Die Wirtschaft Bulgariens seit 1945, Berlin.
Rusinova, S.I. (1966), Gosudarstvennoe ustroistvo sotsialisticheskikh stran evropy, Izdatelstvo Leningradskogo Universiteta, Leningrad.
Smith, A.H. (1983), The Planned Economies of Eastern Europe, Croom Helm, London.
Spetter, H. (1982), The New Economic Reform in Bulgaria: Background, Problems and Prospects of the New Economic Mechanism, Crossroads: A Socio-Political Journal, 9, 122-123.
State Council of P.R.B. (1977), Guidelines for the Protection and Reproduction of the Environment

of the P.R.B., Sofia.

Stoilov, D. (1980), Bulgarskite rezervati-etaloni na nepromenena priroda, Geografiya, 30, 20-25.

Straszewicz, L. (961), Bułgarski przemysł włókienniczy, Przeglad Geograficzny, 33, 663-678.

Taafe, R.N. (1974), Urbanization in Bulgaria: 1946-1970, Etudes Balkaniques, 2-3, 52-54.

Taafe, R.N. (1977), The Impact of Rural-Urban Migration on the Development of Communist Bulgaria, in Population and Migration Trends in Eastern Europe, ed. H.L.Kostanick, Westview, Colorado.

Tishkov, K. (1974), Thermal inversions and industrial pollution of the near-surface air of some depressions in Bulgaria, in Man and Environment, (Studies in geography in Hungary, No.11), Budapest, 197-202.

Tishkov, K. (1980), Rekreatsionite resursi v Staroplaninskata fizikogeografska oblast, Geografiya, 30, 1-4.

Tishkov, K. (1984), Otdikhŭt i turizmŭt - preuspyavasht stopanski otrasŭl, Geografiya, 39, 16-20.

Vanous, J. (1982), East European Economic Slowdown, Problems of Communism, 31, 5.

Vaptsarov, I. (1982), Polezni izkopaemi, in Geografiya na Bŭlgariya, ed. Z.S.Gŭlubŏv, Vol. 1, 44-51.

Venedikov, Y. (1971), Faktori za migratsiyata na selskata mladezhmetodika i osnovni rezultati ot edno anketno prouchvane, Statistika, 18, 23-40.

Volle, J.P. (1979), Croissance urbaine et organisation régionale en Bulgarie, Revue Géographique de l'Est, 19, 103-104.

Zemedelsko Zname (30/3/1978).

Ziapkov, L. (1974), Economic activities influencing the fluvial regime of the Pazardjik and Plovdiv Plains, in Man and Environment (Studies in geography in Hungary, No.11), Budapest, 157-161.

Zwass, A. (1984), The Economies of Eastern Europe in a Time of Change, Macmillan, London.

Zyapkov, L. and Braykov, B. (1981), Uzhnobŭlgarski magistralen kanal, Geografiya, 36, 19-20.

Chapter 5

CZECHOSLOVAKIA

Frank W.Carter

THE CONTEXT OF PLANNING

1945 marked a watershed in Czechoslovakian economic development. Before the Second World War the country had had a free-enterprise economy, and considerable industrial and urban development had occurred, especially in Bohemia and Moravia. Slovakia, in contrast, had remained largely rural and backward (Wanklyn 1954). In 1945, however, the country was liberated chiefly by Russian troops, the German population of about 3,000,000 (out of a total of 15,000,000) fled or was expelled from the towns and the Sudetenland (Luza 1964), and the new Czech government announced the Košice programme, which included the introduction of central economic management (Krejči 1976), though not of a strict or detailed Stalinist type. Key industries, including mining, power, metallurgy and engineering, and the banks were nationalised. Almost a fifth of the agricultural area was seized and redistributed to farm labourers and peasants, and forests became state property (Krejči 1972, pp.1-27). However, the political situation was unstable. The Communists had emerged as the strongest party from the 1946 elections - though without a majority - and in 1948 they established themselves as the ruling group in a constitutional coup d'état, and began at once to implement Stalinist methods and policies (Korbel 1959, pp.198-325). Nationalisation of small businesses and the collectivisation of agriculture struck at the large middle-class, commercially-oriented group in the population - especially in Bohemia and Moravia - and the government took into its hands detailed control over the economic and social development of the country (Feierabend 1952). As Michal (1960, p.1) has

pointed out,
"Czechoslovakia provides, for the first time in
history, a test case of the efficacy of central
planning at a very high stage of
industrialization".
The First Five Year Plan (1949-1953) indicated
the direction which that planning was to take
(Czechoslovakia 1949). Investment was directed
towards heavy industry, and, after the outbreak of
the Korean War in 1950, increased emphasis was
placed upon the manufacture of arms (Mrazek 1960).
Consumer goods were given a much lower priority.
Nevertheless, ambitious targets were set for
increases in production in all sectors of the
economy, many of which proved to be unattainable;
and severe imbalances rapidly developed as a
consequence of the uneven degree of success amongst
industries in achieving planned levels of output
(Olsovsky 1964, p.193). Major adjustments had to be
made to the distribution of investment between
different parts of the economy and to the system of
management in the mid-1950s and again, following a
similar crisis in the economy, in the mid-1960s
(Schaffer 1965; Sik 1965); while the overthrow of
Novotny in the Prague Spring of 1968 was associated
in part with the widespread belief that detailed
planning of the economy by central government had
proved to be unworkable (Golan 1971; Sik 1971).
However, the reforms of the Dubcek era were quickly
suppressed by the Husak government in 1969 and 1970
(Kyn 1975); and Zwass (1984, p.60) has suggested
that Czechoslovakia in the 1970s and 80s has had
opportunities for the "refinement of the steering
system, but no prospects for economic reforms". In
other words, the Czechoslovaks have had the
occasional flirtation with market socialism since
1948, but the Soviet-style Command Economy, with its
emphases upon investment and increased output,
especially of fuel, metallurgical and heavy
engineering products, and later of chemicals, has
been the usual form of management.
Notwithstanding these problems of economic
management some spells of spectacular economic
growth have occurred, especially in the late 1940s,
late 1950s, and in the late 1960s and early 1970s
(Korda 1976), so that output of a wide range of
goods is now much higher than it was before the
Second World War. However, successive Five Year
Plans have contained lower and lower targets for
future growth as the opportunities for 'extensive'
development have dwindled; and increasing attention

has had to be paid to the 'intensive' growth strategy of improving productivity (Zeman and Wanke 1981). Indeed, the rate of growth was so low during the early 1980s (Table 5.1) that Kusin (1982, p.34) was moved to declare that

"with all the emphasis on central control, planning is of decreasing utility in the management of the Czechoslovak economy."

This chapter will examine that statement in the context of the regional, environmental and urban consequences of the economic growth which has occurred since the Second World War.

Table 5.1: Average Annual Increases in National Income in Czechoslovakia, 1951-1985

Period	Increase (percent)
1951 - 1955	8.2
1956 - 1960	6.9
1961 - 1965	1.9
1966 - 1970	7
1971 - 1975	5.6
1976 - 1980	3.7
1981 - 1985	1.7

Sources: _Statistická ročenka Československé socialistické republiky_, various years; Vanous, J. (1982), pp. 2-3.

REGIONAL DEVELOPMENT

(1) The First Phase of Central Planning

Part V of the First Five Year Plan dealt specifically with regional planning (Czechoslovakia 1949, pp.246-249). It envisaged that progress towards regional equality would be achieved by a proper distribution of investment and production according to six rules. Priority was to be given to economically backward regions; productive resources were to be fully utilised in all regions, with preference being given to those with the greatest local supplies of labour, raw materials, power and transport; substantial efforts were to be made to guard against any excessive concentration of investment or production in any region; regions with

fewer opportunities for economic development were to
be used for tourism and workers' recreation centres;
the development of both rural and urban settlement
was to be on modern town and country planning
principles; and systematic investigations were to be
made in all regions to identify their resources and
social needs. A specific section referred to
Slovakia. Gradual transformation of its economic
and social structure was to occur through the
expansion of existing industry, increases in the
productivity of agricultural labour, the wider
distribution of skilled workers, intensive research
into its natural resources, and especially its
minerals, and a great increase in housing,
educational and medical facilities. One of the
largest metallurgical plants in Eastern Europe was
to be built in the eastern part of Slovakia, near to
Košice (Ivanička 1964, pp.11-22).

Until the early 1960s industrialisation was
predominantly extensive in character, and large new
metallurgical, engineering and chemical plants were
constructed to provide a basis for other industrial
development (Kozma 1954). The most active phase of
new plant establishment was between 1949 and 1954
(Figure 5.1a). However, in order that scores of new
factories might be established in Slovakia, South
Bohemia and other less-developed regions production
from the older industrial areas of Prague, Brno,
Duchov, Liberec, Ostrava-Karvina and Ústí nad Labem
also had to be increased, and in particular higher
outputs of coal and electricity were required from
North Bohemia, the major source of Czechoslovakia's
brown coal and lignite, and the Ostrava coalfield
(George 1963). The output of bituminous coal rose
by fifty percent during the 1950s to 26,200,000 tons
in 1960, and that of brown coal by 110 percent to
55,500,000 tons (Czechoslovakia 1984, pp.32-33).

Transport planning was seen to be fundamental
to these attempts to correct the inherited regional
imbalances, and major improvements to the transport
infrastructure were started in the late 1940s. One
of these was the construction of a railway transfer
node at Cierna nad Tisou, on the Soviet border in
Slovakia, which began operation in 1947 (Anon 1975,
pp.30-44). Extensive ramps were built to facilitate
the movement of bulky and liquified goods from the
Soviet broad- to the Czech standard-gauge system.
Another project was the complete reconstruction of
the Košice-Ostrava line, which was completed by
1955, presumably to supply raw materials from the
Ostrava coalfield to the new steel mill (Kansky

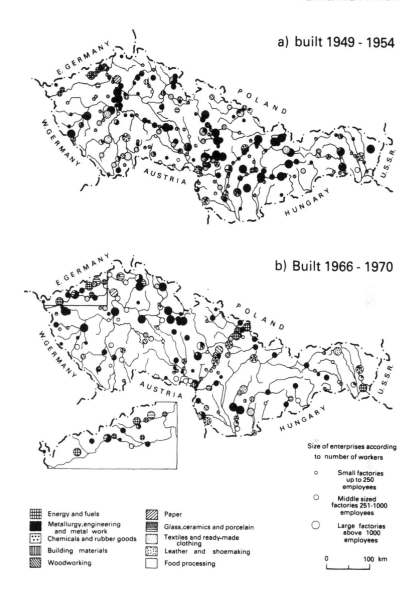

a) built 1949 - 1954

b) Built 1966 - 1970

Size of enterprises according
to number of workers

○   Small factories
     up to 250
     employees

◯   Middle sized
     factories 251-1000
     employees

◯   Large factories
     above 1000
     employees

0   100 km

Energy and fuels

Metallurgy,engineering
and metal work

Chemicals and rubber goods

Building materials

Woodworking

Paper

Glass,ceramics and porcelain

Textiles and ready-made
clothing

Leather and shoemaking

Food processing

**Figure 5.1 New Industrial Enterprises in
Czechoslovakia, 1949-1954 and 1966-1970**

1980). The South Slovak arterial route was also completed in 1955; extensive investment was undertaken in the northern rail links in Bohemia after 1953 in conjunction with the establishment of new brown coal mines; and local lines were built to recreation areas in the Tatra Mountains. Much investment was also directed to electrification. By 1950 the Žilina-Spišská Nová Ves trunk route had been completed; three other trunk lines were electrified over the next decade - from Ústí nad Labem to Kolin in 1958, from Žilina to Košice in 1961, and from Žilina to Prague in 1960; and in all, about 750 kilometres of line were electrified between 1955 and 1960. There was little investment, in contrast, in road transport. Most improvements were of a local nature only, though about 2,000 kilometres of third-class roads were constructed between 1952 and 1960 to increase accessibility to some of the more isolated areas (Czechoslovakia 1962, p.286). However, there was some intensification of the use of the Danube, Labe and Vltava rivers for transport; and the Danube proved to be a particularly valuable link between Czechoslovakia and some Romanian and Soviet ports (Velkobrosky 1953).

The spatial distribution of investment had a great impact on that of population. The years immediately after the war were a period of high natural increase, with high natality in Slovakia and low mortality throughout the country, and Figure 5.2 shows wide regional differences in natural increase, particularly between Slovakia and the Czech Lands (Hanzlík 1967, Pavlik 1959). More particularly, it indicates that it was the most easterly region in Slovakia which had the highest natural increase (of more than twenty per thousand), and the most westerly the lowest. In the Central Bohemian region, in contrast, signs of population stagnation had begun to appear in the 1950s, and the Jicin district of East Bohemia experienced an absolute decrease, thus warning of future problems in the supply of labour. However, when modified by internal migration overall population change was quite different from that occasioned by natural increase (Figure 5.3). For example, not only were many people from the overpopulated Slovakian mountain valleys resettled in the lands left empty by the flight of the Germans, but many Slovaks also migrated to the Bohemian and Moravian industrial centres (George 1947; Sekara 1948; Steers 1948). In particular, the Karvina and Ostrava industrial

districts recorded migration gains, whilst big
losses were experienced in nearby Čadca and Dolný
Kubín, where migration largely offset the effects of
high natural increase (Carter 1970). High migration
gains also occurred in other industrial districts,
such as Česke Budějovice, Jablonec nad Tisou,
Kladno, with its metallurgical and mining
activities, Mladá Boleslav, with its car production
(Hampl 1968), Pardubice, the engineering centre of
Plzen, and the uranium mining town of Příbram. In
Slovakia the main recipients of migrants, besides
the regional capital of Bratislava, were the heavy
engineering town of Banská Bistrica, the
newly-industrialised valleys at Martin, with their
machine industry (Votrubec 1958), the food
processing and engineering town of Nitra, Žiar nad
Hranom, with its non-ferrous smelting, and, of
course, Košice, with its steel mill.

Overall, employment in agriculture declined by
more than a quarter during the 1950s, as that in
mining and manufacturing rose, and the rural
population fell from fifty-one percent of the total
in 1947 to forty percent in 1964. Moreover,
although industry had been expanded in all parts of
the country, a marked shift had occurred in the
distribution of industrial employment. In 1946-7
less than fifteen percent had been in Slovakia, but
by 1961 the figure was 22.6 percent (Häufler 1966,
p.99). In other words, a major structural and
spatial change had been achieved in the
Czechoslovakian economy.

(2) Regional Planning in the 1960s and 1970s

In 1958 a second significant document - the
Town and Country Planning Act - appeared (Vidláková
1977, pp. 84-85). This distinguished between three
types of plan - regional, master and detailed -
which were to shape future spatial planning.
Regional plans were to contain clearly outlined
long-term principles for development. They were to
provide a comprehensive overview of all the
locational, organisational and other characteristics
of the activities in a region, including mining and
industrial enterprises, construction, transport and
water facilities, residential areas and forests.
They were to cover areas of between 300 and 5,000
square kilometres, but these areas did not have to
coincide with administrative districts, especially
if the plans were concerned with natural phenomena,
or industrial agglomerations which covered several
districts, such as that of Ostrava-Karvina, or areas

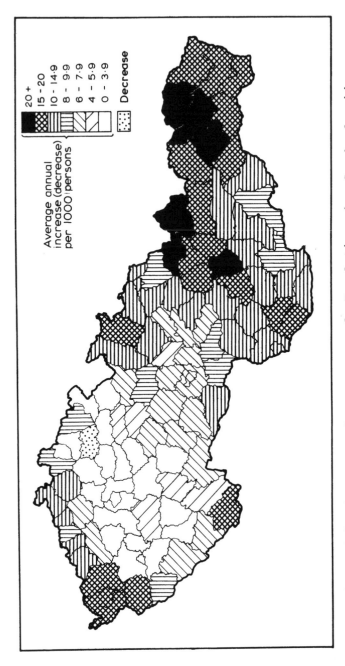

Figure 5.2 The Natural Increase of Population in Czechoslovakia between 1950 and 1959

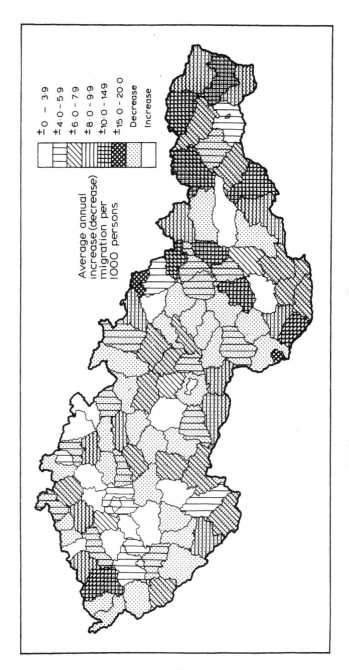

Figure 5.3 Gains and Losses of Population in Czechoslovakia from
Migration between 1950 and 1959

which were linked by common interests, such as the West Bohemian spa towns. Master plans, in contrast, were to stipulate the major principles for the long-term construction or renovation of either whole settlements or parts of them, and they were to take account of both industrial and residential needs for energy, green space, sewage disposal, transport and water supply. The third type of plan, the Detailed Plan, was to refer to particular sites and be governed by such regulations as those dealing with building height and the ratio of built-up to open space. Thus, while regional planning was to regulate the overall economic and social development of areas the other types of plan were intended to deal more specifically with the arrangements within them. Regional plans were to be for five years or for one, and to coincide with the timetable for national economic development, but the other plans were to have no pre-determined completion date, and were to end when projects were complete or modified. Legally, the different types of plan were to remain independent of each other, although parallel in objective, and were to be under the control of different arms of government. In practice, however, connections were to develop between them, particularly where large investments were involved. Furthermore, it was envisaged that the drawing up of each plan would involve considerable coordination between the numerous branches of the economy; and both regional and other plans were always to be subject to possible alteration by central government.

Shortly after the introduction of this new framework two other major changes occurred in the context of planning. Firstly, the administrative division of the country was changed. Administrative divisions are of particular importance for regional planners because they provide the framework for their activities, and in 1949 new units had been created which were thought to be suited to the planned economic development of the country. However, in 1960 this network was amended (Figure 5.4) in an attempt to create an administrative structure which would conform as closely as possible with that of the spatial pattern of economic activity (Häufler 1984, p.378). Post-war ideas about regionalisation had been influenced by the work of local scholars (Dĕdina 1928; Korčák 1934), on the one hand, and by Soviet theory, on the other. However, the Soviet contribution was eventually dismissed as inappropriate on account of the

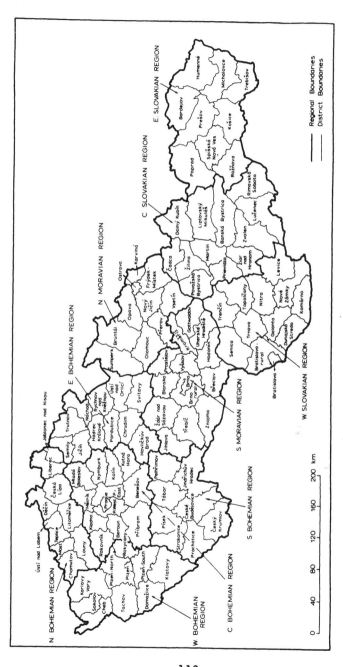

Figure 5.4 The Administrative Division of Czechoslovakia since 1960

difference in scale between the regions envisaged by that theory - which would have treated Czechoslovakia as a single economic area (Blažek 1954) - and those in the Czechoslovakian writings. Before any new regionalisation could be undertaken the relationship between the administrative and economic structures had to be evaluated (Zůrek 1955), and data collected (Střida 1958) with a view to identifying the significant nuclei in the space economy. 135 nuclei were recognised, and from these forty-six foci were chosen, following an analysis of their industrial, population and transport significance. These foci and their hinterlands were then used to delimit large economic regions, seven of which were proposed. However, these findings of the central planning authorities were not applied in full in the new administrative division, which therefore did not reflect accurately the spatial structure of the economy.

Secondly, resources for further extensive growth in the economy were approaching exhaustion, and increasing emphasis was being put upon the need to invest in the most efficient locations for economic activity, rather than throughout the country. Earlier plans for an even distribution of industry had achieved only limited success, and

"after 1960, it became clear that there always were and will be areas with different economic and geographic conditions of development" (Kopačka 1980, pp.334-335). This selectivity in the allocation of industrial investment became marked by the end of the 1960s, and especially as between the Czech and Slovak Republics - a trend which was strengthened after the implementation of the Constitutional Act of the Federative State for two equal nations in 1969 (Calta et al.1983, p.50) - and at the regional scale. Moreover, by that time the government was becoming particularly concerned about the implications of the falling rate of population growth for its industrialisation policy (Elias 1972). Demographic rates in many districts in the Czech Lands were below replacement level, and in Slovakia they were also showing a significant decline. Furthermore, migration from Slovakia to the Czech Lands had diminished considerably, and labour shortages were being experienced in both republics (Novakova-Hribova 1978).

Transport development during the 1960s centred upon the completion of major projects which had been started in the previous decade. In Slovakia regional rail links, such as that between Orlov and

Plaveč, were completed during the early 1960s, whilst in Moravia most rail construction was associated with the large industrial centre of Ostrava. In Bohemia the largest investment was the improvement of the two major nodes of Prague and Ceska Trebova. (The latter is of great importance, for it is the junction of routes connecting Prague, Brno, Ostrava and the Soviet Union via northern Slovakia.) In particular, Prague received money for new bridges and for the reconstruction of the central stations, yards and local lines, all with a view to increasing passenger and freight capacity. Rail links for industry and mining were also improved in Northern Bohemia (Stransky 1963); and over 1,500 kilometres of track were electrified in the 1960s in an effort to free at least one main line across the country from steam locomotion. Investment in road transport, in contrast, continued to suffer from a low priority, and there were few improvements in the network.

During the 1970s, however, a more imaginative approach was adopted towards the transport system (Kansky 1979). Rail continued to be the major mover of freight, but there was greater pressure to use roads for both goods and passenger traffic, and containerisation was also suggested (Zochnak 1979). Increasing attention was paid to pipeline construction. The Brotherhood Pipe, supplying Soviet gas to the Šala refinery in southwest Slovakia, was completed in 1967, and further extensions to the pipeline network were built during the 1970s, as were extensions to the electricity grid. However, less attention was paid to inland navigation problems, although the Danube still carried over a third of the country's waterborne freight. Ideas still persisted in the 1960s about possible links between the Danube, Labe and Oder rivers (Kaspar 1964), and the Labe and Oder systems could have been developed as major foreign trade outlets (Šlampa 1964).

Much of this investment was intended to raise both output and productivity, but there was also an increase of more than 500,000 in industrial employment between 1960 and 1980, and a comparable decline in the number of those in agriculture (Czechoslovakia 1984, pp.24-25). However, changes in the various regions in the country differed widely. For example, between 1967 and 1978 industrial employment increased by a third in Slovakia, and in some districts it doubled, especially those which had been the least

industrialised (Frolov 1978). There was also some
employment growth in the Czech Lands, particularly
in districts with little industry, but the pace was
much slower than in Slovakia (Provaznik 1970), and
decreases in the number of industrial employees
occurred in Prague, Brno, Kladno, Ostrava and Plzeň
(Kopačka 1980, p.336). Comparison of Figures 5.1a
and 5.1b reveals a more concentrated distribution of
new plants in the late 1960s than in tne early
1950s, and one in which they were chiefly located in
the established industrial areas.

(3) Regional Planning in the 1980s

Thus, regional planning had achieved great
changes in the space economy of Czechoslovakia, but
by the late 1970s planners were facing new problems
and technologies. Moreover, study of tne developing
spatial form of the economy had generated a variety
of new insights into its working. Criticisms of the
1960 administrative division of tne country had led
to detailed research on population distribution,
migration and commuting patterns, and their relation
to the delimitation of the hinterlands of economic
centres (Korčák 1961). Regional analyses had been
undertaken of agriculture, industry and settlement
(Ivanicka 1964); and, whilst economists had
concentrated mainly on the study of branch regions,
geographers had became more involved in the
recognition of complex economic regions. These
themes were pursued during the 1970s (Hampl et al
1978), and by the early 1980s socio-economic factors
were also being introduced into regional
delimitation, with the results for Bohemia and
Moravia which are shown in Table 5.2, and similar
work had been started for Slovakia. The results of
all this work confirmed that, despite the regional
policies of the previous thirty years, substantial
differences still persisted in the 1980s between one
part of the country and another; and it would seem,
therefore, that regional policy is likely to
continue to be necessary in the future,
notwithstanding Czechoslovakia's increasing concern
with rationality in the location of investments. In
particular, weaker and stagnating regions will
require assistance, while further development of
their more successful counterparts, usually
embracing large urban agglomerations, may have to be
restrained (Staneková 1983).

It was in the context of these developments
that Town-Planning in Czechoslovakia: Draft Outlook
(Czechoslovakia 1979) laid down a new set of

Table 5.2 Socio-Economic-Geographical Regions in the Czech Lands, 1983

Degree of socio-economic development	Internal economic-geographical differentiations		
	Considerable	Average	Small
High	North Moravian Region	North Bohemian Region	Prague
Average		South Moravian Region	East Bohemian Region
Low	West Bohemian Region	Central Bohemian Region (excl. Prague)	South Bohemian Region

Source: Häufler, V. (1984), p. 379.

strategic principles for future territorial planning
(Nový 1983, p.57), and emphasised that territorial
planning should be seen to be a continuing process,
rather than a once-and-for-all event. The document
approved a three-grade settlement hierarchy of
local, district and zonal tiers, based on a
government plan of 1967. It sought to achieve a
more even distribution of settlement throughout the
country, and identified a total of forty-four areas,
of which thirty-one were on the Czech Lands, which
were to be set aside for future urban development.
It declared that any changes in the settlement
structure should be made with a view to achieving
greater equality, within a rising standard of living
and greater access to cultural, educational and
social facilities, for each region's inhabitants;
and it expressed the hope that the differences in
living standards and achievement between the Czechs,
Slovaks and other national minorities would
disappear as a result of this new and broader
approach to territorial planning. It envisaged that
regional planners would be increasingly concerned
with the place of tertiary and public services in
the settlement system; and it also acknowledged the
need for the protection of the country's natural
environment and historic monuments.

Some progress has been made towards these
goals, at least at the stage of plan preparation,
during the first half of the 1980s, though it has
been through further study of the territorial
structure of industry, and especially of industrial
nodes, rather than through plans for the settlement
system. Many definitions exist of industrial nodes,
but most regional planners agree that the fuller
exploitation of both the natural and social
resources in the regions can only be achieved
through the careful linking of the size and
character of branch plants to the desired degree of
specialisation and the necessary patterns of inter-
or intra-enterprise linkage within industry, and
also to the spatial pattern of settlement.
Sixty-seven industrial nodes have been identified in
Slovakia, of which the five largest - Bratislava,
Košice, Martin-Turany, Považská Bystrica-Púchov and
Dubnica nad Váhom-Ilava - account for a quarter of
the republic's industry, and the sixteen largest for
half (Mládek 1984, p.31). In the Czech Lands
eighty-one nodes, which contain nearly nine-tenths
of the republic's industrial employment, have been
recognised, of which the largest are Prague, Plzeň,
Sokolov, Ústí nad Labem, Pardubice-Hradec Králové,

Brno, Gottwaldov, Olomouc and Ostrava (Mareš 1980 and 1982). It is within this framework that the 'optimum' locations for new industrial branches will be chosen.

But these plans for the ever more careful location of investment could well be upset by future labour shortages. Häufler has stated recently (1984, p.99) that "there is no need to be pessimistic about the future development of Czechoslovakia's population", but reality suggests otherwise. The number of live births has shown a steady decline since the 1974 peak, whilst mortality rose from 170,000 to 185,000 between 1974 and 1983, and abortions have averaged about 125,000 each year. These figures constitute depressing news for both central and regional planners, for by the 1980s there was already insufficient labour for overall needs, and about 20,000 foreign workers were employed in the country, over two-thirds of whom were from Vietnam (Anon 1982, p.41). Future production targets can only be achieved in these circumstances through automation, the use of new technology, and associated increases in labour productivity. Moreover, regional planning is being made more difficult by the continuing variation in the pattern of population growth across the country. Differences persist between the Czech Lands and Slovakia; and in the latter, the northern and eastern districts, which have always been the least-developed areas of the country, now have the country's most rapid rates of natural increase (Häufler 1984, p.97). Population growth in the larger cities of the Czech lands, in contrast, is now very slow, as people appear to be turning rather to the small and middle-sized towns in the more pleasant and less industrialised parts of the country (Musil and Rysavy 1983). Thus, in future adequate supplies of labour may not be available in the areas in which the planners have indicated that industry should expand.

(4) An Assessment of Regional Planning

In general, it is clear that the marked regional differences in the level of development have been much reduced since the late 1940s, and in particular those between Slovakia and the Czech Lands. The structure of employment is now very similar in all regions, and key social indicators show little regional variation. For instance, infant mortality is low throughout the country, and although housing quantity and quality are still inferior in Slovakia, a great levelling up of standards has occurred (Czechoslovakia 1984, p.87). Planners are continuing the effort to reduce differences between urban and rural standards of living, and to restrain suburban growth around the large cities (Musil and Rysavy 1983); and further plans were being considered in the early 1980s to limit the growth of the major agglomerations in the Czech lands - Prague, Brno and Ostrava (Milerski 1982). However, regional policy has not been successful everywhere. For example, despite attempts to resettle West Bohemia following the expulsion of the Germans at the end of the war (Blanc 1963), people are once again moving out of the area, known colloquially as the 'Wild West', and the West Bohemian Regional Planning Committee has admitted that

"The problem of resettling certain areas adjacent to the western border of our state has once again reached a critical situation...The ebbing away of population from these areas is a very serious problem" (Václav 1984, p.8).

One reason for this may be the increased importance of the area for military purposes, as a result of which large areas have been excluded from normal economic and social development. But there are other reasons, and especially a lack of job opportunities and a decline in housing, services and public transport. In the case of industry, government policy maintains that

"The question of job opportunities in industry has been one of the most important issues in the borderlands since World War II, and remains so"

(Václav 1984, p.8), but in reality industry has been stagnating in parts of the region for a long time, and the main aim of planning policy now is to try to maintain the status quo. Moreover, mining and electricity generation have led to a deterioration in the environment. The regional "national committee" has publicly admitted that housing conditions have deteriorated severely in the 'special hardship areas' adjoining the state frontier. Old houses are decaying or have been adapted to form second homes, and construction of new dwellings lags far behind demand. The Regional Planning Committee has stated that

"The housing construction sector has not been complying with its mission in tne past decades, and most building has been constructed in the larger centres in category three areas (that is, those with the least difficult living conditions, lying at least twenty kilometres from the frontier)" (Václav 1984, p.8), rather than in areas where the need is greater. Furthermore, services have suffered. Only eighteen of the 381 'category one' communities, which contain nearly thirty percent of the region, but only four percent of its population, contain a store or workshop; and between 1970 and 1983 the number of grocery and hardware shops declined considerably. Finally, the Committee has admitted that it is disturbed by the reduction in 'bus routes in some frontier districts. In 1980 there were 326 routes with 6,539 services, but by 1984 these had been reduced to 314 and 6,081 respectively, following cuts in sparsely populated districts, to economise on diesel fuel (Václav 1984, p.9). Both workers and schoolchildren have been experiencing increasing difficulty in reaching their places of work, and transport facilities at weekends have become very poor (Anon 1984a).

Thus, regional development has not been without its problems, some of which may be attributable to the failure of the authorities to adopt academics' views of the structure of the space economy and the most appropriate administrative framework for it, but others of which may reflect the limits of even the Command Economy to determine the spatial pattern of development. However, development policies have also had consequences for at least two other major areas - the environment and the pattern of urban settlement - and it is to these that we must now turn.

ENVIRONMENTAL POLICY

Post-war industrial development has had substantial effects upon the natural environment in Czechoslovakia. Of course, industry has been located in Bohemia and Moravia for 500 years, and over the last century and a half these regions have experienced its adverse effects (Carter 1973). But it was not until the socialist development of the country that Czechoslovakia came face to face with the need for an environmental policy. However, during the first two post-war decades Czechoslovakian planners regarded environmental deterioration as an exclusively Western problem and a sure token of the impending collapse of capitalism (Dienes 1974). In this, they took their lead from

Soviet writers, who insisted that, in the protection
of the environment against pollution,
   "a socialist society has undisputed advantages
   over a capitalist one...because in the former
   there is no contradiction between the interests
   of individuals...In a society with public
   ownership of the means of production,
   environmental disruption will invariably be
   accidental"
(Petryanov 1971, pp.42-43). However, state
ownership of resources and productive facilities
means that the government, as Goldman (1971, p.68)
has noted, is generally
   "unable to stand aside as an impartial referee
   between industry and the citizen
   consumer...There is usually an identity of
   interest between factory manager and local
   government official".
The conservation of nature in Czechoslovakia
dates back to 1883, when the first forest reserve
was established (Hadeč 1977, p.18), but it was not
until after the First World War that a ministry of
Education and National Culture took responsibility
for the protection of nature and national monuments.
By 1938 there were 160 nature reserves, and progress
continued after the war with the designation of the
first national park in the Tatra Mountains in 1952.
However, constitutional recognition of tne need to
protect the environment did not occur until 1955
(Czechoslovakia 1955 and 1956), and even then the
laws were rather general. The Protection of Nature
Act, 1956, proclaimed that
   "The state protects nature, its important
   elements and creations, as well as the
   landscape with all its individual character",
but such a decree was far too vague (Maracek and
Koukal 1983, pp.215-217). Furthermore, the
sanctions against those breaking the law were light.
   Greater awareness of the environmental problems
which have been caused by industry did, however,
lead to the passage of four major laws between 1967
and 1977. The first, in 1967, entitled "Measures
for Protecting Air Purity", introduced a new scale
of fines for enterprises which exceeded admissible
air pollution levels. It established a central
authority, under the Ministry of Forestry and Water
Economy, which was responsible for levying these,
paying damages and imposing upper emission limits;
and eight regional inspectorates were set up to
ensure the law's implementation. Monitoring was
made the responsibility of regional and local air

pollution committees.

The second dealt with water pollution. The Water Conservation Law of 1955 had proved to be inadequate to cope with increasing industrial output and the transition to large-scale farming, and in 1963 the government had noted the need for greater attention to pollution, particularly in the principal rivers of the North Bohemian Region (Hruška 1964, p.89). Two years later a further evaluation of the quality of river water was made, and a state norm agreed (Havrda 1966, p.256), but it was not until 1973 that a Water Act was passed to protect both surface and subterranean sources and provide punishments for misuse (Elek 1983). Implementation of the Act fell to the central and regional water inspectorates, the latter of which had been established in 1960.

The third law was designed to protect agricultural land, and especially that of high quality, from transference to other uses. Between 1948 and 1975 the agricultural area had declined by 7.4 percent, while land in urban and other non-rural uses had increased by forty percent (Czechoslovakia 1983, p.284). Under the Agricultural Land Protection Act of 1976 payments are required for land which is withdrawn from farming – payments which must compensate the farming organisation in full for any economic loss which it may suffer, and also the loss which the nation as a whole may be thought to bear as a result of any reduction in the area of agricultural land. (In effect, payments must be adequate to enable the organisation to maintain the same output and economic results as before the transfer of some of its land (Fabry 1979, p.87); and the developer must meet the cost of tne intensification of use of the remaining land, even if the overall efficiency of the economy would be improved by a substitution of other types of production for those of agriculture on it.) Moreover, hop gardens, orchards, vegetable fields and vineyards were 'specially protected'; and only applications for permission to transfer land out of agriculture which concern sites of lower quality, or those which lie within areas zoned for holiday cottages, or areas of fragmented farmland within built-up areas, are likely to be approved (Fabry 1979, pp.84-86).

The fourth law, concerning forests, was passed in 1977. It superseded the Forestry Act of 1960 (Šilar 1979, p.11), and contained safeguards against encroachment by building and damage from industrial pollution. It also stipulated that a fifth of the forested area was to be set aside for recreational or special conservation purposes, including places of exceptional importance for water conservation, woods near large cities, recreation centres for trade union members, and sanatoria and summer camps for children from heavily polluted areas (Karásek 1981).

In all, there were more than 350 regulations in existence concerning the environment by the late 1970s (Kiesewetter 1979), and its protection has been a constant theme in the legal, political and technical literatures since then. To the outsider this plethora of laws may seem impressive, but their application has been far from convincing. For instance, air pollution remains a serious problem. As a result of the emphasis on heavy manufacturing, based on low-quality coal, the emission of sulphur dioxide rose from 1,000,000 tons in 1955 to 3,370,000 in 1982, when Czechoslovakia ranked fifth, after the USSR, Britain and the two Germanies, in Europe's table of polluters (Highton and Chadwick 1982). The Czech Lands, in particular, have suffered from this, and Häufler (1984, p. 69) has admitted that, on average, each square kilometre of them receives twenty-seven tonnes of sulphur dioxide and thirty-seven tonnes of solid matter annually, and that 8.4 percent of the land surface and a third of the population are seriously affected. Comparable figures for Slovakia are 6.3 percent of the surface and 27.3 percent of the population, and lower emission levels of 12.6 tonnes of sulphur dioxide and a similar amount of solid matter have been recorded there. But it is the North Bohemian region which faces the greatest problems for, although it covers only six percent of the country, it produces ten percent of the industrial output, and in 1970 it suffered the highest pollution levels per square kilometre in Europe, with eighty-six tonnes of solid matter and 181 tonnes of sulphur dioxide (Raab 1972, p.20), a position which has changed little since.

Water pollution is also a serious problem in the Czech Lands. The chief sources are cellulose, chemical and food plants, and the River Labe is particularly badly affected. However, the situation is no better in Slovakia, where a recent state publication announced that half of its total river length was classified as "seriously or very seriously" contaminated.

This air and water pollution has affected parts of the country's soil and vegetation cover, and farming, although being one of the main water polluters through the use of fertilisers and pesticides, also suffers from air pollution. Pollution from industry in 1980 caused damage to over half a million hectares of arable land, or twelve percent of the total, and seriously damaged nearly 400,000 hectares of productive forest (**Tribuna** 1983, p.3; **Tvorba** 1982, p.4). Again, the Czech Lands seem to have suffered more than Slovakia because of the greater combustion of brown coal there and the much higher proportion of coniferous trees in the Czech and Moravian forests. Moreover, the increasing use of herbicides and pesticides to combat insects and weeds has led to high concentrations of nitrates in food; there has been contamination of soils by heavy metals in recent years; and opencast coal mining has occurred over wide areas of good agricultural land in North Bohemia. At its worst, air pollution has reached levels which are dangerous to human health; drinking water has been polluted in many urban areas; there is increasing evidence of the pollution of food by chemicals; and public concern is widespread. However, regional planners may have little opportunity to influence the most dangerous developments. For instance, concern was growing in the 1980s over the Gabcikovo-Nagymaros hydro-electric project on the Danube, and environmentalists in both Czechoslovakia and Hungary have become worried about the flora and fauna of a long stretch of the river and the impact that polluted subterranean rivers may have on drinking water supplies (Anon 1984b, p.4). But projects such as this are decided at national and international levels, undermining efforts by local planners to improve the environment. Furthermore, the whole idea of environmental protection is called in question when the state continually emphasises the need for increased industrial output in its desire to catch up with Western European living standards.

URBAN DEVELOPMENT

Czechoslovakia has a long and varied urban history. Between 400 and 50 B.C. Celtic oppidiae were situated on high ground over much of the country - over a dozen of which, including Bratislava, Hostýn and Stradonice, have been

positively identified. From 100 to 400 A.D. Roman
castrae were located along the Danube to guard the
"limes" of the Empire, and small military outposts,
such as that at Trencin, were set up in Slovakia.
During the ninth century the Great Moravian Empire
encouraged a further phase of development in the
valleys, as at Kouřim, Mikulčice and Nitra; between
the tenth and the thirteenth centuries castles and
fortified monasteries were located on strategic
commercial routes, as at Vyšehrad, now a district of
Prague; and, in the Later Middle Ages, several new
towns, such as Brno, Košice and Plzeň, were
established, mainly in connection with mining or
mercantile activity. These formed the basis of
later urbanisation, when eighteenth century
industrial growth created manufacturing centres
based upon natural resources and power. The rapid
urban growth associated with industrialisation was
accompanied by a marked exodus of population from
rural areas, and this continued into the early
twentieth century and resulted in heavy depopulation
in Slovakia and Southern Bohemia (Andrle 1978). As
we have seen, early plans after the Second World War
sought to reverse this flight through the
equalisation of the distribution of industry, and
this has led to a revitalisation of the Slovakian
economy and renewed urban growth there. However,
industrial development has occurred in all parts of
the country, and with it has gone urban expansion on
a large scale, arising not so much from the natural
growth of the population – which has occurred
largely in rural areas – but from migration from
country to town (Kansky 1976).
  Some indication of the development of towns
since 1950 is given in Table 5.3. This shows that
the number of towns has doubled, and that it has
been those with between 50,000 and 100,000
inhabitants which have experienced the largest
proportional growth of any group. Moreover, there
are now five cities – Prague, Bratislava, Brno,
Košice and Ostrava – with over 200,000 inhabitants.
However, the future of smaller settlements has also
been of concern. Since the 1940s 1,240 factories
and nearly fifteen percent of the employment in the
secondary sector have been put into places with less
than a thousand inhabitants, in an attempt to
discourage any further exodus from rural areas
(Mareš 1978), while communities of between one and
five thousand people now contain over 300 industrial
plants and nearly one third of the industrial labour
force (Nový 1983, p.30), with the result that, as

Table 5.3: Numbers of Towns in Czechoslovakia

Population	1950	1960	1970	1983
Above 200,000	2	4	4	5
100-200,000	3	1	2	2
50- 99,999	6	9	12	25
20- 49,999	24	33	41	62
10- 19,999	58	72	84	115
5- 9,999	12	12	13	16
Total	105	131	156	225

Source: Statistická ročenka Československé socialistické republiky for relevant years

Table 5.4: Second Home Development in Czechoslovakia, 1945-76

Year	Czech Lands Number	Percent of Total	Slovakia Number	Percent of Total	Czecho-slovak Total
1945	40,178	100	-	-	40,178
1955	62,487	100	-	-	62,487
1965	108,925	95.5	5,085	4.5	114,010
1970	127,877	93	9,625	7	137,502
1972	156,402	94	9,844	6	166,246
1976	203,850	90	22,649	10	226,499

Sources: Anon (1972); Anon (1974); Otrubová (1980), pp. 129-143.

the post-war period has progressed, immigration to the cities has waned. It should also be noted that there have been marked regional contrasts in urban growth. For instance, it is the Prague region which has had the lowest absolute and relative growth in urban population over the period – perhaps reflecting the emphasis on investment in other parts of the country – while the greatest proportional increases in the number of towns have occurred in the Eastern Slovakian region, which is centred upon Košice, and in West Bohemia. At present just over half of the country's population is urban, but there is still a marked difference between the republics. In the Czech Lands in 1980 urban dwellers constituted two thirds of the total (Čtrnact 1983), compared with about a fifth in Slovakia.

Unfortunately, this urban development has not been without its problems, and one of the most important of these has been housing. Priority has been given to workers' accommodation, in communities defined as those

"in which the working classes are in a majority and where at least sixty-five percent of the population receive wages or salaries"

(Votrubec 1960, p.265), but in 1970 official documents admitted that there was a shortfall of nearly 700,000 dwellings. A decade later the same sources claimed that the gap had dropped to just over a quarter of a million (Franek 1982, p.43), but, as Musgrove (1984, p.92) has stated, "these statistics should be treated with caution". There are three major reasons for this deficit. Firstly, migration from rural to urban areas was very great during the 1950s and 60s, when the main receiving areas were Prague, Ostrava-karvina, Bratislava and Košice (Bašovský 1973). Secondly, housing has been accorded a lower priority than industrial growth throughout the post-war period by central government; and thirdly, the provision of land for those people wishing to build their own houses in towns and cities has been inadequate. (However, that is not to say that private house building has not occurred at all, for much has taken place in rural areas, not least for second homes.)

More particularly, there have been problems in Prague and Bratislava. In Prague planners have faced a conflict between the need for new housing schemes in the old town centre and the preservation of its character. There has also been a loss of dwellings as small apartments have been demolished or improved. For every four new dwellings completed between 1960 and 1973, one was lost (Andrle et al 1981). Much of Prague's new housing is in new 'neighbourhood unit' estates of multi-storey blocks which have been built around the perimeter of the city on greenfield sites. Amongst these are the "South-Western" suburb, with 120,000 inhabitants, the "Southern" suburb, with a population of 100,000, and the "Northern" suburb, in which a further 120,000 people live (Carter 1979, p.451).

In Bratislava local planners have authorised construction of about 3,000 new apartments each year, and these have also been mainly in multi-storey blocks. But they have been built at the expense of parks and other green space, so that, according to one observer, "Bratislava is a disjointed high-rise sprawl" (Economist 1985, p.51). Typical is the vast Petrzalka suburb, where about 100,000 people were moved into an estate which was far from complete, and where complaints about poor finishing, leaky windows and cracked walls, and about inadequate numbers of shops and services, have been commonplace.

It is of some interest to note that, although housing has been socialised, with no houseowner allowed to let his property for profit (Krèjči 1972, p.23), the housing market still contains significant elements of a class nature, which pose problems for the authorities. Szelenyi (1983, p.42) has noted that

"housing [has] never entirely lost its market character, and that differences between households, both in their actual housing and in their chances of acquiring any desired kind of housing, including housing of good quality [have] continued to depend on their social status".

Secondly, there has been a rapid and considerable development of second homes by the growing urban population, which enjoys shorter working hours and longer paid holidays than in the past. In particular, these have increased in popularity since the introduction of the two-day 'English vikend' in the early 1970s, and the wider ownership of private cars (Gardavský 1971 and 1979). However, early efforts to control their location and standard were inadequate, and more recently, according to Musgrove (1984, p.92), planners have not been able to prevent

"losses from the housing stock that have arisen from sales of rural houses for leisure use as second homes".

The level of demand for second homes appears to differ widely between the two republics, and Gardavský believes that this may be related to their contrasting economic and settlement histories. Over a third of the Czechs live in settlements of more than 20,000, which has proved to be a critical level for second-home demand, compared with only a tenth of the Slovaks. Thus, it was on the Czech Lands that the number of second homes grew rapidly up to the mid-1970s, when new planning laws restricted further development, rather than in Slovakia (Table 5.4). However, even within the republics marked regional contrasts exist in second home densities. High concentrations are found around Prague (Gardavsky 1969) and in Southern and Northern Moravia, around Brno and Ostrava respectively, and forty-one percent of those in Slovakia are located in the Western Region, especially around Bratislava (Otrubová 1980).

Housing shortages in urban areas have led to a great increase in commuting. By 1970 a quarter of the total workforce, or 2,300,000 people, were considered to be commuters. (That is, they were travelling more than eighteen kilometres to work by train or ten by 'bus (Demek and Střida 1971, p.202).) Commuters accounted for fifty-four percent of all rail passengers and forty-four of those travelling by road. The highest levels of commuting were recorded in Slovakia (Pivovarov 1970, p.75), followed by the South Moravian region, but much lower levels were noted in the western parts of the country. Planners have realised that much time is being lost in the journey to work and have been urged to reduce the number and length of such trips, and some successes have been achieved. In Prague public transport has received considerable investment. Two lines of the underground metro system have been completed, and a third was under construction in the mid-1980s. Suburban and country 'bus routes now focus on the termini of the lines, and, as a result, travel within the city centre has been made much easier and quicker (Slepicka 1984). But serious problems also exist. For example, planners in Bratislava are trying to develop a new road system across the Danube at a time when the most immediate need for commuters is for more 'buses and trams during the rush hour in order to relieve the overcrowding of the existing vehicles (Economist 1985, p.51).

CONCLUSION

Economic development in Czechoslovakia since 1945 has been responsible for a transformation of the space economy. The old contrasts in the standard of living and degree of urbanisation between the Czech and Slovak lands have been much reduced, and these changes have brought with them a greater homogeneity of social attitudes, if not of language and national identity. These achievements may be credited in large part to the policies and system of central planning which have been in operation since the late 1940s. However, it was noted at the outset of this essay that doubt was being cast once again in the 1980s on the appropriateness of Czechoslovakia's rigid planning system for the management of its economy (Kusin 1982, p.34), and there are clear reasons to extend this scepticism to the area of regional planning. In particular, the planners do not appear to have brought under control such important consequences of economic development as pollution, housing shortages in the towns and long-distance commuting, each of which has shown a marked regional incidence. Furthermore, there are at least two major areas of the country - Northern and Western Bohemia - in which interlocking problems of an economic, environmental and, in the case of Western Bohemia, social nature have persisted. Nor has central planning been able to move the economy on from its dependence upon heavy industry, which ties the pattern of development to resource-based locations, and from what has become old-fashioned engineering in the traditional industrial areas, to more advanced engineering and high-technology industries. Indeed, it is rather difficult to see how, given their institutionalised and traditional role within the structure of government and planning in Czechoslovakia, the older industries can be forced into decline so that new, advanced ones may take an increasing share of the meagre supplies of labour, and become established. Furthermore, given the clear preference of the Czechs in particular for small and medium-sized towns, rather than the existing industrial agglomerations, it may be more difficult to obtain labour for all activities, both old and new, in those agglomerations in future. If the backwardness of Czech industry is overcome, it may be in the small historic towns, and in the more attractive environments, that this will be achieved, and if this were to occur the map of population and production in Czechoslovakia might undergo changes in the next forty years which would prove to be at least the equal, though very different, from tnose of the last forty.

REFERNCES

Andrle, A. (1978), Vyvoj Ceskoslovenskych mest 1869-1970, Geograficky Casopis, 30, 126-149.
Andrle, A., Pojer, M. and Kučera, K. (1981), Survey of Dwelling Stock Decreases in Czechoslovakia, Terplan, Prague.
Anon (1972), Soupis objektu individualni rekreace, Česka statistika, 12.
Anon (1974), Supis objektov individualnej rekreacie v SSR podl'a stavu k 31.12.72, Statisticke informacie.
Anon (1975), 30 (Tricet) let socialisticke dopravy ČSSR, Nakl. Dopravy a Spoju, Prague.
Anon (1982), Foreign Workers, Czechoslovak Life, 10, 41.
Anon (1984a), People Moving Out of the West Bohemian Borderland, Radio Free Europe Research, 9/11, 14.
Anon (1984b), Rectors are blue about the Danube, Times Higher Educational Supplement, 26th. October, p.4.
Bašovský, O. (1973), Pohyb obyvatelstva a regionálna štruktúra ČSSR, Acta Geographica Universitatis Comenianae, 12, 98.
Blanc, A. (1963), Le probleme des regions frontières: le cas de Tachov, Revue géographique de l'Est, 3, 155-165.
Blažek, M. (1954), K otázkám rajonovani v Československu, Politická ekonomie, 5, 18-21.
Calta, V., Hašové, H, and Klimplová, H. (1983), Socialist Czechoslovakia, Orbis, Prague.
Carter, F.W. (1970), Czechoslovakia's North Moravian Region: A Geographical Appraisal, Revue Géographique de l'Est, 1-2, 57-71.
Carter, F.W. (1973), The industrial development of Prague, 1800-1850, Slavonic and East European Review, 11, 243-275.
Carter, F.W. (1979), Prague and Sofia: An Analysis of Their Changing Internal City Structure, in The Socialist City: Spatial Structure and Urban Policy, ed. R.A.French and F.E.I.Hamilton, Wiley and Sons, Chichester, pp.425-459.
Čtrnact, P. (1983), Urbanizace v ČSR ve výslednich sčitaní lidu 1961-1980, Studia

Czechoslovakia

Geographica, 81, 55-71.
Czechoslovakia (1949), The First Czechoslovak Economic Five-Year Plan: Act and Government Memorandum, Ministry of Information and Public Culture, Prague.
Czechoslovakia (1955), Government Decree No. 1/1955 Zb.
Czechoslovakia (1956), Government Decree No. 40/1956 Sb.
Czechoslovakia (1962), Statisticka Rocenka ČSSR 1962, Federalni Statisticky Urad, Prague.
Czechoslovakia (1983), Statisticka Rocenka ČSSR 1983, Federalni Statisticky Urad, Prague.
Czechoslovakia (1984), Statisticka Rocenka ČSSR 1984, Federalni Statisticky Urad, Prague.
Dědina, V. (1928), Regionální členění Československa, Sborník Československske Společnosti Zeměpisné, 35, 89-92.
Demek, J. and Střida, M. (1972), Geography of Czechoslovakia, Academia, Prague.
Dienes, L. (1974), Environmental Disruption in Eastern Europe, in Environmental Deterioration in the Soviet Union and Eastern Europe, ed. I.Volgyes, Praeger, New York, pp. 141-158.
Economist (20/4/1985), 51.
Elek, T. (1983), Chránene vodnohospodárske oblasti v prírodnom a životnom prostredí, Životné Prostredie, 17, 157-161.
Elias, A. (1972), Manpower trends in Czechoslovakia 1950-1990, Government Printing Office, Washington D.C.
Fabry, (1979), Protection of Agricultural Land, Bulletin of Czechoslovak Law, 18, 82-91.
Feierabend, L.K. (1952), Agricultural cooperatives in Czechoslovakia, Mid-European Studies Center, New York.
Franek, J. (1982), Housing in Czechoslovakia, Research Institute for Building and Architecture, Prague.
Frolov, V.V. (1978), Nektorie izmeneniya v territorialnoi strukture promishlennosti evropeiskih stran SEV i Ch.S.S.R. pod vliyaniem mezhdunarodnogo sotsialisticheskogo razdeleniya truda, Acta Universitatis Carolinae: Geographica, XIII, 27-35.
Gardavský, V. (1969), Recreational hinterland of a city, taking Prague as an example, Acta Universitatis Carolinae: Geographica, 1, 3-29.
Gardavský, V. (1971), K problematice vymezování rekreačních zázemí měst, Problémy geografického výskumu, pp.325-330.

133

Czechoslovakia

Gardavský, V. (1979), Second Homes in Czechoslovakia, in Second Homes: Curse or Blessing, ed. J.T.Coppock, Pergamon, Oxford, pp.63-74.

George, P. (1947), The new settlement policy in Czechoslovakia, Slavonic and East European Review, 26, 60-68.

George, P. (1963), L'industrialisation de la Slovaquie, Revue géographique de l'Est, 3, 145-153.

Golan, G. (1971), The Czechoslovak Reform Movement: Communism in Crisis 1962-1968, Cambridge U.P.

Goldman, M.L. (1971), Environmental Disruption in the Soviet Union, in Man's Impact on the Environment, ed. T.R.Dewyler, McGraw-Hill, New York, pp.61-75.

Hadeč, E. (1977), The conservation of nature, in Landscape and Man in Socialist Czechoslovakia, ed. O.Vidláková, Orbis, Prague, pp.17-33.

Hampl, M. (1968), Complex economic geographical differentiation of environment, Acta Universitatis Carolinae: Geographica, 2, 19-49.

Hampl, M., Ježek, J. and Kuhnl, K. (1978), Sociálnegeografická regionalizace ČSR, Acta Demographica, 2.

Hanzlík, J. (1967), Vývoj obyvatelstva na Slovensku v obdobi 1869-1961, Geografický Časopis, XIX, 3-30.

Häufler, V. (1966), Changes in the Geographical Distribution of Population in Czechoslovakia, Academia, Prague.

Häufler, V. (1984), Ekonomická geografie Československu, Academia, Prague.

Havrda, V. (1966), Rozmístění zdrojů znečištení a čistota toků Severočeského kraje, Sborník Československe Společnosti Zeměpisné, 71, 256.

Highton, N.H. and Chadwick, M.J. (1982), The effects of changing patterns of energy use on sulfur emissions and depositions in Europe, Ambio, 11, 326.

Hruška, E. (1964), Tvorba a ochrana krajiny jako životního prostředí, Sborník Československe Společnosti Zeměpisné, 69, 89.

Ivanička, I. (1964), The Geography of the Region of the East-Slovakian Iron-works, Acta Geologica et Geographica Universitatis Comenianae: Geographica, 4, 428pp.

Kansky, K.J. (1976), Urbanization under socialism: the case of Czechoslovakia, Praeger, New York.

Kansky, K.J. (1979), Recent Progress in Transportation Research and Instruction in

Czechoslovakia, East Central Europe/L'Europe du Centre-Est, 6, 85-92.

Kansky, K.J. (1980), Regional transport development and policies in Czechoslovakia since 1945, in East European Transport: Regions and Modes, ed. B.Mieczkowski, Nijhoff, The Hague, pp.147-164.

Karásek, O. (1981), Forests and Man's Health, Czechoslovak Life, 7, 6-7.

Kaspar, J. (1964), K problematice kanalu D-O-L a tretiho zeleznicniho tahu, Doprava, 6, 377-381.

Kiesewetter, Z. (1979), Exploitation and protection of natural resources and their impact on human environment, Bulletin of Czechoslovak Law, 18, 77-81.

Kopačka, L. (1980), Some Economic-Geographical Aspects of the Development of Czechoslovak Industry after the Year 1945, Historicka Geografie, 19, 321-375.

Korbel, J. (1959), The Communist Subversion of Czechoslovakia, 1938-1948, Princeton U.P.

Korčák, J. (1934), Regionální členění Československu, Statistický obzor, 15, 70-77.

Korčák, J. (1961), Immigratsionnaya baza cheshkich gorodov, Problems of Economic Regions, 27, 233-242.

Korda, B. (1975), L'economia cecoslovacca dopo la reforma, L'Est, 1, 9-45.

Kozma, P. (1954), Hutni průmysl a rudne doly, technicky pokrok v Gottwaldove petiletce, SNTL, Prague.

Krejči, J. (1972), Social Change and Stratification in Postwar Czechoslovakia, Macmillan, London.

Krejči, J. (1976), The Czechoslovak economy during the years of systematic transformation: 1945-1949, Jahrbuch der Wirtscaft Osteuropas, 7, 297-344.

Kusin, V.V. (1982), Husak's Czechoslovakia and Economic Stagnation, Problems of Communism, XXXI, 24-37.

Kyn, O. (1975), Czechoslovakia, in The New Economic Systems of Eastern Europe, ed. H.H.Hohmann, M.C.Kaser and K.C.Thalheim, University of California Press, Berkeley.

Luza, R. (1964), The transfer of Sudeten Germans: a study of Czech-German relations, 1933-1962, New York Press, New York.

Maracek, J. and Koukal, A. (1983), Nektere aktualni problemy pravni upravy ochrany prirody v ČSR, Zivotne prostredie, 17, 215-217.

Czechoslovakia

Mareš, J. (1978), Vliv industrializace na rozvoj mest, Studia Geographica, 47, 67-72.

Mareš, J. (1980), Geografický potenciál průmysl ČSR, Studia Geographica, 69, 17-23.

Mareš, J. (1982), Gravitační území průmyslových míst v ČSR, Sborník Československé Společnosti Zeměpisné, 87, 105-109.

Michal, J.M. (1960), Central Planning in Czechoslovakia, Stanford U.P.

Milerski, O. (1982), Vymezeni aglomeraci v ČSR z hlediska potreb oblastniho planovani, Sborník Československé Společnosti Zeměpisné, 87, 185-195.

Mládek, J. (1984), The Study of Industrial Nodes in Slovakia, Acta Geographica Universitatis Comenianae, 24, 29-39.

Mrazek, O. (1960), 15 let rozvoje znarodneneho průmysl ČSSR, SNTL, Prague.

Musgrove, S. (1984), Housing in Czechoslovakia, Housing Review, 33, 91-93.

Musil, J. and Rysavy, Z. (1983), Urban and regional processes under capitalism and socialism: a case study from Czechoslovakia, International Journal of Urban and Regional Research, 7, 495-527.

Novakova-Hribova, B. (1978), Zemeny ve vyvoji obyvatelstva CSR v obdobi 1961-1970 (stanovene pomoci statistickych jednotek), Studia Geographica, 47, 37-77.

Nový, O. (1983), Town and Country Development in Czechoslovakia, Orbis, Prague.

Olsovsky, R. (1964), Survey of Economic Development of the Czechoslovak Socialist Republic from 1945 to 1960, Czechoslovak Economic Papers, 3, 175-200.

Otubová, E. (1980), Priestorové rozloženie chát na Slovensku so špecifickým zameraním na chaty obyvatel'ov, Acta Geographica Universitatis Comenianae, 18, 129-143.

Pavlik, Z. (1959), Dynamika hospodářsko-společenské struktury obyvatelstva českých zemí, Demografie, 1, 145-155.

Petryanov, I. (1971), Public Greed? No! Public Weal!, Soviet Life, 12, 42-43.

Pivovarov, Y.L. (1958), Nektoryje osobennosti socialisticheskoj rekonstrukcii ostravskogo rajona Chechoslovakii, Izvestiya Akademmi Nauk SSSR, (Seriya geograficheskaya), 3, 71-75.

Pivovarov, Y.L. (1970), Commuting as an Aspect of Population Geography in the Socialist Countries, in Recent population Movements in the East European Countries, ed. B.Sárfalvi, Akadémiai Kiadó, Budapest, pp.73-76.

136

Provaznik, J. (1970), Ekonomické výrovnavanie českých krajín a Slovenska, Plánované hospodářství, 4, 21-27.

Raab, P. (1972), Současný stav znečištění, in Ochrana čistoty ovzduší v ČSSR, ed. I.Novák, MLVH, Prague.

Schaffer, H.G. (1965), Czechoslovakia's New Economic Model, Problems of Communism, XIV, 31-40.

Sik, O. (1965), Economic Planning and Management in Czechoslovakia, Orbis, Prague.

Sik, O. (1971), Reform und Restauration in der tschechoslowakischen Wirtschaft, Zeitschrift für Ostforschung, 20, 401-428.

Šilar, J. (1979), The Forestry Act of 1977, Bulletin of Czechoslovak Law, 18.

Šlampa, O. (1964), Polish Sea Ports and Czechoslovak Foreign Trade, Sborník Československé Společnosti zeměpisné (Congress Supplement), 169-174.

Slepicka, L. (1984), Dilemata prazske dopravy: Kdy budeme cestovat do zamestnani rychleji a pohodlneji?, Hospodářské Noviny, 13, 8.

Staneková, E. (1983), Úloha infraštruktury v územnom rozvoji, Ekonomický Časopis, 31, 859-866.

Steers, J.A. (1948), The middle people: resettlement in Czechoslovakia, Geographical Journal, 112, 28-42.

Stransky, K. (1963), Srediska nakladni zeleznicni dopravy v Severoceskem kraji, Sborník Československé Společnosti zeměpisné, 68, 45-48.

Střda, M. (1958), Voprosy ekonomicheskogo rajonirovaniya Chechoslovakii, Izvestiya Akademmi Nauk SSSR (Seriya geograficheskaya), 5, 50-59.

Szelenyi, I. (1983), Urban Inequalities under State Socialism, Oxford U.P.

Tvorba (17/3/1982).

Václav, J. (1984), Život při západní hranici, Hospodářské Noviny, 9, 8.

Vanous, J. (1982), East European Economic Slowdown, Problems of Communism, XXXI, 1-19.

Velkobrosky, K. (1953), Ceskoslovenska ricni plavba a jeji spoje do namornich pristavu, Doprava,1 199-203, 220-224, 243-246.

Vidláková, O. (1977), Public administration and legal regulation of the human environment, in Landscape and Man in Socialist Czechoslovakia, Orbis, Prague, pp.81-111.

Votrubec, C. (1958), Vyvoj Československych měst v letech 1950-1956, Sborník Československé Společnosti Zeměpisné, 63, 137-147.

Czechoslovakia

Votrubec, C. (1960), Geographical problems of building towns and workers' settlements in Czechoslovakia, Sborník Československé Společnosti Zeměpisné, 65, 262-267.

Wanklyn, H. (1954), Czechoslovakia, Philip, London.

Zeman, E. and Wanke, R. (1981), On the threshold of the 7th Five-Year Plan, Czechoslovak Life, 1, 3.

Zochnak, J. Vplyv pravnej regulacie na rozvoj kontejnerizacie v československom dopravnom systeme, Pravny Obzor, 62, 203-210.

Žurek, O. (1955), K otázkám ekonomického rajonování v ČSSR, Plánované hospodářství, 4, 51-60.

Zwass, A. (1984), The Economies of Eastern Europe in a Time of Change, Macmillan, London.

Chapter 6

THE GERMAN DEMOCRATIC REPUBLIC

R.E.H.Mellor

THE CONTEXT OF PLANNING

The German Democratic Republic (GDR) is like no other country in Eastern Europe. Not only is it an entirely new creation of the post-war settlement, requiring to adapt its economy to new orientations and scales of activity, but it is the only country whose population has declined during the post-war period. Moreover, unlike much of Eastern Europe, it was highly developed before 1939, with commercial agriculture, a substantial industrial base, a highly urbanised population and a well-developed infrastructure. Thus, it has been adjustment, including spatial adjustment, rather than development, which has been the key issue for the GDR, and it is this issue which will be examined below with regard to the industrial, agricultural, transport, territorial (regional) and settlement patterns, together with the associated problems of environmental protection.

The German Democratic Republic (GDR) emerged from the division of the Reich by the Allied powers in 1945. The Allies grouped existing local government areas together in a rather arbitrary fashion to form occupation zones. The old provinces of central Germany were crudely lumped together to form the Soviet Occupation Zone, and a four-power regime was set up in Berlin. Moreover, the problems which this created for the GDR were exacerbated by the equally arbitrary definition of Poland's western boundary along the Oder and Neisse rivers, and the transfer of the port of Stettin (Szczecin) to that country.

It had been originally agreed that Germany would be managed by the four powers as a social and economic whole, but practice in the Western zones

quickly became quite different from that in the
Soviet. The currency reform, which was considered
vital to the re-establishment of economic health in
the Western zones, and the decision to establish a
market economy there, brought the final break in
1948. The Soviet Union reacted by testing the
resolve of the Western powers to stay in Berlin by
blockading their sectors of the city, and the
following year saw the emergence of the two post-war
German states. The Western powers created a federal
republic, whereas in the Soviet Zone the German
Democratic Republic appeared - a centralised state
with a planned economy in the image of the people's
republics of the Eastern bloc. The already closely
guarded boundary between the Western and the Soviet
zones became a virtually-closed inter-German
frontier.

Before 1945 the Reich had been a closely
integrated economic and social unit, but this was
completely disrupted. Central Germany was cut off
from the territory that had passed to Poland, and it
was also isolated from West Germany. The GDR
consequently inherited an unbalanced economic
structure. Its large engineering and metal-working
industry had until then been overwhelmingly
dependent on raw metal from the Ruhr, in the west,
and Silesia, in the east, and these areas had also
been its principal sources of hard coal. The
important chemical industry of the Elbe-Saale basin
and the Saxon textile industry were separated from
their major markets in West Germany; and the
destruction by wartime bombing (though less serious
than in West Germany), and the rapacious reparations
dismantling by the Russians, further accentuated the
imbalances in the economy.

The GDR also inherited a serious population
problem. The area of the present republic had had a
population of 16,700,000 in 1939, but at least
4,500,000 refugees arrived during a two-year period
immediately after the war, and by 1947 the
population had reached 19,100,000. Most of the
refugees were settled in the poorer and remoter
country districts. However, since then the
population has declined, with an especially rapid
fall to 17,080,000 in 1961, as both local residents
and the refugees moved to West Germany. About
3,000,000 people left the GDR, most of whom were in
the most fertile and productive age groups, and in
1961 the rate of 'illegal' emigration, or
Republikflucht, reached 300,000. Such a loss could
not be tolerated by the government of the GDR; the

inter-German frontier was barricaded, and West Berlin was isolated by the Wall which was built around it. Thereafter there was a slight recovery in the population total, but it fell back again to 16,950,000 in 1973 and to 16,700,000 in 1982. Prospects for an upturn are not promising, and the GDR is among the very few countries of the world with a shrinking population.

This drain on the younger age groups intensified the already unfortunate age and sex composition of the population. The small number in the working age groups was further depleted, and there were acute difficulties in manning industry. (The West German solution of importing foreign labour was unacceptable in the socialist bloc.) At the same time, those of pensionable age, amongst which the number of women greatly exceeded that of men, were a steadily growing proportion of the total population. These were especially acute problems through the 1960s and 1970s, though since the late 1970s the proportion of people in the working age groups has begun to rise slightly. However, the long-term prospects are not good, for the proportion of children is now lower than at any time since 1945. Manpower planning continues to be extremely difficult, for the highly irregular shape to the age-sex pyramid means that the numbers in any particular age group fluctuate substantially from year to year (Figure 6.1). As the age-specific birth rate has fallen, attempts have been made through material incentives to stimulate its growth, but the results have not been encouraging.

INDUSTRIAL ADJUSTMENT AND DEVELOPMENT

The post-war shift to a state-owned, centrally-planned economy required considerable industrial and agricultural remodelling, and this problem was compounded by the need to develop a spatial structure for the now separate economy, as well as the difficulties entailed in its self-inflicted reluctance to trade with West Germany on the pre-war pattern. Pressures were also put on the GDR to trade to a greater extent than formerly with Eastern Europe and the Soviet Union, though an unrealistic level of autarky was also sought, and the task of rebuilding the economy was further increased as a result of the Soviet Union's plunder of the infrastructure for reparations. Dismantling did not end until 1953, and the value of equipment

141

The German Democratic Republic

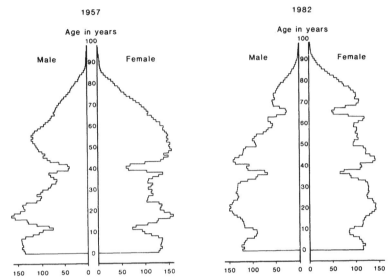

Figure 6.1 Population Pyramids for the GDR for 1957 and 1982. Note the wide range in the size of cohorts between closely adjacent age groups.
Source: Statistiches Jahrbuch der DDR

taken by the Soviet Union has been estimated at almost 16,000 million dollars, or over fifty percent more than the Russians had claimed at the Yalta conference. Some industries were almost eliminated, and a wide range of those that were left retained only between twenty-five and forty percent of their pre-war capacity. Metallurgy, chemicals and engineering were particularly hard hit.

Reconstruction began with typical Stalinist planning objectives. The Eastern European people's democracies were being pressed to be self-sufficient – an aim more realisable in the Soviet Union than by any of them. Before 1939 the area of the GDR had supplied only seven percent of the iron and steel output of the Reich, although it contained thirty-two percent of the population, and it drew most of its raw metal from the Ruhr or Silesia. Although the territory lacked suitable coal and ore, an ambitious programme to develop iron and steel making was instituted in 1950. In effect, this meant a new beginning, since eighty-five percent of the rolled-steel, eighty percent of the crude-steel, fifty-six of the steel-casting and fifty percent of the cast-iron capacities had been dismantled. As early as 1946 smelting had been restarted at the small Unterwellenborn works, and a year later its steel rolling mills had been repaired. By 1949 steel was also coming again from the Hennigsdorf plant, and in 1949 three more small plants were restarted. The main project in the new programme was the construction of a full-cycle iron and steel combine near Fürstenberg on the Oder. This was a greenfield site, initially named Stalinstadt. Ore was to be brought principally by rail from the Ukraine, over a thousand kilometres away, and coke from Czech and Polish Silesia and from the Soviet Donbass. However, the rail links proved inadequate, and the Oder waterway made relatively little contribution to transport. The original capacity of Eisenkombinat Ost was planned at 500,000 tonnes, and later this was increased to over a million, although subsequently much of the promised development was postponed until the mid-1960s. Nevertheless, it is now the largest industrial unit in the GDR, and is closely linked to other metallurgical plants.

Originally the 'matching' Eisenkombinat West at Calbe was intended to use the local ores, though poor in iron and rather acidic, from the Harz and Thüringen Mountains, and coke produced from lignite in Lusatia, where a large cokery had started production near Lauchhammer in 1955. However, by the late 1960s this steel plant had been abandoned, ostensibly because the ore deposits were exhausted (although its ore had in fact been brought from Czechoslovakia). More important, however, had been the unsuitability of the lignite coke which had been used, and the recognition during the 1960s that the GDR could obtain better quality raw metal more conveniently and less expensively through intra-bloc trade.

Self-sufficiency proved to be equally difficult to achieve in the sphere of energy supply. Other than a copious endowment of lignite, the GDR is poor in energy resources. For instance, the extraction of bituminous coal around Oelsnitz and Zwickau, where the deposits were nearing exhaustion, was finally abandoned in 1977, and hard coal deposits under the North German Plain lie at depths which are too great to be exploited. The oil and gas deposits in the north of West Germany lap over into the GDR in the Altmark around Salzwedel, where they have been worked, and the small deposits in Mecklenburg were exploited with Soviet aid. However, the GDR depends largely on imports for its oil, and these come chiefly from the Soviet Union to Schwedt through the Friendship Pipeline. Natural gas will also be drawn in large quantities from the Soviet Union on completion of a pipeline from the southern Urals; and, as the transport system is modernised and petroleum-based chemicals replace those based on lignite, demand for hydro-carbons will rise, making the economy increasingly dependent on outside suppliers.

The GDR is the world's largest producer of lignite, a friable soft coal, poor in heat value and rich in ash, which is best converted into electric current near the mines. Electrification on a large scale has thus typified central Germany since early this century, and has been expanded since the Second World War by large new lignite-fired stations, as well as by the harnessing of the modest sources of hydro-electric power, and by the building of nuclear stations at Rheinsberg near Berlin, at Lubmin on the Baltic and near Stendal, with Soviet aid. The GDR is an important participant in the COMECON Mir electricity grid.

Self-sufficiency has also proved to be an equally untenable goal for the manufacturing industries of the GDR. The domestic market has been too small and too poor to support industries where large economies of scale are the key to success, and capacity has actually exceeded home needs in several branches of chemicals and engineering despite reparations dismantling. At the same time, the shift away from an interest in consumer goods has left several industries and factories, such as the large Saxon textile mills, underutilised, lacking both home and export market opportunities.

The policy of autarky was dropped after Stalin's death, but incorporation within the Soviet sphere produced further change as the GDR tuned its economy to new trading patterns. One difficulty was that the DIN system of industrial standards, which had been in operation in the GDR, proved to be too rigorous for some other East European countries, and so a new set was devised which was closer to the Soviet GOST system. This made trade between the GDR and COMECON partners easier, but worked to the detriment of inter-German trade and trade with the West in general.

Soviet influence upon the chemical industry has also left it in a rather backward state. Early in the century the Elbe-Saale basin of central Germany had emerged as a major concentration of heavy chemical production, and under the National Socialists the industry grew substantially as synthetic substances were used to reduce Germany's dependence on imports. Although marked for reparations the Soviet authorities found it hard to re-establish dismantled plants on new sites in their own country (though some synthetic rubber and petrol plants were successfully moved), and so eventually it was considered better to retain plants _in situ_ and work them with local labour as 'Soviet companies', _Sowjetische Aktiengesellschaften_, under highly advantageous financial conditions. Eventually fifty-two percent of the capacity of the chemical industry in the GDR was under the control of such companies, but early in 1954 these plants were sold back to the Germans. The industry received a boost after 1958 through the emphasis on 'chemicalisation' by Khrushchev, in his efforts to modernise the Soviet economy. However, this once-leading sector has fallen behind West German industry technologically, and this is reflected in the slow switch from a lignite to an oil raw material base, with the former accounting for forty percent of the industry's raw materials in the GDR compared to only five percent in the Federal Republic.

Nevertheless, as COMECON has become a more effective body, agreements on specialisation and trade, with more sophisticated financial arrangements, have helped to ease several of the GDR's economic dilemmas. In particular, the encouragement to trade has helped to solve the problems of raw material and energy supplies after the fiasco of Stalinist autarky. The concept of specialisation has favoured countries like Czechoslovakia, Poland and the USSR, which have well-developed iron and steel industries, as they supplied those without, such as the GDR. In the same way, bituminous coal can be more readily imported from Czechoslovakia, Poland and the USSR than won from the country's own meagre deposits. Acceptance of trade with countries outside the socialist bloc has also enabled the GDR to cover some of its energy requirements by importing crude petroleum, notably from Egypt, Iraq and Syria, and so reduce its dependence on the Soviet Union from about ninety-five percent in 1960 to around eighty-eight percent in the early 1980s.

From the Soviet point of view, the GDR is of particular importance for its high technology industries, notably chemicals, electronics, precision engineering and optics (represented especially by Zeiss at Jena). Under the specialisation agreements all these industries have been given priority, but the GDR also manufactures equipment for working and processing lignite, for beet sugar production and for cement-making. It has also become the major supplier of railway coaches – particularly those for dual-gauge running – and for specialised freight vehicles like refrigerator wagons. The GDR is the principal producer in the socialist bloc of roller bearings, and a notable contributor of printing machinery. It has also taken advantage of the rising demand for consumer goods in Eastern Europe. Since the early 1970s the production of domestic appliances, for example, has been greatly expanded, and these goods are even sold as "Made in Germany" through West German mail order stores, under their own house labels.

The modernisation and 'socialisation' of industry have given rise to a number of problems of a spatial nature. For instance, in the industrial districts of Saxony, such as those around Karl-Marx-Stadt (Chemnitz), where there were a great number of very small firms before 1945, these units have been merged under state ownership into larger and reputedly more effectively organised enterprises. This has involved considerable short distance relocation, as also have the efforts to segregate industry where small units have been spread among housing or other urban land uses. However, many workers, and particularly women and older people, have been reluctant to travel to the new sites, and have not sought alternative employment. This has been a serious loss in view of the manpower shortage. Moreover, a large proportion of these very small firms were in the consumer-good industries, which have been eclipsed by the growth of capital-good manufacture, and thus the manpower problem has been complicated by the need for extensive retraining. In order to contain the amount of relocation needed, new units have been formed by grouping together existing plants, with carefully co-ordinated inter-plant transport. Another serious problem has been posed by the exhaustion of natural resources in the south of the country and the need to find alternative work for miners, particularly around Zwickau and in the Geiseltal. Brown coal workers have been found employment in other fields, but abandonment of bituminous coal mining has presented a much greater challenge, which has been tackled chiefly by introducing new industries and giving adequate retraining.

NEW PATTERNS IN FARMING

The new social and economic system has had a considerable impact on farming. Land reform was initiated immediately after the Soviet occupation in districts where there were estates of over one hundred hectares, and so primarily affected Brandenburg and Mecklenburg; and pressure was also brought against peasants with holdings of over twenty hectares. Confiscated land was shared out among both local farm workers and refugees, who were termed 'new peasants', but the move was not very successful, and perhaps intentionally so. The new farmers were beset by various constraints, generally lacking access to capital and being without managerial experience. The rather hastily defined holdings, with a lack of suitable buildings and equipment, were far from easy to work; and the refugees, who had no local farming experience, made a mediocre showing. By 1950 over a fifth of the new holdings had been abandoned; and in 1951, when this was forbidden, a wave of disillusioned 'new peasants' fled to West Germany. Those who remained found no alternative but to take part in collectivisation. Some former es'ates were converted into state farms, or Volkseigene Güter (VEG), on the model of the Soviet sovkhoz.

Collectivisation was spread over the years 1952 to 1960. Initially three types of collective, or landwirtschaftliche Produktionsgenossenschaft (LPG), were instituted. Type I was regarded as an introductory phase, with only the communal working of land. Type II was a brief transitional phase before full collectivisation was attained; and Type III contained those farms which were fully collectivised. This last stage was reached most quickly wherever large estates had been common, but the smaller peasant farmers of the south were reluctant to enter collectives, and a long struggle ensued. Since the completion of collectivisation, pressure has been applied to create larger units. Between 1960 and 1975 collectives fell in number from 19,300 to 4,600, and by 1983 had declined to 3,900. In 1960 the average size of an LPG was 280 hectares, and by 1983 this had risen to 1,354 hectares. At the same time, the number of state farms fell from 669 to 478. There has also been an emphasis upon the closer association of farms, and individual farms have been encouraged to specialise in either arable or livestock, and to undertake industrial processing of their products. Efforts have also been made to remodel the rural landscape, in order to bring the conditions and standards of living of farm dwellers closer to those of townspeople, with 'agrarian towns' being built to serve particularly large farms.

It has been state policy to retain a high level of self-sufficiency in foodstuffs, and this level has varied between seventy-two and eighty-two percent. What is more, this has been achieved from an agricultural area of only 0.4 hectares per citizen. There was little unused land to take into cultivation, to offset a loss of 240,000 hectares which occurred between 1950 and 1970, and consequently emphasis has been placed rather on improvements in yields. However, since 1970 about 2,200 hectares of wasteland has been reclaimed each year; 4,500 hectares of agriculturally useful land was won from the 138,000 hectares of reconstituted land on old lignite workings between 1971 and 1978; and a further small net gain has been made by re-organising holdings, field boundaries and tracks. Re-organisation of farming has led, as in most industrial countries, to a fall in the proportion of the population employed. In 1950 27.9 percent of the labour force worked in agriculture and forestry, but by 1983 this had fallen to 10.6. The agricultural labour force has also been ageing for many years, but since 1975 there has been some success in attracting young people into the countryside.

THE TRANSPORT SYSTEM

As with manufacturing, the transport system was also affected both by the wartime rundown and the subsequent reparations. Through dismantling, the length of multiple track on the railways was reduced from thirty-seven to ten percent of the total, and some cross-country railways in the north were completely removed. About half the rolling stock and locomotives, as well as some repair workshops, were taken. Route length fell from 18,500 kilometres to 14,215 in the early 1950s, but has since recovered somewhat to 14,323 in 1983.

Pre-war movement in the _Reich_ had been principally on an east-west axis, but this was cut by the division of Germany, and both new states have had to reorient their patterns of road and rail traffic. In the GDR this new pattern has been most marked on the railways. Since the late 1960s, reconstruction of the badly rundown system has been resolutely tackled. Second or multiple track is being put back on most of the 7,500 kilometres of mainline, and new signalling systems introduced, in part to replace the labour-intensive Soviet-style dispatcher system, which was used after 1945. Electrification of the main freight lines which link the southern industrial districts together was undertaken in the 1950s and 1960s, creating the Sachsenring; and plans now foresee electrification outside this system, including electric traction directly into Berlin. Steam traction has been replaced almost entirely by diesel locomotives, mostly supplied from Hungary or the USSR.

The altered spatial pattern of the economy has demanded several important additions and adjustments to the rail network. Out of over forty railways which crossed the new inter-German border in 1945, only five remain in use, and some of these are only for freight traffic. The Berlin outer ring railway, which had been begun before 1914, was completed during the 1950s, thus allowing internal traffic in the GDR to avoid passing through West Berlin. A high-capacity mainline has been created from Rostock to the southern industrial districts; and there have been major alterations to allow easier flows of freight through junctions where the general direction of traffic has changed. Lastly, one new line has been built to avoid trains on internal GDR services having to run for a few kilometres through West German territory.

The GDR is important as a transit land in international railway traffic. Train ferries via Sassnitz and Warnemünde handle traffic from Scandinavia, whilst most traffic from Western Europe to Poland and the Soviet Union crosses it, and will do so increasingly as railway container traffic across the Siberian landbridge increases.

Railways carry a higher proportion of traffic in the GDR, where road haulage has been slow to develop, than in West Germany. This may reflect the existence in Eastern Europe, as in the Soviet Union, of a strong railway lobby, but the inadequate lorry park and the poor state of the roads have also held back road haulage, and the ownership of motor cars is appreciably lower than in Western Europe. The overwhelming proportion of commercial vehicles have had to be imported, chiefly from Czechoslovakia and the Soviet Union; and little major work was done on the road network until the late 1960s. However, the seventy-four kilometres of motorway begun in the

1930s between Dresden and Leipzig were completed in
1971; the Berlin outer orbital motorway has also
been completed in association with the building of a
motorway to Rostock; plans exist to finish the
projected pre-war Leipzig-Magdeburg motorway; and
the Berlin-Hamburg motorway has been under
construction, with the help of West German finance.
There has also been an improvement of other main
roads, but problems have arisen because
lignite-based tar is less durable than tar from
bituminous coal, though this situation should
improve as a larger volume of tar is derived from
oil refining. The objective is now to concentrate
all hauls of less than eighty kilometres on road
transport and to close many minor railways.
      The new boundaries of the GDR caused
considerable disruption to inland waterways.
Traffic from Hamburg to the rest of West Germany
virtually ceased rather than pass through the GDR
via the Elbe and Mittelland Canal, and this route
has been replaced by the costly construction in West
Germany of the Elbe Lateral Canal. In the GDR the
Paretz-Nieder-Neuendorf Canal was built to avoid
having to pass through West Berlin; a canal suitable
for 1,350-tonne barges from Rostock to the Elbe was
proposed, though it is unlikely to be built; and
there are important proposals to make the Saale
suitable for 1,350-tonne barges as far as Halle, to
provide water transport to Leipzig, and generally to
improve Elbe and Oder navigation. It is also
intended to make waterways capable of taking modern
pushtug units. A considerable transit traffic of
barges to Western Europe from Poland and
Czechoslovakia takes place across GDR waterways.
      The Soviet Military Administration did not
allow the GDR to have any sea-going vessel until
1950. However, by 1983 it had the third largest
fleet in COMECON, comprising 173 vessels of 659,739
NRT, of modern home construction or from other
COMECON countries. The loss of the main Baltic
port, Stettin, to Poland made it necessary to
develop another, and Rostock, which offered better
long-term prospects than Wismar, was chosen. It has
been developed on a major scale, with a passenger
terminal at Warnemünde and an oil terminal at the
Breitling. Container facilities have been added
since 1976. It handles three-quarters of the total
tonnage of the GDR ports of Rostock, Stralsund and
Wismar, and has competed strongly with Poland's
Baltic ports. In particular, it is more convenient
for shipments from Czechoslovakia and Hungary than

any of the Polish ports, though it has not completely usurped Hamburg for Czechoslovak trade.

TERRITORIAL PLANNING

The broad changes at national level in the organisation of the economy and society of the GDR have been accompanied by changes at the regional level, and these, in turn, have been reflected in territorial planning. This has followed the pattern of the Soviet Union, with at least three emphases. Firstly, there has been an attempt to equalise the the level of development both between one region and another, and between town and country. Secondly, towns have been perceived to be 'proletarian centres', and as such have been the preferred form of settlement, around which the economy and society have been organised; and thirdly, while each region has some activities that it can carry out better than any other, with a consequent degree of local specialisation, the GDR has made a great effort to encourage diversification of highly-specialised local economies.

However, some features of territorial planning in the GDR do differ from the Soviet model. Having inherited an already advanced industrial economy and a well-organised and effective agriculture, it has not faced either a general or a regional development problem comparable with that of Russia, where much of the territory was grossly underdeveloped at the time of the Revolution. Again, with a well developed transport network and a much more compact territory, where even axial distances are small, economy in transport - a key interest in the USSR - has been of far less concern; and, with an advanced economy but a serious labour shortage, much attention has been given to improving the rational use of labour and increasing its productivity.

In 1945-1946 the Allied powers divided Germany into large states, or **Länder**, in the belief that the reconstituted German nation-state would eventually be a federal or confederal structure. These **Länder** form the framework of the German Federal Republic, but in the Soviet Zone they rapidly lost their role, and in 1952 were replaced by fifteen **Bezirke** including East Berlin (Figure 6.2). Each of these is centred on a major town, most of which are industrial. **Bezirk** administrations play a significant role in the planning process, applying the broad policies laid down by the State Planning

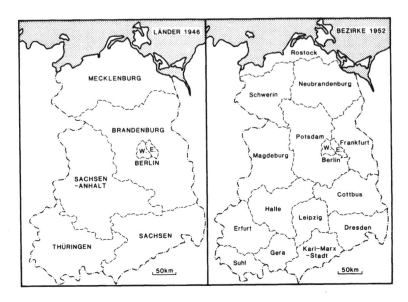

Figure 6.2 The Administrative Divisions of the GDR. The radical reorganisation, with the replacement of the Länder which were set up in 1945-1946 by the Bezirke which were modelled on Soviet units, was an important move in the process of administrative centralisation. The lower tiers of local government (Kreise and Gemeinden) survived, though in reduced numbers.

Commission to the detailed character of their own areas.

The basic problem of territorial planning has been the need to bring the economic structure and living standards of the predominantly agricultural north and centre up to the level of the industrial south (Figure 6.3). Moreover, the northern districts have contained the main labour reserves, for the reorganisation and mechanisation of agriculture have provided a pool of labour in addition to that already present among the underemployed refugee population. Industrial expansion in the south would have allowed the intensification of the existing industrial agglomerations and brought substantial returns on investment in the short run, but it would have required the recruitment of some of this northern labour, and associated infrastructural expenditure.

152

Thus, in the long run, everything has commended a shift of investment priorities to the structurally weak northern areas, even though this would have involved greater initial costs and a longer lead time before economic growth could have commenced; and much industrial growth has occurred there.

For example, four shipbuilding yards in the Baltic ports have been expanded, and maritime equipment is manufactured for them in inland towns, one instance of which has been the production of nautical electronic equipment in association with the research facilities of the University at Greifswald. Development has also proceeded through so-called 'investment complexes' at Neubrandenburg and Schwerin, where engineering, food manufacture and plastic processing are the main branches. Light industry has been encouraged in small towns, producing furniture, much of which is for export, grain and milk products; and the supply of energy has been augmented by the nuclear power plant at Lubmin near Greifswald.

The most striking transformation has been in the Frankfurt Bezirk, where two large industrial developments have been sited. The small town of Schwedt was selected as the site for a large refinery at the terminus of the oil pipeline from Russia and later a line from Rostock, while the town of Eisenhuttenstadt near Fürstenberg has been built around its steelworks. Both these projects were placed on the new eastern frontier as a conscious locational choice, for those sites were not only the nearest to the principal raw material supplies, but also enabled the East Germans to emphasise the stability of the Oder-Neisse border. Elsewhere in the Bezirk a rolling mill has been expanded at Finow, and a crane works has been built at Eberswalde, a tyre plant at Fürstenwalde and a semi-conductor factory at Frankfurt. Industries have also been developed in the rural northern parts of Potsdam Bezirk, with energy requirements being met by the nuclear generating station at Rheinsberg; and a similar programme has been instituted for the neglected northern areas of Magdeburg Bezirk - the Letzlinger Heide and the Altmark. The potential of this predominantly agricultural area has been increased by the discovery of natural gas near Salzwedel, and there are plans to build a nuclear power station near Stendal. Magdeburg Bezirk already has a flourishing food industry, producing over twenty-five percent of the GDR's beet sugar. Another of the central Bezirke, Cottbus, has

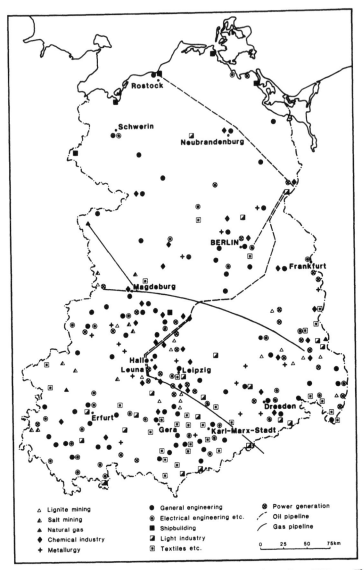

Figure 6.3 Mining and Manufacturing in the GDR. The contrast between the north and south of the country should be noted.
Sources: <u>Atlas</u> <u>Deutsche</u> <u>Demokratische</u> <u>Republik</u>, Karte 33, Haack, Gotha 1979; <u>Geographic</u> <u>Manual</u> <u>GDR</u>, Verlag Zeit im Bild, Berlin 1979.

benefited from the restructuring of the GDR's economy. It contains sixty percent of the national lignite reserves; more than thirty-five percent of the total energy requirements of the GDR are now supplied from it; and its role has become steadily more important as the older fields around Halle and Leipzig have been exhausted and as electricity generation has been greatly expanded in enlarged and new lignite-fired power stations, such as Boxberg, Lübbenau and Vetschau. The lignite is also used to produce a range of chemicals, as in the Schwarze Pumpe complex near Lauchhammer. As a result of these developments there has been an inflow of labour, and large residential complexes have been developed, such as Neu-Hoyerswerda, though some labour has also been made available by the re-organisation of the textile industry of Lusatia.

Nevertheless, despite the spread of industries to the agricultural areas of the north and centre, the southern _Bezirke_ remain the focus of GDR industry, where they have posed special territorial planning problems. Erfurt, Gera, Halle, Karl-Marx-Stadt, Leipzig and Suhl _Bezirke_ together contain some thirty-nine percent of the GDR, but they account for fifty-seven percent of the population and contribute sixty-four percent of the industrial production. One of the most serious problems in these areas has been the labour shortage, but planners have also been anxious to avoid the infrastructural costs which would arise if workers were brought in from other areas. Thus, the emphasis has been on the intensification and rationalisation of production, and the transfer of labour from declining to expanding industries. One important element of planning in these districts has been the regrouping of the existing plants into more effective units, especially by eliminating the older, smaller and least efficient - a process which has often gone hand-in-hand with the segregation of industry from residences in such towns as Karl-Marx-Stadt and Leipzig.

The major industrial agglomerations within the central and southern _Bezirke_ cover about fifteen percent of the GDR and contain roughly fifty percent of its industrial workers, providing at least half of the industrial output. Several still show the considerable local specialisation which had emerged well before the Second World War and which it has been thought wise not to dilute unduly. Examples are the electrical engineering industry of Berlin, the fuel, energy and chemical industries of the

Halle and Leipzig districts, and instrument making in Dresden. Indeed, the continuity of the industries in their former locations in Halle and Leipzig **Bezirke** has encouraged the growth of interrelationships between them on a large scale, similar to the Soviet concept of the 'territorial production complex'. Furthermore, these industrial nodes have been expanded in many cases by related developments. A typical case has been the big sulphuric acid plant at Coswig, on the northern fringe of the main chemical area, which rectifies one of the imbalances which had been created in the industry by the division of Germany and supplies a high demand market using local raw materials. Another has been the shift in the chemical industry from a lignite to a petroleum base, which was the reason for building the big Leuna II plant at Merseburg. The raw materials for this plant are brought by pipeline from Schwedt, in the case of oil, and from Czechoslovakia, in the case of natural gas. The increased labour needs of the chemical industry of Halle **Bezirk** have been catered for by the construction of the new town of Halle-Neustadt. On the other hand, some industries have been run down. For instance, the shift of textile manufacture from Karl-Marx-Stadt **Bezirk,** where it had accounted for three-quarters of all production, to other districts, and its general decline as part of the programme for correcting the 'disproportions' arising from the division of Germany, have been followed by the conversion of its premises for use by the electronics and engineering trades. Similarly, there has been considerable rationalisation as a result of the integration of some hundred widely-scattered hosiery plants in the Limbach-Oberfrohna district.

Other problems have arisen in the southern **Bezirke** over the development of agriculture. For example, the tradition in many districts of farmers seeking some employment, either part-time or seasonally, in industry, such as in the sugar mills around Zeitz, over the winter, has no longer been acceptable. The formation of effective LPGs has also posed problems in areas in which farmland exists only in relatively small parcels amid forest and woodlands, and where steeply sloping fields and awkward access have made mechanisation difficult, as in the Mittelgebirge.

The isolation of West Berlin has also been a difficulty for the GDR. The original four-power intent had been to manage Berlin as a single unit, but division has meant that planning and development have largely gone separate ways in the eastern and western sectors. The central district of East Berlin has problems of access, being surrounded on three sides by the divisive but self-inflicted Wall; and its commercial quarter has changed considerably in comparison with pre-war times as the new post-war economic system has developed. One feature has been the restoration of some residential use, in pursuit of the Eastern bloc's desire to avoid the 'dead heart' syndrome it so much despises in cities of the Western World. New housing on the neighbourhood principle has replaced the old tenement blocks and courtyards of the traditional Berlin Mietskaserne, though industrial building methods have unfortunately created almost as much uniformity as they have replaced. Moreover, compared to the glitter and ebullience of West Berlin, East Berlin makes a rather drab, even deserted, impression. As elsewhere, much attention has been given to separating industry and housing, and this has complemented the desire to form larger and more modern industrial units. In particular, an attempt has been made to link enterprises in Berlin with those elsewhere in the GDR, and to shift plants needing extensive space out of the city. New industries have been introduced to form a better balance, but future development will concentrate on technical improvements in existing plants. Berlin is particularly important for electrical engineering and electronics, but its other long established industries, like clothing, food, printing and textiles, have also been encouraged. Furthermore, attention has been given to drawing together its scattered research and educational facilities, as well as to developing major new health-care complexes, such as that at Berlin-Buch.

SETTLEMENT PLANNING

The new economic and social policies since the war have also resulted in considerable changes in the pattern of settlement. Particular attention has been given to towns, which have been seen as the 'most economic and culturally rich form of settlement', and efforts have been made to make them 'national in form and socialist in content'. Restriction of the private ownership of land and property has presented the opportunity for replanning and redevelopment, but unfortunately neither the material resources nor the creative talent have been sufficient to take full advantage of this situation. Berlin, Dresden, Leipzig and Magdeburg all suffered as a result of being major wartime targets for aerial bombardment, and other towns were badly damaged in ground attack, but, unlike in West Germany, large areas which had been cleared of rubble and ruins in the GDR were to lie for several years as open spaces before rebuilding commenced.

Much of the resources devoted to rebuilding in the GDR was concentrated first in the reconstruction of town centres in the flamboyant style of Stalinist Russia, but some new industrial towns, most notably Stalinstadt (later Eisenhüttenstadt), were also begun. After the mid-1950s, perhaps to lessen civil tensions, emphasis shifted more to housing, particularly in places where industrial development was occurring, like Halle-Neustadt, Neu-Hoyerswerda, Rostock and Schwedt, with the tempo growing as prefabricated building methods were introduced. New housing of this period was monotonous and poorly equipped, and has been severely criticised. However, having shed the straitjacket of Stalinist orthodoxy, some of the newer city centre projects, like the Strasse der Nationen in Karl-Marx-Stadt, compare favourably with the West, and some of the most interesting work has occurred in East Berlin.

After the mid-1960s reorganisation of the building industry greater concern was shown over design and construction methods. Planning became more sophisticated, and greater attention was given to fundamental changes in the pattern of settlement. Major new projects were begun, and attention was devoted to rebuilding some of the national monuments which had been destroyed during the war, notably the old city of Dresden. After 1973 interest shifted once more to housing, with the improvement of existing dwellings and provision of better amenities in new housing. The monotony of housing schemes was overcome by the provision of more variety in house types, and the growing use of private cars also began to be recognised. Since 1976 there has even been encouragement for private house building and improvements to the older housing stock.

Table 6.1 reflects the shift in the distribution of population which has followed from the changing emphases in industrial development and the reorganisation of the countryside. Urban population has risen both as a proportion of the total and in absolute numbers, but the proportion of

Table 6.1: The Distribution of Population by
Community Size in the GDR

	1939	1950	1983
Total population (millions)	16.74	18.36	16.7

Community Size	Percentage of Total Population		
Large towns (over 100,000)	31.6	20.7	26.1
Medium towns (20,000-100,000)	13.7	18.4	22.7
Small towns (5,000-20,000)	13.8	18.1	26.4
Country towns (2,000-5,000)	10.8	13.7	11.3
Rural communes (below 2,000)	30.1	29.1	23.5

Sources: Kaberman (1961); Statistisches Jahrbuch
der DDR, various years.

people living in the largest towns, of over 100,000
people, has fallen. Of the fifteen in this
category, five still have populations below those of
1939, whereas only two towns with pre-war
populations of less than 100,000 - Rostock and
Schwerin - have exceeded that figure. Those
remaining below their 1939 populations were all
major wartime targets. Most marked has been the
rise in the share of the medium-sized towns, of
between 20,000 and 100,000 people, although
seventeen of these still have populations which are
smaller than before the war. In this group are new
industrial centres, like Eisenhüttenstadt,
Hoyerswerda and Schwedt, and the seats of the
Bezirke, where much new housing has been available.
There have also been increases in the shares of
the population in towns of between 5,000 and 20,000

people and in the so-called 'country towns' of 2,000 to 5,000. This has been in part the outcome of the formation of new farming units and of the plans to create 'agrarian towns', (Agrärstadte), similar to the Soviet agrogoroda. The proportion of population classed as rural, that is, living in communes (Gemeinden) with less than 2,000 people, has consequently fallen from thirty percent in 1939 to just over twenty-three in 1983 - but it is still well above the eight percent for West Germany. However, strong control over development in the GDR has prevented the alarming 'suburbanisation' of the countryside that has taken place there.

During the 1950s internal migration was dominated by the movement of refugees from rural districts, particularly in the north, where they had first settled, to towns, where there were better employment prospects. However, subsequent adjustments in industrial structure have been followed by different patterns of movement. For instance, movement from the older industrial districts in the south has been generated by the rundown of some industries, although this drift has been contained by introducing new activities. Migrants from all over the country have moved to the industrial centres, with people from the older lignite mining districts of Halle and Leipzig going to the new mining communities of Lusatia, to Eisenhüttenstadt and to Schwedt. The northern districts have generally lost population, though some people from industrial districts in the south have been attracted to new industries associated with the maritime activities of Rostock and the other ports; and, as the seat of government, Berlin has attracted between 7,000 and 10,000 immigrants each year. Many people seeking employment in Berlin are, however, forced to live in towns around the outskirts of the city, thus contributing to the gain by migration of Potsdam Bezirk.

This migration has created one difficulty to which no solution has been found. The mining areas of Lusatia lie across the homeland of the Slavonic Sorbian minority. During the 1950s their cultural organisation, Domowina, did much to promote the ethnic identify of the Sorbs, and was supported by Wilhelm Pieck, who was born in Lusatia. However, his successors have taken less interest in the Sorbian question, and the position of the minority (which is of uncertain number, but possibly between 70,000 and 100,000) has been weakened by revisions to the Constitution. Fears have been expressed that an influx of essentially German workers will endanger an already fragile ethnic society, and this may have important consequences for international relations, for the fortunes of this Slavonic people are carefully monitored in Czechoslovakia, Poland and Yugoslavia.

THE ENVIRONMENTAL CHALLENGE

The growth of industry since the early 1950s has increased the need for environmental protection. One of the most pressing aspects of the problem arises from the Republic's demands for water, both for industrial and domestic use, and for the disposal of noxious effluent from the chemical industry. The annual volume of water available is between 15,000 and 17,000 million cubic metres, though in a wet year this may rise to 30,000 million, or fall to 6,000 to 8,000 million in a dry one. At the same time the annual consumption has risen from around 5,000 million cubic metres in the early 1950s to just short of 9,000 million in 1970; is expected to exceed 10,000 million during the 1980s, and to be over 17,000 million by the year 2000. Fifty-eight percent is derived from river water, twenty-one percent from lakes and reservoirs, eighteen percent from groundwater, and the remainder comes from springs. Three-quarters of the water is used by industry - a quarter alone by chemical manufacturing and a tenth by mining and metallurgy. Thus, it is not surprising that there has been an emphasis on rationalising and, if possible, reducing industrial water consumption. Agriculture takes between eleven and fourteen percent, but its demands are also rising, for increasing use is being made of artificial watering, especially on the fertile but dry loessic country of Saxony-Anhalt and Thüringen, in the rainshadow of the Harz and Thüringer Wald, and in the drier areas of Brandenburg. The domestic use of water accounts for little more than ten percent of total consumption.

Increases in the water supply to the agglomerations in the southern **Bezirke** have been achieved principally through the construction of reservoirs in the Erzgebirge, on the edge of the Lusatian lignite fields and on the Helme and Unstrut in the Thüringer Wald. Some of these have been formed out of old lignite workings. Supplies to industry around Bitterfeld, Dessau, Halle, Leipzig, Leuna and Magdeburg have been augmented from groundwater reserves in the Elbaue near Prentzsch, in the Annaburger Heide near Torgau, in the Letzlinger Heide north of Magdeburg, and from the Bodetal reservoir system in the eastern Harz. It has been stressed that new industrial developments with heavy demands for water must be carefully located to make the most economical use of the available resources.

An equally pressing problem has been the effective disposal of effluents. It has been stressed that the temperature of cooling water should be reduced substantially before it is fed into rivers, but that it is preferable that such water should be recycled. Attention has been given to extracting undesirable elements such as acids, albumen and fats, and special measures have been taken to remove alkalis, phenols and sulphides. In the potash and salt mining districts there has been the extra problem of controlling the flow of salty solutions into rivers, though quite a lot runs away into West Germany along the Aller and Werra. Chemical plants are the main source of pollutants, but sugar beet refineries are also significant contributors, and one synthetic rubber plant can cause more pollution than a town of two million people.

Once worked out, large opencast lignite workings become a devastated landscape, and their rehabilitation is costly and complex. However, German law has always been rigorous in its requirement for the restitution of the surface after mining. The primary task is to establish a suitable vegetation cover, but this depends very much on the materials which have been left by the miners, and the ease with which a new soil structure can develop. The aim is usually to return as much of the land as possible to farming, though it is common for a considerable proportion to be afforested, at least initially. Some pits are, however, allowed to flood or are filled artificially, and in some instances it is necessary to realign the drainage pattern. Moreover, the combined effect of mining and of the extraction of groundwater from the pits may create extensive cones of exhaustion of the groundwater, and these have been severely detrimental to farming, especially in Halle Bezirk. Water-table problems have also been created by the exploitation of some gravel deposits for aggregate.

During the Second World War and in the early post-war years little was done to control undesirable gaseous emissions from the chemical industry. This problem is most serious during still-air conditions, when fogs build up near the big chemicals plants in Bitterfeld, Halle and Merseburg in the Elbe-Saale basin, and also seriously affect Leipzig and district. Not until the 1960s was the problem resolutely tackled, and it is said that the situation will be further improved as industry substitutes natural gas and petroleum as raw materials for lignite. Factories also cause serious pollution in basins in hillier areas, one example of which is the synthetic fibre plant at Rudolstadt-Schwarza, which emits sulphurous fumes.

Lastly, there is one problem to which no immediate solution appears to be available, namely the growing damage by acid rain to vegetation and water quality. This is now a widespread affliction, which extends well beyond the boundaries of the GDR and calls for concerted international action, but it is exacerbated in Central Europe by the general pattern of air movement, which brings contaminated air from the west. The challenge is of major importance, since forests cover twenty-seven percent of the GDR and are important for drainage, shelter and protection against soil erosion, quite apart from their value as timber; and the problem has been made no easier by the need to restore large areas which were ruthlessly clear-felled in the reparations period.

THE TWO GERMANYS

Thus, the GDR has been obliged to adapt its inherited pattern of production and settlement to fit its post-war geo-political context, and much has been achieved at the same time as it has continued to raise output and to remain the richest of the East European states in terms of gross national product per capita. However, it may be too soon to declare that the period of adjustment in the space economy is at an end, for the close cultural and historical ties between the GDR and West Germany are potentially stronger than any of the country's links with its allies in Eastern Europe. Even now no other COMECON member has, for example, anything like the special agreements covering trade between the two Germanys, and although much post-war development in the GDR has tipped the balance of the spatial pattern towards the east of its territory, while the western areas have been consciously neglected, there unquestionably remains a special relationship between the two states. Formal relations between the Germanys are deeply affected by the pressures of the two blocs in which they find themselves as a consequence of events since 1939, but there is also an important, if unquantifiable, bond which continues to hold the Germans together as a people, as it has done previously when they have been divided. It would nevertheless be unreal to deny that, with strikingly different social and economic systems in East and West, and new distributions of economic activity and trading links, two Germanys do now exist, and that any chance of political reunification, which was so much debated in the 1950s and 1960s, is as far away as ever it has been since 1945.

SELECT BIBLIOGRAPHY

Anordnung über die Ordnung der Planung der Volkswirtschaft der DDR 1981 bis 1985 (1980), Teil P - Territorialplanung. Planung des Umweltschutzes Gesetzblatt der Deutschen Demokratischen Republik Sonderdruck 1020, Berlin.

Broll, W. (1969), Die ökonomische Bedeutung der DDR for die RGW-Staaten, Osteuropa-Wirtschaft 14, 24-41.

Bruns, W. (1978), Deutsch-deutsche Beziehungen - Pramissen, Probleme, Perspektiven, Opladen.

Catudal, H.M. (1978), The Diplomacy of the Quadripartite Agreement on Berlin, Berlin.

Ehlermann, C-D. et al. (1978), Handelspartner DDR - Innerdeutsche Wirshaftsbeziehungen, Schriftenreihe Europäische Wirtschaft 76.

Gresillon, M. (1974), Les relations ville-industrie : le complexe de Halle, RAD, Annales de Géografie 83, 260-283.

Jacob, G. (1961), Zur Problematik der ökonomischen Rayonierung in der DDR, Geog. Berichte 7, 123-130.

Jacob, G. et al. (1976), Beiträge zur territorialen Produktionsstruktur, Wissenschaftliche Abhandlungen der Geog. Gesellschaft der DDR 13.

Kaberman, H. (1961), Die Bevolkerung des Sowjetischen Besatzungsgebietes - Bestands - und Strukturveranderungen 1950-1957, Bundesminister für Gesamtdeutsche Fragen, Bonn.

Kohl, H. et al. (1974), Die Bezirke der Deustchen Demokratischen Republik - Ökonomische Geographie, Gotha.

Kohl, H. et al. (1976), Ökonomische Geographie der Deutsche Demokratischen Republik, Gotha.

Kohl, H. et al. (1978), Complex territorial changes in old industrial areas of the German Democratic Republik, in Industrial Change = International Experience and Public Policy, ed. F.E.I. Hamilton, London.

Kozlov, I.D. (1973), Zur Integration der DDR in der Energiewirschaft der RGW-Länder, Petermanns Mitteilungen 117, 1-16.

Leptin, G. (1970), Die Deutsche Wirtscahft nach 1945 = ein Ost-West Vergleich, Opladen

Leptin, G. (1976), Die Rolle der DDR in Osteuropa. Deutsche Gesellschaft für Osteuropakunde, Berlin.

Leser, H. (ed.) (1976), Bundesrepublik Deutscheland = Deutsche Demokratische Republik. Teil IV Thematische Karten zur Welt von Heute, Kiel.

Ludemann, H. et al. (1984), German Democratic Republik - Regional Structure and Development, GeoJournal 1.

Ludz, P. et al. (1979), DDR-Handbuch, Bundesminister for Innerdeutche Beziehungen, Bonn.

McCauley, M. (ed.) (1983), The German Democratic Republic since 1945, London.

Mellor, R.E.H. (1978), The Two Germanies, London.

Mitteilung der Staatlichen Zentralverwaltung für Statistik der DDR über die Durchführung des Volkswirtschaftsplanes 1983 (1984), Dokumente zur Politik der DDR 1, Berlin.

Mitzscherling, P. et al. (1977), DDR-Wirtschaft = eine Bestandsaufnahme. Deutsches Institut for Wirtschaftsforschung, Berlin.

Neef, E. (ed.) (1977), Sozialistische Landeskultur = Unweltgestaltung = Umweltschutz, Leipzig.

Pritzel, K.(1966), Die wirtschaftliche Integration der sowjetischen Besatzungszone Deutschlands in den Ostblock, 2nd ed., Bonn.

Raumordnungspolitik in der DDR - Planung, Productionsstruktur, Wohlstandsverteilung (1978), DIW-Wochenbericht 45, 223-251.

Rupp, F. (1951), Die Reparationsleistungen der sowjetischen Besatzungszone, Bonner Berichte aus Mittel = und Ostduetschland, Bonn.

Schmidt-Renner, G. et al. (1961), Wirtschaftsterritorium Deutsche Demokratische Republik, Berlin.

The German Democratic Republic

Stams, W. (1968), Der Aufbau von Dresden – Planung einer sozialistiischen Grossstadt, *Geog. Berichte* 13, 175-205.

Werner, F. (1972), *Zur Raumordnung in der DDR*, Berlin.

Chapter 7

HUNGARY

Paul A. Compton

THE CONTEXT OF PLANNING

Planned, as opposed to unregulated, development
has been the path chosen by Hungary since the
consolidation of communist control in 1949. As a
result its society is highly ordered, but it has
tended to lack the innovative spirit associated with
individual initiative. Planning was first applied
to the economy, where it involved the abolition of
market relationships and the elimination of the
independent decision-making function of the various
units of production. Within a short period it
became synonymous with a system of tight control
which spread rapidly to embrace most other areas of
society. More recently, however, a spirit of
'liberalism' has been rekindled, and there has been
some retreat from central planning. Although the
objectives of socio-economic development are still
formulated in five-year plans, these are implemented
today through fiscal measures and incentives, rather
than by orders from higher to lower authorities, and
in this Hungary differs very significantly from the
other communist countries of Eastern Europe. The
first section of this chapter outlines in more
detail these two contrasting styles of economic
management, while subsequent sections show how the
priorities of the planners have been expressed in
the context of the country's regional, settlement
and environmental problems.

NATIONAL ECONOMIC PLANNING

(1) The Centrally Planned Economy, 1950 to 1967
The years immediately after 1945 were a period
of reconstruction and of the introduction of a

167

completely new system of economic planning – that
approved by the Soviet Union, and one which at least
at first took no account of Hungarian conditions.
However, its introduction was not altogether
unwelcome to the Hungarian people for pre-war
capitalism was judged to have failed to overcome the
country's problems of backwardness, and a strong
central planning apparatus seemed to offer the most
effective means of modernisation.

The years immediately after 1945 constituted a
period of consolidation of the new system. The
large landed estates were broken up and distributed
amongst the peasantry; banks and larger private
companies were nationalised; and the state gained an
increasingly pivotal role in the economy as smaller
private commercial concerns were squeezed out of
existence. By the beginning of the First Five Year
Plan in 1950 the system of centralised control was
fully established, and it remained the mechanism for
achieving the broad objectives of economic and
social policy, set out in subsequent three and
five-year plans, until the end of 1967. The aim of
the First Five Year Plan was the maximisation of the
rate of economic growth through forced, heavy
industrialisation. It was strongly autarkic in
conception, and depended largely on massive
transfers of manpower and capital from agriculture
to industry. Separate institutions of state,
organised in a broadly hierarchical manner but
sometimes with overlapping functions, controlled in
great detail the activities of 750 enterprises. The
National Planning Office played a key role in this
structure, and was responsible for drawing up
detailed material plans within the limits laid down
by the National Economic Commission. Production
plans geared to a set of national economic
indicators were prepared on a quarterly or annual
basis for individual enterprises, setting out the
levels of investment and spending, and establishing
the amounts of energy, raw materials and manpower to
be used in achieving the production targets. To
simplify the mechanism, enterprises were grouped
horizontally by production type, and directives were
transmitted via the responsible department within
the branch ministries.

Although this system was cumbersome, it did
offer some advantages, at least initially. It
permitted the adoption of a long, as opposed to a
short, term perspective, and it was this, together
with the concentration of resources, which made
possible development projects which could not

otherwise have been realised. Moreover, its rigid chain of command permitted the utilisation of largely untrained manpower in lower and middle managerial positions - something which could never have been contemplated in a system based on individual initiative. What is more, the achievements of this form of planning were impressive. Per capita national income increased at an annual rate of six percent between 1950 and 1967; the value of industrial output quadrupled; and the proportion of the labour force engaged in agriculture dropped from just over half to around one quarter.

The disadvantages of central planning, however, soon came to outweigh the advantages. Market prices had no role to play within the system, and the only requirement for the state sector was that total sales revenue should balance costs, thus creating a complex system of cross subsidies which were offset by the low prices which were paid by the state for agricultural deliveries. Inter-enterprise prices, rather than reflecting actual costs and allocating resources efficiently, therefore came to act largely as accounting devices within the planning mechanism. As for the consumer, the price of industrial goods was kept artificially high, and the price of food, housing and transport, artificially low. Agricultural production stagnated.

Similarly, export prices were divorced from actual production costs. Intra-COMECON trade was based on a price structure fixed in 1951, while exports necessitated a complex system of variable exchange rates, generally at substantially higher levels than the official one. Moreover, enterprises were not permitted to trade directly with their foreign partner, but had to buy and sell through a foreign trade company, at domestic producer prices, and were thus sheltered from the need to adapt to changed international circumstances. The one area in which prices exerted a direct bearing on individual decisions was in the retail sphere, but these were fixed in order to control consumer demand rather than to influence supply.

Thus, the central planning system shielded enterprises from those forces which would have stimulated more efficient economic activity, and they came to see their function as one of merely fulfilling or overfulfilling the production targets set for them. The elimination of any real system of value encouraged costly projects of doubtful viability, and technological innovation was neglected. Much investment was frequently tied up in unfinished projects. Targets were fulfilled in the easiest possible manner - by the production of unsaleable goods which went into grossly inflated stocks, or by the wasteful use of expensive raw materials - while the quality and variety of products, notably for the consumer market, deteriorated. The response of the planning authorities to these deficiencies was greater regulation of production through the transmission of increasingly detailed directives and orders.

Even after the pace of industrialisation was relaxed and bonuses introduced to stimulate a greater sensitivity to the costs of production, the over-centralised system of planning still proved to be incompatible with attempts to intensify production and stimulate greater flexibility. Despite quite radical modifications, such as the amalgamation of small production units into larger enterprises and trusts, and the taxation of assets to promote their more efficient utilisation, the basic weaknesses continued to assert themselves. For instance, even though the degree of supervision from the centre was relaxed, enterprises were still not responsible for their own investment decisions, the procurement of their materials or the disposal of their products, though their net income was guaranteed provided they kept within the prescribed targets. Moreover, shortages of a whole range of goods were also an ever-present problem and enterprises found that it was in their interests to hoard manpower, investment and raw materials (Kornai 1981). But new problems were also emerging in the economy. Firstly, the large reserves of manpower, on which the extensive phase of industrialisation had been based, had been largely exhausted by the late 1950s, and further progress could only come through the raising of efficiency and productivity; and secondly, the planning mechanism required ever more information to function effectively, and the tasks which it had to perform were becoming increasingly complex. As a result, it had become widely accepted by the mid-1960s that the system was in need of radical reform.

(2) The New Economic Mechanism (NEM)

While Hungary was not alone in reforming its system of central planning in the late 1960s, the NEM went further than the reforms in neighbouring countries by actually eliminating some of the more important functions that had been performed centrally. Since its introduction the National Planning Office has still drawn up the one- and five-year plans - setting out the objectives of economic and social development - but these are now treated as guidelines, and are implemented through incentives and indirect measures. Compulsory directives to enterprises, setting production and other targets, were abolished. Thus, enterprises have gained considerable independence from the central apparatus, and have been made more responsive to the dictates of the market. Furthermore, a portion of their profits may now be put into their own development funds which, with their newly-granted right to raise bank credits, has given enterprises considerable freedom over investment decisions. Only the most major investments are now determined centrally. Moreover, profits may also be used to raise wages within certain limits, as well as to pay bonuses, and the more profitable companies are now better able to attract labour. The price system has also been made more flexible, and fixed prices for many items were abolished. Recognising the fact that about fifty percent of national income is dependent on foreign trade, and that one third of it is with the West, many enterprises are now permitted to trade directly with their foreign partners, rather than through the intermediary of a foreign trade enterprise.

Although the 1970s saw some movement away from the spirit of the reform, partly in response to such problems as the very rapid rate of labour turnover which developed as individuals sought to maximise their incomes by moving from one job to another, and partly as a result of the more difficult trading climate, the commitment to the reform was reasserted after 1979. Almost all the subsidies and special taxes which were introduced during the previous decade to protect vulnerable areas of domestic manufacturing were abolished, and funds are no longer made available, at least officially, to rescue inefficient enterprises from bankruptcy. Changes in employment legislation have also made it easier to dismiss workers in the interests of efficiency. A beginning was also made to the process of aligning the Hungarian price system with that of world markets, and a single exchange rate and partially convertible Forint were established against the main western currencies. Membership of the IMF and World Bank has helped to underwrite this change by ensuring credits. One consequence of this has been that hard currency trade has been simplified, and in particular tourism from the West has benefited from the abolition of the system of compulsory currency exchange. In addition, the scope for business initiative has been widened, and individuals and enterprises now have the right to create small companies and co-operatives in the fields of industry, commerce and services. Commercial activities which were formerly undertaken by local councils have been leased under tender to private operators, and the renting of the productive assets of state-owned enterprises to groups of employees outside normal working hours has been encouraged.

It has been said that the success of the NEM has been its ability to prevent the sort of deterioration in the Hungarian economy which occurred in other communist countries during the 1970s (Marrese 1980). Such an assessment may appear rather lukewarm, given the fact that those were years of rising prosperity in the country, but it must be acknowledged that fundamental weaknesses persist within the Mechanism, notably the low level of accountability of economic decision making, the reluctance of enterprises to innovate, the persistence of overinvestment and the growth in the size of the hard currency debt. It is too early to judge whether the most recent reforms will be successful in overcoming these deficiencies.

REGIONAL DEVELOPMENT AND PLANNING

(1) The Regional Problem
     Post-war planning, in the various forms which it has taken, has had to contend with severe imbalances in the spatial structure of the Hungarian economy. Between 1867, the year of the Compromise with Austria, and the outbreak of the First World War, the economic development of the country had been impressive. However, its effects were highly localised, and generated no more than islands of development within a general sea of agrarian backwardness. Moreover, the regional disparities which had been created were further aggravated when the dismemberment of Greater Hungary at the Peace Settlement in 1919 stripped the country of its middle-rank towns, left Budapest as an overdominant primate city, and largely separated the sources of raw materials, now in neighbouring countries, from the centres of manufacturing. Little was achieved during the short and troubled inter-war years to

remedy these imbalances.

The first post-war census of 1949 showed that Budapest, with its 1,500,000 inhabitants, accounted for forty-seven percent of the entire urban population of the country and was more than ten times the size of the second city, Szeged. It also contained fifty-four percent of the country's industrial employment. The only other significant areas of industrial activity lay along the Middle Mountains, running from Borsod County in the north of the country to Zala County in the southwest, where the country's basic industries were located, and where a substantial manufacturing sector had grown up in association with them in and around the city of Miskolc. (The area forms a discontinuous 'densely settled zone' to the northeast and southwest of Budapest in Figure 7.1.) Other important urban settlements included Györ, the commercial centre of the Little Plain, Pécs, with its neighbouring coalfield, Szeged and Debrecen, but the rest of the country was backward and totally agrarian. Of course, many regions were intrinsically unsuitable for non-agricultural activities, but others possessed labour reserves, good communications, abundant water supply or other advantages which could have been used as a basis for development. Furthermore, equity demanded the raising of the standard of living in the more backward areas, perhaps through investment in public utilities, and a reduction in their relative isolation; and the problems of most rural areas were capable of mitigation through the creation of a prosperous agriculture.

(2) Regional Planning Policy in the Centrally Planned Economy

From the outset the stated aim of regional policy was the decentralisation of industry from existing concentrations, together with the strengthening of the agricultural sector. The initial years of economic planning, however, had the reverse effect, for the First Five Year Plan (1950-1954) emphasised sectoral, rather than regional, aspects of industrialisation. Moreover, the drive for self-sufficiency, with its emphasis on coal mining and the basic producer industries, inevitably concentrated investment in the existing resource-oriented locations of the Middle Mountains and the Pecs region, while the growth in other types of manufacturing was achieved most easily by investing in Budapest, with its existing factories,

Hungary

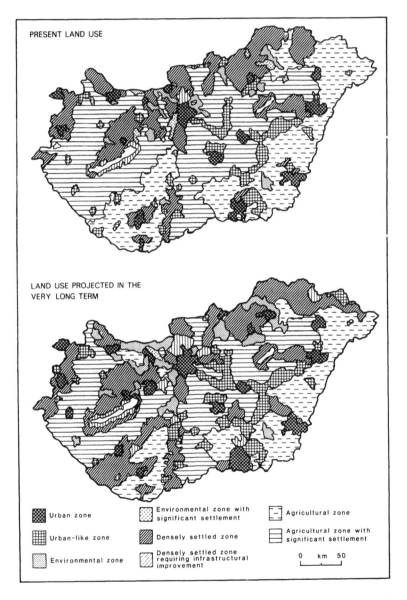

PRESENT LAND USE

LAND USE PROJECTED IN THE
VERY LONG TERM

Urban zone

Urban-like zone

Environmental zone

Environmental zone with
significant settlement

Densely settled zone

Densely settled zone
requiring infrastructural
improvement

Agricultural zone

Agricultural zone with
significant settlement

0   km   50

Figure 7.1 The Present and Planned Patterns of Land
Use in Hungary

developed infrastructure and nodal position in the transport network.

Five new socialist towns were created during the First Five Year Plan - Ajka, Dunaújváros, Komló, Oroszlány and Várpalota - but the choice of sites ran counter to the aims of regional policy. With the exception of Dunaújváros, all were in existing industrial areas, and the choice of that town seemed to indicate a perverse attempt to ignore the constraints of the natural resource endowment in the drive for self sufficiency. The town was built around a new integrated iron and steel combine, but from the start the efficiency of the plant was compromised by its dependence on imported raw materials. Although, owing to other locational advantages, Dunaújváros has now emerged as the most successful of the new socialist towns, it is doubtful whether it would have been started in any other than the special circumstances prevailing in the early 1950s. Similarly, the vast increase in aluminium production during the early 1950s, although justifiable on the basis of domestic bauxite reserves, only made sense in the context of economic autarky, for the electricity which was generated locally for the smelting process proved to be extremely expensive.

While the pace of industrialisation was being forced, agriculture was losing capital, to the obvious detriment of rural areas and the forty-nine percent of the population who depended on the agrarian economy for their livelihood in 1949. Even after the pace of industrialisation was moderated in 1954, investment continued to be placed in existing industrial areas, and the substantial gap between the opportunities and living standards in the industrially developed and the backward agrarian regions had widened further by 1960. The one beneficial outcome of the first decade of central planning was a weakening of the dominant position of Budapest in the country's industry.

It was only during the Second Five Year Plan (1961-65), as a more capital intensive form of development was embarked upon, that the problems of the backward agrarian areas were more fully grasped. Fiscal and investment policy began to favour them, and efforts were made to move some industries from Budapest, including those deemed to be unsuitable to an urban environment because of the pollution they cause, those employing unskilled and semi-skilled labour, and those with obsolete plant (Bora 1976). Although half the total investment during the period

175

occurred in the established industrial regions outside Budapest, the policy of decentralisation achieved some notable results, and by 1968 200,000 new industrial jobs had been created in the backward agrarian regions in the less capital-intensive branches of engineering, in light manufacturing and, above all, in food processing. Even though these regions only received a quarter of the investment, their non-agricultural employment was more than doubled during the 1960s, and a more balanced territorial structure of industry began to emerge (Table 7.1).

Table 7.1: Changes in the Spatial Structure of Industry in Hungary, 1956/60 to 1970

	Investment 1956-70	Growth in Industrial Manpower 1960=100	Proportion of National Industrial Manpower	
			1960	1970
Budapest	22.5	105	44	34
Existing industrialised areas	52	137	36	38
Under-industrialised areas	25.5	199	20	28
Hungary	100	134	100	100

Source: Bora (1976)

However, the policy of favouring the backward regions was not without its critics. While the location of new industrial plants in, for example, the towns and villages of the Great Plain was clearly desirable on social grounds, it did involve more expenditure than would have been the case in the established industrial regions, and especially Budapest, because of the need to provide expensive infrastructure and to train labour (Dienes 1973). Enterprises were unhappy at being required to relocate branches and undertake new developments outside Budapest, and where possible did so in towns and villages within easy reach of the capital. The consequence was that the Budapest agglomeration mushroomed, and this in turn created further problems.

Nevertheless, within a period of twenty years, Hungarian society had been transformed by this economic development. The labour-intensive nature of the forced industrialisation of the 1950s depended upon the utilisation of surplus rural manpower and generated extraordinarily high rates of long-distance internal migration, as well as commuting. In little more than a decade the proportion of the active labour force in agriculture dropped from around fifty-five to forty percent, and peasants were obliged to adopt entirely new life styles in the industrial areas. However, the problems of adjustment were considerable, not only for the individuals concerned, but also for the settlements which received them. Budapest faced a particularly severe crisis in housing, urban transport and services, and the other provincial cities had to cope with similar difficulties. It was only during the 1970s that the central and local authorities began to come to terms with them.

(3) Regional Planning Policy under the NEM
The economic reform of 1968 not only marked a new direction in national economic planning but also initiated a strengthening of regional policy. Two directives were approved by the Council of Ministers in 1971. One, the National Regional Plan Conception, was concerned with regional policy per se, while the other, the National Settlement Development Strategy, was concerned with the closely related issue of the settlement network. Both directives have the force of law, though they really only serve as broad guidelines, and the detailed content and implementation has been left to the institutions which are more specifically involved with planning - the Ministry of Construction and Urban Development, the county and city councils and the Scientific and Planning Institute of Urban Construction (VATI). In accordance with the spirit of the NEM, the regional development plans associated with the directives have been implemented indirectly through a range of fiscal measures, incentives, subsidies and a zoning policy, and may be likened to the Structure Plans which are drawn up by County and Regional Councils in the United

Kingdom. Only the location of the most important investments is now determined centrally. The plans are of varying duration, ranging from the medium term - typically of ten years duration - to the very long term of up to fifty years. They also vary in their geographical coverage, and include plans which relate to limited areas with special planning needs, such as those for the Balaton area and the declining coalfields, comprehensive plans for economic planning districts, and national plans with a strong regional content, such as the housing programme. However, before discussing the content of these directives, and the plans based upon them, in more detail, it is appropriate to outline the basic principles which have governed Hungarian regional planning in recent years.

As Kóródi (1976) has stated, regional planning in Hungary contains both economic and social components. In general terms it seeks the rational utilisation of the natural and human resources of the country within a spatial structure of the forces of production which serves the interests of the population. More particularly, it is based on a series of premises. For example, economic activities should be sited at the most advantageous locations, although not so as to prejudice the development of backward regions. Decisions about the location of industrial plant should be based on objective criteria and a satisfactory compromise between the interests of the enterprise involved and the wider concerns of society. The regional and local mix of plants should be such as to ensure the efficient use of infrastructure as well as a balance of employment opportunities for men and women. Cooperative and state farms should be encouraged to pay due regard to soil and topographic conditions, and land of doubtful profitability should be taken out of cultivation, perhaps for afforestation, although not before alternative employment has been created in the areas affected. The tourist and recreational potential of the country should be fully tapped, but not to the detriment of the natural environment. The improvement of the country's infrastructure should be given greater priority, following its relative neglect during the 1950s and 1960s. In particular, villages should have all-weather connections with the trunk and secondary road systems, the rail network should be rationalised, and uneconomic traffic should be transferred to the roads. Public utilities should be extended to the more backward regions, and by these means geographical disparities in living conditions should be reduced.

(4) The National Regional Plan Conception (NRPC)

The Ministry of Construction and Urban Development commissioned the Scientific and Planning Institute for Urban Construction in 1975 to prepare the NRPC, and the proposals were published in 1980. According to the terms of reference, the Institute was required to make recommendations about the future spatial development of the energy, transport and utilities networks, the siting of new industry, the improvement of the settlement network, and measures for the protection of the environment. The plan was prepared in close co-operation with various interested bodies - government ministries, research institutes and the universities - and is 'self regulating' in the sense that it is designed to be sensitive to changing regional circumstances. It has been described as a plan not only for the regional development of the economy but for society at large (Baráth 1981).

The plan is built around the central assumption that regional economic and demographic characteristics will play the decisive role in future planning, although the natural endowments of the environment will continue to be significant. The demographic prognosis within it is rather bleak, for the population is expected to decline from 10,700,000 to 10,200,000 through natural decrease between the early 1980s and 2000, and the manpower situation is unlikely to improve in the foreseeable future. The urban population, however, will continue to grow, and should reach three quarters of the total by 2020, giving rise to a marked territorial differentiation between the more dynamic urbanised regions and the dominantly rural areas, where steep population decline may be expected. Internal migration and long-distance commuting will continue to moderate as the spatial pattern of production stabilises. The structure of employment is also expected to undergo radical change as the tertiary and quaternary sectors expand at the expense of basic manufacturing and agriculture, although most of this change will be accommodated within the normal processes of recruitment to, and retirement from, the labour force.

The NRPC strategy is based on greater territorial co-ordination and the more effective division of labour at national, regional and local levels. At the national level the economic and cultural life of the country is to be strengthened by the co-ordinated development of Budapest and its agglomeration. At the regional scale a more even distribution of urban settlements is to be achieved by the development of the productive and service functions of an increasing number of settlements, with the aim of raising the number of towns and cities from the 109 in the 1980s to around 200; and, at the local level it is intended to encourage a greater functional unity between individual settlements and their surrounding hinterlands.

The NRPC is a compromise between four contending models of regional development, each with its own strengths and weaknesses. The first is the continuation of the policy of concentrated development of previous decades, which would have the disadvantage of raising regional tensions and continuing the under-utilisation of local resources. The second is based on the development of those subsidiary areas which are already linked to regions of concentrated socio-economic activity, and would lead to a better utilisation of local resources, but only in the medium term. The third is one in which existing tendencies towards agglomeration would be strengthened through the encouragement of a more effective division of labour between higher-order centres and their surrounding agglomeration zones, but this would have a very detrimental effect on backward areas; and the fourth would concentrate development on those backward areas. However, it would be the least efficient in improving national income and the general standard of living.

The compromise between the models is expressed in the three guiding principles of the NRPC. The first principle demands the effective utilisation of local resources in the regions, with agriculture and agrarian-industrial activities carrying the same weight as mining and manufacturing in the development process. Geographically, the implementation of this principle will involve the extension of the Budapest region through the recognition of three separate zones for complex development - the immediate vicinity of the capital, including sixty settlements; an intermediate zone in which Dabas, Gödöllö, Monor, Ráckeve, Százhalombatta and Vác would be the main centres; and an outer zone which would include those towns which are at present somewhat deficient in tertiary and quaternary functions as a consequence of their proximity to Budapest, namely Czegléd, Dunaújváros, Hatvan, Jászberény, Salgótarján, Székesfehérvár and

Tatabánya. Further expansion of the main provincial poles is also envisaged, and, in particular, the regional cities of Debrecen, Györ, Miskolc, Pécs and Szeged, and their agglomeraton zones; the Great Plain centres of Békéscsaba-Békés-Gyula, Kecskemét, Nyiregyháza and Szolnok; and the Transdanubian towns of Kaposvár, Sopron, Székesféhervár, Szombathely and Veszprém. In addition, this first principle envisages the formation of three belts of urban growth along the main axes of infrastructural provision - the line of the Danube between Esztergom and Györ, that between Dunaújváros and Mohács, and the existing north-east to south-west zone of development associated with the Middle Mountains. The counties of Bács Kiskun, Baranya, Békés, Csongrád and Hajdú-Bihar will remain primarily areas of intensive agriculture.

The second basic principle of the NRPC is the transformation of the traditional radial structure of communications, centred on Budapest, into a more flexible 'open mesh' system. Such a development would yield considerable advantages, and the potential of the east-west zone - linking the towns of Debrecen, Dunaújváros, Székesféhervár, Szombathely, Szolnok and Veszprém - could be more fully exploited through the integration of the local energy, transport and water networks, and the construction of a new bridge across the Danube to the south of Budapest. The Zagyva valley, between Kisvárda and Záhony, together with the corridor linking Budapest, Kecskemét and Szeged, would form secondary zones of development, while the Balaton region and the area lying between the cities of Kaposvár, Nagykanizsa, Pécs and Zalaegerseg would constitute two further belts of dynamic growth.

The third principle is the evening up of the rates of economic growth in the various regions, with the aim of diminishing the number of retarded areas. This requires that more attention be given to the border regions in the south-west and north-east of the country, and that Borsod and Szabolcs-Szatmár Counties should be given particular priority in view of their high rates of population growth. It also requires that the policy of investing in the towns of the Alföld as 'islands of development' should be modified to embrace the intervening areas as well; and it envisages that western Transdanubia and the lower Danube valley will be developed.

The implications of the three principles of the NRPC for land use change at the macro-scale are

181

summarised in Figure 7.1. The main axes of development along the line of the Danube and the Middle Mountains appear clearly. However, the creation of an 'open mesh' structure should prevent over-expansion of the main centres of population and provide considerable flexibility with regard to future land-use planning. The NRPC envisages no more than a modest increase in the extent of the built-up area, for future development will involve the more effective and intensive use of existing settlements, and will not be at the expense of the agricultural area. Nonetheless, the amount of agricultural land will decline as marginal areas are taken out of cultivation, chiefly for afforestation, until at least 2020. The expansion of mining activities and the growing need for water storage will also cause some encroachment (Table 7.2).

At the local scale the NRPC seeks to create a harmonious mix of functions within a structured spatial framework. Micro-regions form the basic planning unit at this scale, and five types have been recognised according to the range of their functions. The most advanced are invariably urban districts, whose industrial, agricultural or recreational functions are important at the national level, while the most backward are entirely lacking in any form of 'urban life-style' or economic base for such a development. Planning aims at progressively increasing the complexity of the more developed micro-regions and at initiating urbanising processes in the remainder. Functional service regions - linking settlements with their hinterlands - will also have a part to play in the development process.

However, the NRPC is only a plan conception, and its recommendations must be implemented at the levels of more detailed planning. For instance, the general content of the NRPC is incorporated into medium- and long-term national plans, while recommendations about land use are carried into effect in county development plans. The NRPC's guiding principles also serve as the basis for the determination of regional development budgets. In short, the NRPC has set out the basis for the extension of both the social and technical infrastructure - thereby providing a context for socio-economic development - but it is not a detailed plan for that development.

Table 7.2: Planned Land Use Change in Hungary

(in thousand km^2)

		1980	Long-term Plan for 2000	Very Long-term Plan for 2015-2020
Inner Areas	Residential	n.a.	2.25	2.40
	Institutional	n.a.	0.29	0.45
	Industrial	n.a.	0.42	0.53
	Communications	n.a.	0.43	0.60
	Agriculture	n.a.	0.15	0.20
	Other	n.a.	0.53	0.80
	Total	2.99	4.07	4.98
Outer Areas in non- agricultural use	Water	n.a.	4.00	4.14
	Communications	n.a.	1.09	1.25
	Other infrastructure	n.a.	0.03	0.05
	Recreation	n.a.	0.15	0.30
	Other	n.a.	0.76	0.75
	Total	7.06	6.03	6.49
Forest and Reeds		16.37	17.27	18.63
Agricultural		66.62	65.67	62.94
Total		93.03	93.03	93.03

Sources: Baráth (1981); Mezögadasági és Éllemiszeripári Miniszterium (1981)

(5) The National Settlement Development Strategy
(NSDS)
Although the National Settlement Development
Strategy forms an integral part of the NRPC, it is
appropriate to consider it separately for, unlike
the NRPC, it has been implemented in an on-going
fashion since the early 1970s, and the stage has
already been reached where fundamental modifications
to some of its basic policies are being suggested.
The Strategy was designed to rectify the
deficiencies that had for long been apparent in the
settlement system. The Great Plain, for example,
had been served by a rudimentary network of 'urban'
centres, many of which were really no more than very
large villages, and there was a general deficiency
of urban functions and services outside Budapest and
the other major centres of population. The NSDS is
regarded as a policy for social justice, and is one
means of eliminating the substantial differences in
living standards and access to services and public
utilities which had grown up as a result of the
uneven economic development of earlier decades. It
is also seen as helping to stabilise the regional
distribution of population, and thereby alleviating
the housing and public transport problems created by
the heavy in-migration to the cities during the
1950s and 1960s.
The NSDS represents the tailoring of
Christaller's Central Place model to the special
requirements of a socialist economy and society.
Over 1100 settlements were included in the Strategy,
and each was assigned to a particular level of the
settlement hierarchy. In its first published form,
in 1971, it recognised a hierarchy of three tiers in
addition to Budapest - an upper tier consisting of
three orders, a middle tier of two orders and a
lower tier, again with three orders. Population
targets were established for each of the orders, and
each settlement was supposed to serve its own
population and that of its surrounding hinterland
with functions appropriate to its position in the
hierarchy. The spatial representation of the
hierarchy is shown in Figure 7.2 and is discussed in
more detail elsewhere (Compton 1984).
During the 1970s the Strategy was implemented
as a prescriptive plan and did much to promote the
development of the five regional centres - Debrecen,
Györ, Miskolcs, Pécs and Szeged - into effective
'counterpoles' to Budapest. The county towns also
prospered, while the growth of service provision and
public utilities in a number of former villages in

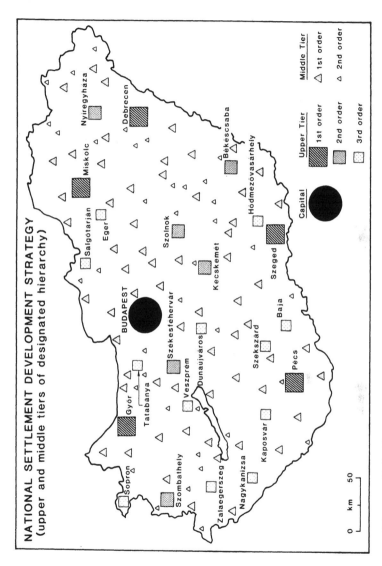

Figure 7.2 The National Settlement Development Strategy of Hungary

185

the middle tier was sufficient to warrant their promotion to urban status. In contrast to these favourable trends, however, the targets for many of the settlements in the middle tier and for most of those in the lower tier were not achieved, and the relative level of development of the villages which were left out of the NSDS altogether declined even further.

Moreover, the NSDS was increasingly criticised during the 1970s for encouraging a more centralised pattern of development than had been intended. Not only did it exclude two thirds of all the settlements but, because administrative and financial responsibility was exercised hierarchically, the regional cities and county towns of the upper tier were developed at the expense of the smaller towns and larger villages. As Enyedi (1983) has pointed out, eighty percent of the development funds administered by district councils in 1980 were controlled by the central exchequer. It is, therefore, not altogether surprising that large-scale residential developments and the bulk of sectoral investments have been placed in the larger towns and cities, and that during the late 1970s and early 1980s settlements in which forty-seven percent of the population resided received only ten percent of development funds. In short, under the NSDS there was a trend towards the concentration of population and facilities in the larger settlements.

It has also been suggested that the hierarchical structure of the System, with its population targets and prescribed functions, is too rigid and cannot be adapted easily to the changing character of the space economy. For example, the special needs of the agglomerations which were forming, particularly around Budapest, were not recognised, nor was the necessity for forging links between central places and their zones of attraction. Moreover, there were instances of neighbouring settlements being assigned to the same level of the hierarchy, and thereby encouraged to compete rather than to co-ordinate their activities, while many settlements in the middle and lower tiers were so under-developed that the necessary functions could never be created from locally-generated resources.

In response to these criticisms modifications were announced to the Strategy in 1981. The changes included the abandonment of population targets, the reduction of the number of hierarchical orders from nine to seven, and the shifting of the focus of development to the medium sized and smaller centres. Investment in the regional and county cities has been reduced accordingly. Greater co-ordination within given hierarchical orders is to be encouraged, and the particular needs of the Budapest agglomeration have been recognised by the designation of six new nodal centres within it. But, while the 1981 modifications have gone some way towards meeting the immediate criticisms, many doubts remain. Foremost among them is the problem of the villages, and the 1,500,000 people in them, which have been left out of the NSDS. The amalgamation of cooperative farms has led to the closure of farm offices in many of them; the village school network has been replaced by a system of district schools; health care facilities have been centralised; village shops have been closed; and the number of independent village councils has been drastically reduced, with the consequence that village people now face worse living conditions than they did in 1971, when the Strategy was launched.

But the Strategy has also been subject to more fundamental questioning. For example, doubt has been thrown on the need for a policy in which the details of settlement development are spelt out, and on whether this should be at the local, regional or national scale. Questions have been raised as to what particular model of settlement development should be followed - whether it should be one based only on a hierarchical system of service centres, or on centres and their zones of attraction, or on a dichotomy of towns and villages - and uncertainty has been expressed as to whether a hierarchical system is necessary to ensure the effective spatial distribution of service centres. A comprehensive research programme, sponsored by the Ministry of Construction and Urban Development, was set up in 1981 to provide answers to these questions, and it has become clear that a decentralised model, based on the harmonious development of centres together with their zones of attraction rather than one based on centres only, has become the favoured strategy for the future. The local administrative framework of the country was restructured at the beginning of 1984 in anticipation of this change, and the former dichotomy between rural and urban districts eliminated with the abolition of the rural district councils. Local administration now consists of two tiers - Budapest and nineteen counties, which form the upper tier, and 142 urban settlements and large villages together with their zones of attraction,

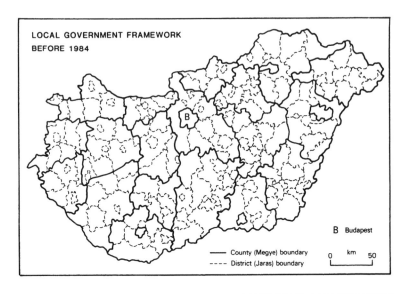

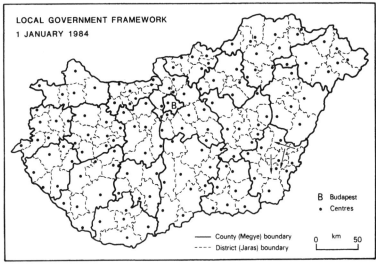

Figure 7.3 The Administrative Divisions of Hungary

which are the lower tier (Figure 7.3). The creation of 142 lower-tier councils of equal rank has not only reduced the status of the five regional cities but also the other higher-order centres in the NSDS, thus implying that their claim on the central development fund will be accorded a lower priority in future, while conversely the right of smaller settlements to assistance has been enhanced. Moreover, an administrative system, based on functional settlement regions, which links central places with their surrounding rural hinterlands, should also be more effective in extending the develoment process to the large number of people still living in the small villages (Daróczi 1980).

PROTECTION OF THE ENVIRONMENT AND OF LAND

Generally speaking, economic development has taken precedence over other considerations in post-war Hungary, and the natural environment may have suffered as a consequence. Of late, however, the authorities, like those in many other countries, have begun to appreciate the role which the natural environment plays in society. An Act for the Protection of the Human Environment was passed in 1976, and a National Authority for Environmental Protection and Nature Conservation was set up in 1980 (Tardy 1984). Active steps are being taken to reduce the levels of water and air pollution, and areas of special environmental interest, including five international biosphere reserves, are now protected. A system of national parks is being created to conserve both the cultural and natural heritage of the country, and the chief of these are the Hortobagy National Park, embracing the most typical remaining 'puszta' region of the Great Plain, and the Bukk Mountains National Park.

Many of the rivers in Hungary are moderately or highly polluted, in part because they are already dirty before they enter the country, but also because considerable further pollution occurs within Hungary through the discharge of inadequately treated sewage. The Danube is particularly badly affected below Budapest and also to the south of Dunaújváros, and the Sajo river system of northern Hungary, which carries effluent discharged in Slovakia, is further polluted as it passes through the Miskolc industrial region. On balance, however, the overall quality of river water does not deteriorate in Hungary, and water leaving the country is as clean as that entering.

Lake Balaton is a particularly significant example of a valuable natural asset under environmental stress and of the attempts to remedy such problems. The Lake and its surroundings have been designated as the 'Balaton Recreation Area' and are subject to special environmental protection measures. However, in spite of this there are problems of incipient eutrophication caused by the excessive use of the lake for recreation and by modern agricultural practices in its catchmemt (Bora 1984). Recreation grew in a largely unregulated fashion during the 1960s and 1970s, and there was widespread construction of second homes on the lake-side. The provision of mains sewerage, in contrast, lagged far behind, and sewage was increasingly discharged into the lake. As for agriculture, viticulture on the hillsides overlooking the lake has contributed to a high rate of sedimentation, and the indiscriminate use of artificial fertilisers and pesticides, together with the disposal of liquid slurry from factory-farm livestock-rearing units, has built-up nitrogen, potassium and other toxic substances in the water. As yet eutrophication is only serious in limited areas, but if unchecked the whole of the lake could die. This would lead to drastic economic and social effects in the areas around the lake, for Balaton is the sole location in Hungary for mass water-side recreation. Thus, the prime concern is to arrest the process of eutrophication and to improve the quality of the lake water; and it is clear that remedial action will be expensive and may entail the raising of extra revenue from lake users. Above all, the discharge of insufficiently treated effluent into the lake will have to cease; constraints have already been placed on new building around the lake to prevent further overloading of the existing sewage system; and cooperative and state farms are being encouraged to moderate their use of chemicals. Those polluting the lake, both individuals and public concerns, now face stiff fines.

Land policy is chiefly concerned to preserve the agricultural area of the country and to reduce the rate of conversion to other uses. Encroachment was particularly rapid during the 1950s, and, although the Land Protection Act of 1961 reduced the rate of loss, this was only temporary, for the process again accelerated during the 1970s. Furthermore, although some loss of agricultural land is to be expected, the areas thus alienated have not always been used effectively, and their transfer has meant a diminution of agriculture's export-earning potential, all of which has prompted a reassessment of the economic and social value of agricultural land.

The problem of land conversion arises largely from the division of the administrative areas of settlements into inner and outer zones. The inner zones have traditionally embraced the built-up area, together with extensive tracts which are designated for non-agricultural development. Outer areas, on the other hand, are predominantly composed of agricultural land, but may also include land for recreation, household plots and gardens. The problem of encroachment arises because, whereas the value of land in inner areas is determined by market factors, in outer areas the land market is not free, land values are fixed according to agricultural quality, and those values are set at unrealistically low levels. As a result, institutions and enterprises which are seeking land for development have scrambled for the cheaper land in the outer areas despite the availability of sites in the inner zones (Daróczi 1984).

This problem was tackled in 1977 in an amendment to the Land Protection Act. Under this, the conversion of tracts of less than ten hectares in the outer areas to non-agricultural activities now requires the permission of a Land Office, while that of the Ministry of Agriculture and Food is needed for areas in excess of that figure. A conversion tax was also introduced for the use of the higher qualities of agricultural land, and this was extended to all qualities in 1981. Proceeds from the tax have been split between the Development Funds of the County Councils and a national Land Protection Fund. Under the 1977 and 1981 amendments some of the less intensively used inner areas have been re-zoned, becoming part of the outer zones, and in the future it is anticipated that most development will be excluded from them (Table 7.2). Nevertheless, as Daroczi points out, these measures do not amount to a comprehensive land protection policy, and serious discussion in the mid-1980s of the content of a putative Code for Land and Urban Development, and of the possibility of a radical revaluation of agricultural land, both suggested that the authorities were aware of continuing difficulties in the protection of agricultural land.

THE CHANGING ROLE OF PLANNING

We may summarise the development of spatial and environmental policy in Hungary since the Second World War by noting that, although the elimination of regional imbalances in the levels of development and standards of living was an objective of the First Five Year Plan, the primacy which was given to maximising the rate of economic growth had the effect of widening these disparities still further, and that the first effective action to tackle the regional problem was delayed until the early 1960s. It was not until this time that the more intensive use of labour, capital and raw materials supplanted the extensive phase of economic development, and that effectiveness and efficiency were reintroduced as criteria in assessing economic performance, in an evolution of policy which culminated in the New Economic Mechanism in 1968, and which, in turn, reinforced the regional dimension of economic development. The principles governing the development of the settlement network (NSDS) and the National Regional Plan Conception were published by the Council of Ministers in 1971, and although the NSDS was implemented as a prescriptive plan, and subject to much criticism, it had achieved some success by the early 1980s in neutralising the economic and cultural dominance of Budapest by deflecting development into the main provincial towns. However, this success was bought largely at the expense of the smaller towns and villages, and the Strategy underwent further modification during the 1980s with a view to spreading the available development funds across the whole range of settlements. In contrast, the details of the NRPC, which will serve as the blue-print for all future regional development, were only completed in 1981.

As Hungarian society has become more complex, so the nature and tasks of planning have changed. During the 1950s planning was virtually synonymous with programmes to spread industry more widely across the country, but in more recent years the emphasis has become one of improving the country's infrastructure and expanding service provision in the interests of the population at large. At the same time concern about the deterioration of the environment has grown rapidly amongst the public. Moreover, there are signs that Hungary will soon enter the post-industrial phase of development, for the numbers employed in basic and manufacturing industry are already beginning to drop, while the tertiary and quaternary sectors are growing in importance. Up to now the planning system in Hungary appears to have been sufficiently flexible to cope with the changes which have occurred, and has been more successful in this than those in many of the other countries in Eastern Europe. It will be of considerable interest to see whether it can cope with the even greater changes which seem likely in the years ahead.

REFERENCES

Baráth, E. (1981), Az országos területrendezési tervkoncepcio, Városépités, 5-18.

Bora, G. (1976), Changes in the spatial structure of Hungarian industry and the determinants of industrial location, in Regional Development and Planning, ed. Compton, P.A. and Pecsi, M., Akadémiai Kiadó, Budapest, 117-126.

Bora, G. (1984), Environmental management in the Lake Balaton region, in Environmental Management: British and Hungarian Case Studies, ed. Compton, P.A. and Pecsi, M., Akadémiai Kiadó, Budapest, 91-108.

Compton, P.A. (1984), Hungary, the national settlement development strategy, Cities, 1, 374-386.

Daróczi, E. (1980), Administrative and financial frameworks for urban development in Hungary, in Development of Settlement Systems, ed. Enyedi, G. and Meszaros, J., Akadémiai Kiadó, Budapest, 41-54.

Daróczi, E. (1984), The protection of agricultural land on the urban fringe : the case of Veszprem City, in Environmental Management : British and Hungarian Case Studies, ed. Compton, P.A. and Pecsi, M., Akadémiai Kiadó, Budapest, 51-74.

Dienes, L. (1973), The Budapest agglomeration and Hungarian industry : a spatial dilemma, Geographical Review, 63, 356-377.

Enyedi, G. (1983), A magyar település hálozat átalakulása, Magyar Tudomány, 5, 341-352.

Kornai, J. (1981), Economics of Shortage, Elsevier, Amsterdam.

Kóródi, J. (1976), Regional development policy and regional planning in Hungary, in Regional Development and Planning, ed. Compton, P.A. and Pecsi, M., Akadémiai Kiadó, Budapest, 25-34.

Marrese, M. (1980), The Hungarian economy : prospects for the 1980s, in Economic Reform in

Eastern Europe and Prospects for the 1980s, ed. Economics Directorate and Information Directorate NATO, Pergamon, Oxford, 183-201.

Mezögazdasági és Éllemiszeripári Miniszterium (1981), Országos föklügyi és térkepészeti Hivatala, Budapest.

Tardy, J. (1984), Geographical trends in environmental protection research in Hungary, in Geographical Essays in Hungary 1984, ed. Enyedi, G. and Pecsi, M., Geographical Research Institute, Hungarian Academy of Sciences, Budapest, 165-178.

Chapter 8

POLAND

Andrew H. Dawson

THE CONTEXT OF PLANNING

     Planning in Poland since the Second World War
has been a fragmented activity. Aims and methods
which were adopted during the mid-1940s were greatly
altered by 1950. Major innovations with respect to
spatial planning were made in the 1960s, and these
in turn were much developed and amended during the
1970s.   A wholesale reorganisation of   planning
authorities took place in 1975.   Some of these
changes reflected the influence of the Soviet Union,
some were a response to growing public awareness in
Poland and elsewhere about such issues as pollution
and the loss of good agricultural land, but others
followed moments of severe crisis in the management
of the economy.   In spite of substantial economic
growth, popular discontent in Poland led to the fall
of governments in 1956, 1970 and 1980, and to major
shifts of policy, and the crisis of 1980-1983
brought the economy to the point of   external
bankruptcy and internal collapse.   Thus, Polish
planning   in   the   post-war   years has   been
characterised by a series of brief periods, each of
which has been distinctive in its aims and approach.
However, so brief have they been that none of the
long-run plans for the space economy of the country
have been able to run their course, and all have
been overtaken in mid-term by some radical
redirection of policy. In brief, planning in Poland
has had to cope with one of the most dynamic
environments among the countries of Eastern Europe,
and therefore this chapter will outline the way in
which regional, urban, land-use and environmental
planning have developed since 1945 by focussing upon
each of these short periods, concluding with an
assessment of what has been achieved and an

indication of the problems which await solution.

POST-WAR RECONSTRUCTION

Between the end of the fighting and 1949 the overriding priority was to make good the wartime damage. Almost two-fifths of the fixed assets of the country had been destroyed or removed (Karpiński 1964, p. 15), and damage was especially great in Warsaw, in the northeast and southeast, and in those parts of the Northern and Western Territories which had been inhabited by Germans. Thus, for example, thirty-five percent of industrial buildings had been destroyed in the country as a whole, but in Warsaw the figure was fifty-four percent. Similarly, less than half of the country's stock of industrial prime movers had survived, and in Warsaw only a quarter (Główny Urząd Statystyczny 1967a, p. xxvi). All parts of Poland had suffered substantial losses of farm buildings, equipment and livestock, housing, transport facilities and other forms of infrastructure.

As the Russian and Polish forces moved westwards across the country, fundamental changes and decisions occurred which have affected the economy ever since. For instance, all agricultural holdings which were larger than a hundred hectares, or which included more than fifty hectares of arable land, or which had belonged to Germans, and almost all forests were seized. Ten million hectares, or about a third of the present area of Poland, fell into the hands of the state by these means. Some was redistributed among peasant farmers, thus allowing the establishment of 813,000 new farms and the extension of 254,000 others, but much of that in the Northern and Western Territories remained in state ownership. Nevertheless, the effect was to strengthen the peasant element within central and eastern areas of the country, where privately-owned small farms became almost the only form of agricultural landownership, and in the country as a whole, where in 1950 eighty-five percent of the agricultural land was held by private farmers, three-quarters of which was in holdings of between three and fourteen hectares (Główny Urząd Statystyczny 1968, pp. 217, 233). Thus, small peasant holdings of the type which were discussed in Chapter 2 were preserved, most of which were organised as mixed, rather than specialist, enterprises, with a substantial element of

196

self-sufficiency for the farmer and his family. They possessed little equipment, and employed primitive methods of production. A second major change was that which affected the mining and manufacturing industries and services. Almost all large and medium sized industry, and all mineral resources, public transport, banking and foreign trade were declared to be in public ownership. Thirdly, great movements of people took place from the eastern territories, which had been taken by the USSR, and also from central and southern Poland, to the Western and Northern lands. This migration was largely of younger people, and as a result marked contrasts developed between the demographic structure of those lands and the rest of the country. For example, rates of natural growth were a third or more higher in the areas of immigration throughout the 1950s, with consequences for the structure of the population and the demands for employment, housing and communal facilities, which have lasted much longer.

The recovery of production after the war was impressive. By the end of the Plan for Economic Reconstruction in 1949 the outputs of coal, steel, machinery, industrial chemicals, cement, fertilisers, sugar beet and some other products were all far in excess of the 1938 levels. However, those of cars, radios, bricks, meat, milk and cereals were still well below the pre-war level. Nevertheless, the outputs of 'group A' goods – producer goods – and of those for consumption – 'group B' goods – as a whole grew at the same rate between 1946 and 1950 (Główny Urząd Statystyczny 1964, pp. xxx-xxxvi) (Table 8.1).

Physical planning, which had been relatively well developed in Poland in comparison with most of the other countries of Eastern Europe before the war, resumed. A Central Spatial Planning Office was established in 1945, and under the Physical Planning Act of 1946 three levels of spatial planning authorities – national, regional (województwo) and local (powiat) – were established. Work began on a National Spatial Plan, and it was intended that each of the fourteen regions, or voivodships, would draw up more detailed plans in accordance with it. Similarly, the several hundred powiaty were each to have a plan which would accord with that of their voivodship, thus establishing a coherent and integrated blueprint for the long-term development of the country.

Poland

Table 8.1: Indices of Achievement of the Polish Economy, 1938-1980

	1938	1946	1949	1956	1970	1979
Population (millions)	34.8	23.6	24.6	28.1	32.7	35.4
Proportion in towns (percent)	30	34	36.2	44.9	52.2	58.2
Proportion dependent on agriculture (percent)	60.0[1]	-	47.1[2]	-	29.8	22.5
Output of Selected Products						
Cereals (million tonnes)	12.5[3]	5.1	11.9	12.1	16.3[3]	17.9[3]
Sugar Beet (million tonnes)	2.8[3]	3	4.8	6.4	13.6[3]	15.3[3]
Meat (thousand tonnes)	967	337	843	1529	2207	3265
Milk (million litres)	10	3.3	7.1	10	14.5	16.4
Coal (million tonnes)	38	47	74	95	140	201
Steel (million tonnes)	1.4	1.2	2.3	5	11.8	19.2
Sulphuric Acid (thousand tonnes)	189	124	276	481	1901	2983
Nitrogen and Phosphate Fertilisers (thousand tonnes)	86	63	148	299	1629	2417
Cement (million tonnes)	1.7[4]	1.4	2.3	4	12.2	19.2
Bricks (millions)	1820	513	1253	2786	3660	2276
Machine tools (thousands)	4.3[4]	1.6	5.4	16.9	36.3	39.3
Cars (thousand)	1.9	-	-	5.8	64.2	350
Radios (thousand)	142	-	66	499	987	2661

1 1931   2 1950   3 Five-year averages for 1934-8, 1966-70, 1975-9   4 1937

Sources: Główny Urząd Statystyczny (1966), pp. 38-39; (1980), pp. XXXII-XXXIII

An outline of a National Spatial Plan, which was based upon the pre-war ideas of Chmielewski and Syrkus, was drawn up in 1947. In it the space economy was conceived as being a series of specialised production points, or nodes, which were linked together by bands or corridors of transport facilities. Junctions of the bands occurred at existing centres of production or indicated potential centres, and development was intended to take place along the bands and at the junctions (Figure 8.1a). It was envisaged that the nodes would form a hierarchy, after the manner of that described by Christaller (1933). In advocating this conception, the authors of the plan argued that it would facilitate the linking of the Western and Northern Territories to the rest of the country, thus obliterating the effects of the pre-war international frontiers, and would indicate those regions in which the settlement network, and indeed the whole economy, required development. Three large new centres of manufacturing industry were to be established in the northwest, northeast and southeast of the country, where there was little alternative employment to that in farming and, in the case of the northeast and southeast, substantial overpopulation in the countryside (Malisz 1974, pp. 16-25). Conversely, manufacturing industry in the highly-developed and congested Upper Silesian coalfield was not to be extended if it could be undertaken satisfactorily in other parts of Poland. The Plan was to be carried out over twenty-five years. Post-war reconstruction was expected to take five, and that was to be followed by two ten-year periods of, first, the industrialisation of the country, and, second, the development of the hierarchical series of service centres.

In addition to the Central Planning Office, voivodship offices were set up, and work began on plans for the Upper Silesian and Wałbrzych coalfields, the Gdańsk Bay littoral, the cities of Łódź and Warsaw, together with their environs, and some rural areas. Town planning also began again, and by the end of the 1940s about four hundred settlements had been provided with master plans in sketch form (Zaremba 1966, pp. 276-277). That for Warsaw was of particular interest. It did not envisage that the population would recover to its pre-war level of 1,289,000, but that it would reach only 800,000 by the mid-1960s. It aimed to do away with the gross overcrowding and congestion of building which had been allowed to develop during

Poland

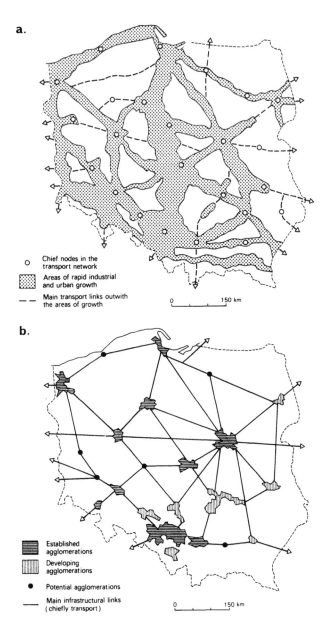

a.

○ Chief nodes in the
   transport network

▨ Areas of rapid industrial
   and urban growth

－ － Main transport links outwith
      the areas of growth

0   150 km

b.

▤ Established
   agglomerations

▥ Developing
   agglomerations

● Potential agglomerations

── Main infrastructural links
    (chiefly transport)

0   150 km

Figure 8.1   National   Spatial   Plans   for   the
Development of Poland in (a) 1947 and (b) 1970

the nineteenth century in the inner city - if necessary by knocking down some of the few surviving buildings - to segregate the major land uses, and to provide green 'wedges' between industrial and residential zones. The city centre was to be restored to its former status as the major location of services and administration, and the Vistula valley was to become a large green area for recreation (Prezydium 1965, p. 46).

Thus, there was much plan-making once the war was over, but the inherited pattern of development could not be altered greatly during the short period of reconstruction, and great contrasts still existed in the level of economic development between one part of the country and another in 1950. In particular, medium-sized and large towns were thinly spread over the country except in Upper Silesia, dependence upon agriculture (Figure 8.2a) and the pressure of rural population on the land were both greatest in the southeast and centre, and lowest in the Northern and Western Territories, and the availability of houseroom (Figure 8.3a) showed a very similar pattern with the highest values in the north and west, and the greatest overcrowding in the south and east. Nor could much be achieved to alter the form of the urban areas, for there was great resistance to suggestions for the demolition of yet further property so soon after the wartime destruction, and few resources were available for the laying out of urban parks and recreational areas.

Moreover, the time which was required to implement these plans was denied. As relations between the USSR and the western powers deteriorated at the end of the 1940s, the Russians strengthened their control over Poland, and Soviet aims and systems of planning were introduced. The spatial planners were criticised for drawing up long-run plans at a time when the economic Plan for Reconstruction only covered three years, and because they had indicated targets for the future growth of towns and cities in spite of the fact that the economic plan had included few details about the future location of new industries. In other words, spatial and economic planning had been operating independently of each other in several fundamental respects, and economists charged the spatial planners with creating unrealistic and idealistic blueprints for a far distant future. However, these criticisms were probably little more than a pretext which allowed the Polish authorities to abolish the

Poland

a.

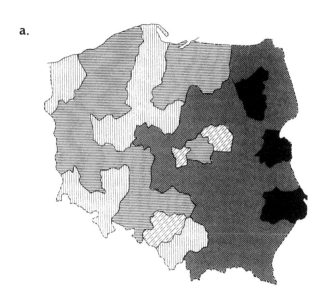

b.

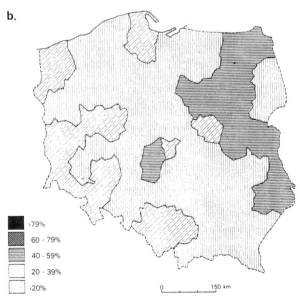

>79%

60 - 79%

40 - 59%

20 - 39%

<20%

0   150 km

Figure 8.2 The Proportion of the Population Dependent on Agriculture in Poland in (a) 1950 and (b) 1980

central and voivodship planning offices - for which
there were no equivalents in the Soviet Union - in
1949, and to suppress the Polish tradition of
imaginative spatial planning, as the country entered
a period of Stalinist control.

THE SIX YEAR PLAN, 1950-1955

The period between 1949 and 1956, and
especially between 1949 and 1954, was Stalinist in
both aim and method. The aim was the rapid
industrialisation of the country, and Soviet systems
of economic planning and management were introduced,
including the establishment of government ministries
for each industry and of a strong, central, economic
planning agency, the State Economic Planning
Commission. A medium-term Six Year National Plan
was approved 'for building the foundations of
socialism', and this was to be followed by five-year
plans which were to run simultaneously with those in
the USSR. Almost all the remaining privately-owned
manufacturing and trade were abolished. A
determined effort was made to collectivise
agriculture, and much greater attention was given to
the output of producer, than of consumer, goods. A
highly ambitious programme of investment in industry
was adopted, which included a thousand new mines and
factories, and this was to be financed in part by
the compulsory deliveries of grain and meat from
peasant farms at low prices, which began in 1952.
The provision of new housing in the cites - which
fell almost entirely into the hands of central
government - was to be meagre. In other words, the
economic development of Poland was set to follow a
path very similar to that of the Soviet Union during
the 1930s, and it was not until the Poznań riots of
1956 and the reinstatement of Wladyslaw Gomułka as
First Secretary of the Polish United Workers Party
(the Communist Party) that significant changes were
made.
The effect of the Six Year Plan was marked.
Although about half of the new factories which had
been envisaged had to be cancelled when the Plan was
found to be too ambitious, and many others were not
completed until the late 1950s (Wróbel and Zawadzki
1966, pp. 435-436), industrial output rose rapidly,
with the increase in producer goods exceeding that
of items for consumption, and a million more people
- an increase of over fifty percent - were employed
in mining and manufacturing between 1949 and 1956.

Poland

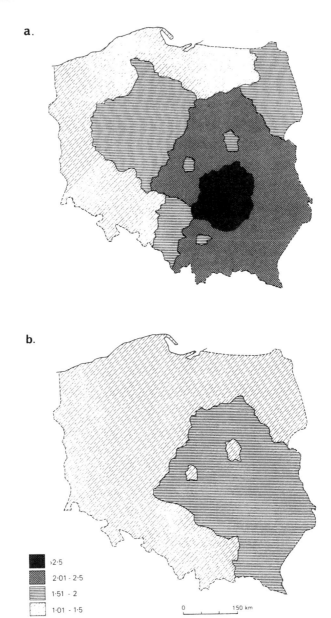

a.

b.

>2·5
2·01 - 2·5
1·51 - 2
1·01 - 1·5

0   150 km

Figure 8.3 Numbers of People per Room in Housing in
Poland in (a) 1950 and (b) 1970

Much of these increases occurred in the existing industrial areas, but major new investments included the Nowa Huta steelworks near Kraków, in a region in which industry had been only weakly developed in the past, and the Warsaw steel mill. As a result, urban population also grew rapidly, rising from 8,900,000 in 1949 to 12,600,000 in 1956. That of Warsaw, which had already reached 800,000 in 1950, had exceeded a million by the end of the period. However, the most spectacular growth of industrial employment and urban population during the 1950s occurred not in such major industrial centres as Łódź or Upper Silesia, but in some parts of the country which hitherto had been dominantly rural. In particular, eastern Poland's share of industrial employment increased despite the large overall growth during the period, and population increases in towns such as Białystok, Rzeszów, Stalowa Wola and Tarnów were at twice the national rate for urban areas, or more. Nevertheless, the growth of urban population might have been even greater, for housing received relatively little investment. Between 1950 and 1955 only 3.7 dwellings were completed in the towns each year on average per thousand people (Główny Urząd Statystyczny 1963, p. 185), and the shortage of urban housing was severe. Despite an almost static number of people in agriculture over that period, the rural population grew in many parts of the country, and the number of those commuting to work in the towns increased sharply (Lijewski 1977, p. 230).

Following the abolition of the voivodship planning offices, spatial planning during the Six Year period was much reduced. Nevertheless, it was not absent, for the Six Year Plan did contain a number of broad, spatial objectives, of which the raising of the level of industrialisation in tne central and eastern parts of the country was one. About a third of the new factories were to be placed in areas outwith the old industrial regions, and thus opportunity was to be taken of the possibility of raising industrial output with the aid of surplus rural labour. Indeed, it was intended that eventually there would be an even or uniform distribution of industry across the country so that the whole population would have access to industrial employment. However, no national spatial plan was produced to replace that which had been sketched out during the Period of Reconstruction, only about a third of the country was covered by regional planning of any sort – chiefly areas in which rapid

industrial and urban growth was to occur - and only
in the case of one of the fourteen areas so covered
- Upper Silesia - was a plan completed and approved
during the Six Year Plan period (Zaremba 1966, p.
280).

The Upper Silesian Plan was drawn up by a
committee appointed by the State Planning
Commission. It was based upon the principles of
fully developing the productive resources of the
region, and in particular of increasing the output
of its coal and metalliferous ores, while limiting
the growth of, and gradually decentralising,
manufacturing, which was not directly dependent upon
local raw materials. It was also intended to
improve the living conditions in the region through
the reconstruction of some of the towns, the
reduction of pollution and the reclamation of waste
land. Under the Plan, which covered only a part of
the voivodship of Katowice, the region was divided
into area A - the densely-developed industrial and
urban core covering about seven hundred square
kilometres, in which mining and metallurgy were
concentrated, and which had a population of about
1,250,000 and 310,000 mining and manufacturing jobs
- and area B around it. Area B covered about 1,700
square kilometres, and was much less intensively
developed, with a population of about 300,000 and
80,000 industrial jobs. Further growth of
population and employment in area A was to be
discouraged in view of its problems of subsidence,
water shortage and pollution, but now that the whole
area was in the hands of a single state for the
first time since industrialisation there had begun,
the opportunity was to be taken of allowing some
localised urban expansion in order to create a clear
hierarchy of service centres. Katowice was selected
to become the focus for the whole region, while
Bytom, Gliwice and Sosnowiec were to be secondary
centres. Nevertheless, most new developments, and
in particular housing on a large scale, were to be
sited in area B (Kotela 1966, pp. 119-127). During
the Six Year Plan period three new towns were begun
in area B, as were several dormitory settlements on
the edge of the built-up area. However, it proved
to be beyond the power, or willingness, of the
authorities to prevent further growth within area A
(Table 8.2). Between 1949 and 1960 the number of
industrial plants there increased from about 1,100
to about 1,800, while employment rose by about a
quarter. This growth was in part a reflection of
the intention to expand mining and those industries

which were dependent upon the mineral resources of
the area. However, it may also have reflected the
attraction of Upper Silesia to industrial ministries
which were under pressure to achieve their output
targets, and which preferred to make use of the
skilled workforce there rather than to employ people
from rural areas who had no experience of factory
work. In short, industrial ministries may have been
able to flout the aims of the regional plan in the
same way as their equivalents in the Soviet Union
have been alleged to have done (see Chapter 2).
Population increase, on the other hand, was
relatively small; the percentage growth of both
employment and population in area B was three times
as great as in area A (Table 8.2); and on all three
criteria area A advanced less rapidly than the
country as a whole.

Table 8.2: Industrial and Population Growth in
Upper Silesia 1949-1960 (percent)

	Increase in the number of industrial plants 1949-1960	Increase in industrial employment 1949-1960	Increase in the population in towns 1949-1960
Poland	81	69	35
Upper Silesia			
Area A	64	23	13
Area B	66	70	43

Source: Główny Urząd Statystyczny (1967b), Tables 1
and 5.

Town planning continued during the Six Year
Plan, but it could no longer be related to spatial
plans at the regional and national scales. Rather,
it was based upon information of an economic nature,
such as the future demand for labour in each town,
which was supplied by the central, economic
planners. Town plans were also drawn up according
to the Town Planning Standards of 1951 - a body of
regulations closely related to those in use in the
Soviet Union (Malisz 1966, p. 65). One aim of the

regulations, and of the associated plans, was to ensure that housing and other development would incur as few servicing costs as possible. Thus, high-density residential development, usually in blocks of flats of between three and five storeys, was the norm. Malisz has since described these densities as excessive (1966, p. 65), while Kotela (1966, p. 176) has claimed somewhat disingenuously that the monumental, Russian style in which such housing was built had been adopted for "no good reason". It is also of relevance to note that the Standards did not deal with at least two areas which had been of interest to Polish town planners during the Period of Reconstruction but which had played little or no part in Soviet urban development up to that time, namely, the redevelopment of substantial areas and the design of areas within cities at a scale larger than that of the individual street block.

Nonetheless, some patterns for large-scale urban developments had to be drawn up, for, although much town growth consisted of little more than the addition of new blocks to the outskirts of existing settlements, several new towns were begun. The largest of these was Nowa Huta, which was to accommodate the workers of the Lenin steelworks. Although only seven kilometres from Kraków, it was intended that the new town should be independent of it, with a full range of services (although no provision was made in the plan for a church). The initial population target was 100,000, and the ground plan was of a formal and regular nature, with tree-lined avenues radiating from a central square containing a statue of Lenin. Another new town was that at Tychy, to the south of Katowice. This settlement was to be a dormitory in area B of Upper Silesia for people working in area A, and most of the early building was of blocks of flats on a roughly grid-iron plan around the railway station. However, provision was also made for some manufacturing industry. The town was to be completed by 1980, when it was expected to house 130,000 people (Kotela 1966, p. 124). As a result of the combination of formal street plans with the massive style of architecture the urban developments of the period, whether they be in the new towns or in the parts of Warsaw which were rebuilt at that time, such as Marszałkowska, are readily recognisable.

However, it should be noted that other projects which were undertaken during the early 1950s were of a quite different character. One was the rebuilding of the historic cores of Warsaw and Gdańsk. Using the record of Canaletto's paintings the old town of Warsaw, and areas around it, were painstakingly restored in order to assert that the Polish nation would not succumb to the wartime attempt to destroy its material culture. Secondly, no less than five national parks were established during that period, thus bringing the total in the country by 1956 to six. One of these - that in the Pieniny Mountains - had been designated originally in 1932, but it was re-established and enlarged in 1954, and others were set up in the Babia Góra, Holy Cross and Tatry Mountains, and at Ojców.

THE GOMUŁKA PERIOD, 1956-1970

The return to power of Gomułka in 1956 was followed by some significant changes in the methods by which Polish economic development was to be achieved. The overall aim of the period was a 'more proportional development of the whole national economy', and there was to be greater emphasis upon the production of consumer goods and on the improvement of the standard of living (Jachniak-Ganguly 1978, p. 64). Farmers were allowed to leave the collective farms, and almost all did so immediately. The proportion of 'non-productive' investment in the total was raised, at least initially, and official interest in regional planning revived slowly. However, the reformist character of the Gomułka Government was short-lived. As the 1960s progressed, the earlier emphases on accumulation rather than consumption, on 'productive' rather than other investment, and on basic rather than consumer industries were reasserted. Popular discontent with Poland's economic performance became widespread, and the Gomułka period ended, as had that of the Six Year Plan, with the outbreak of popular disturbances, and a change of government.

The economic achievements of the period were substantial (Table 8.1). The output of basic chemicals rose fourfold, that of cement trebled, those of steel and machine tools doubled, and coal production increased by a half. There were also large increases in the output of cars, radios and other consumer durables. Employment in mining and manufacturing rose from 2,900,000 in 1956 to 4,300,000 in 1970, and that in services from

2,000,000 to 3,400,000. The proportion of the population living in the towns came to exceed fifty percent. Agricultural output also increased, though not by as much as that of manufacturing, and there was a further slight fall in the number of people working on farms. By the end of the period only about a third of the Polish labour force was working in agriculture.

However, these major changes in the structure of the economy took place very largely in the absence of spatial planning. In spite of the acceptance of the need for long-term, perspective planning in the late 1950s, the re-establishment of the voivodship planning offices in 1959, the passage of a Spatial Planning Act in 1961, and the setting up of a special board in 1967 to prepare a spatial plan for the whole country, the emphasis throughout the period remained on economic, rather than spatial planning. Furthermore, the industrial ministries retained the initiative in decisions about the location of new investment, and the voivodship plans which were drawn up lacked the framework of a national spatial plan to guide them. Only at the local level did spatial planning proceed throughout the period.

Fundamental to what spatial planning did occur during the Gomułka years was the long-term plan for economic expansion. The first of these covered the period from 1961 to 1980. It set out further substantial increases in industrial output, especially in relation to the exploitation of the country's raw material base and the production of capital goods, but the output of consumer goods was also to double per capita, and agriculture was to become more intensive. More particularly, the output of chemicals was set to increase more than tenfold, those of electricity and thermal power and of machinery more than sixfold, and those of building materials and metals fourfold, but food, footwear and leather production were only expected to grow by between two and three times (Secomski 1966, pp. 452-457). No spatial plan was prepared, but three principles of location were incorporated into the economic plan, at least for the siting of investments during its early years. These were the need to make use of the natural resources of each voivodship, to limit migration by building new plants where local supplies of manpower were available, and thus reduce the demand for new housing and associated 'non-productive' investment, and thirdly, to reduce the greatest differences between the levels of development in the various parts of the country, but only within 'economically reasonable limits' (Wróbel and Zawadzki 1966, p. 439). Some authors (Hamilton 1982, Zimon 1979) have accepted the claim that this amounted to a New Location Policy, and have recognised in these aims a marked retreat from the Six Year Plan's aim of uniform industrialisation of the country. But it should be emphasised that the three principles specifically included industrial growth in rural areas which possessed labour supplies or mineral resources, and it would appear that, to that extent, the emphases of development, both economic and spatial, were not very different under Gomułka from those which had been accepted between 1950 and 1956.

Spatial planning at the voivodship level began again within this long-term framework. Voivodship plans were based upon figures supplied by the central, economic planners about future investment and the likely demand for labour in each voivodship and town. They were expected to designate broad areas in which particular activities, such as industry, agriculture or tourism, would be dominant, and to show the general arrangement of communications and the service and settlement hierarchy, but they were to be drawn up at the relatively small scales of 1:100,000 or 1:200,000, and were not intended to indicate the detailed zoning of land for individual purposes. That was to continue to be the role of the local plans, although these were not to be drawn up in conformity with the voivodship plans. Thus, all the country was to be covered by Master Plans, as they were known, at the voivodship level, each of which had to be approved by central government, and all towns were to have local Master Plans, while more detailed plans were to be produced for areas which were either about to be the sites of major new developments, such as the copper mining area around Lubin in Lower Silesia, or which posed complex problems of development coordination, such as the Gdańsk-Gdynia conurbation.

Some impression of the thinking behind the voivodship plans which were drawn up may be gained by an examination of those for Katowice and Kraków. In the case of the Upper Silesian industrial area (in Katowice voivodship) the target populations for 1980 (Table 8.3) seem to indicate that the earlier policies of permitting only modest growth in the core of the area, and of deflecting growth to the new towns and other peripheral settlements, such as Jaworzno and Oświęcim, were to continue.

Poland

Table 8.3: Population Targets for Some Towns in
Poland during the Long-term Plan 1961-1980
(thousands)

	Population in 1960	Planned Population for 1980
All towns in Poland	14,200	21,600
Upper Silesia		
Major service centres Area A		
Katowice	270	300
Bytom	183	185
Gliwice	150	160
Sosnowice	132	150
Other towns in Area A		
Chorzów	147	160
Ruda Śląska	132	155
Zabrze	190	205
New towns in Area B		
Pyskowice	22	40
Tychy	50	120
Industrial towns in Area B		
Jaworzno	53	72
Leszczyny	8	28
Oświęcim	31	100
Kraków voivodship		
Kraków	481	750
Nowy Targ	17	30
Tarnów	71	105

Source: Kotela, C. (1966), pp. 113-114.

Conversely, in the neighbouring Kraków voivodship, where very high rates of demographic increase had been experienced after the war and where the workforce was expected to increase substantially over the period, many towns were planned to receive major industrial investments, and to grow accordingly, even if this involved much migration from the rural areas. Indeed, a large part of the voivodship, including the areas with coal, ores and other valuable minerals, was designated as an industrial zone in which most of the labour force would be in industrial employment. The mountainous areas, in contrast, were to be a recreational zone, and a small part of the voivodship was to be dominated by agriculture. Within this agricultural zone - which included almost all of the area covered by good quality soils - a large area was marked out for intensive forms of production. These zones were not intended to be exclusive, but to indicate the priorities which should be adopted in decisions about the type of investment within them, and in some areas there was overlap between zones. For example, some areas of good soil within the industrial zone were, notwithstanding that overall zonation, also to be areas of intensive agriculture. The plan also indicated the transport network which would be necessary to link the different zones, and the pattern of housing and green belts in areas of industrial development.

The Gomułka period also saw the adoption of new ideas with regard to town planning and architecture, and a growing concern over the environment. Heavy Russian styles of building were replaced by lighter, more functional forms. Tower blocks of flats of eight or ten storeys appeared, decorated with balconies, and new residential areas were laid out on more sinuous and informal road patterns. The contrast in Nowa Huta, for example, between the centre of the town and its more recent suburbs is particularly marked. Four more national parks were established; the reclamation of land which had been damaged by mining began on a small scale in 1967; there was legislation in the 1960s to regulate the pollution of the atmosphere and water bodies; and it was decided to discourage further sporadic, dispersed housebuilding in rural areas, especially on more fertile soils.

However, in spite of all these initiatives, spatial and environmental planning continued to face serious problems during the Gomułka period. The National Spatial Plan was not completed until 1972, and so voivodship Master Plans could not be coordinated fully at the national scale. Moreover, all major investment decisions were made by central government, and were based primarily on economic, and not spatial, advice. As a result, voivodship planning authorities were called on neither to initiate nor steer development to any great extent, and their role was largely to react to decisions made by central government, either in the form of the Planning Commission or the industrial ministries. Indeed, their strongest power was the right to refuse permission for developments which did not accord with their plans. In other words, they were little different from the strategic planning authorities in the United Kingdom after 1968 or many other mixed economies. What is more, much of the investment was in the form of expansions to existing factories, often at a scale which was within the remit of their managers, and therefore escaped the attention of the planning authorities at all levels. Nevertheless, the spatial pattern of economic development did undergo marked changes during the Gomułka period. There was a general growth of towns, a reduction in the proportion of the population dependent on agriculture, and in the density of agricultural population on the land, and the amount of houseroom per capita increased; and in all these matters the central and eastern parts of the country progressed faster than the more developed. The changed pattern of houseroom may be seen from a comparison of Figures 8.3a and 8.3b. However, the considerable economic growth which had permitted these changes had been accompanied by a great increase in the pollution of the environment, for it was economic growth rather than environmental protection which had been emphasised, and the penalties which were imposed upon industrial polluters were slight in relation to the costs involved in its prevention (Fullenback 1981, pp. 30-33).

THE GIEREK PERIOD, 1970-1980

The immediate cause of the fall of Gomułka in 1970, and of his replacement by Edward Gierek, was rioting over proposals to increase the prices of food. However, discontent with the performance of the economy as a whole had been building up during the 1960s, and the new government responded to this by making important changes in the methods of

economic management. Agriculture was relieved of
the requirement to make compulsory deliveries, and
the prices paid to farmers - though not those paid
by the public - were raised in an attempt to
encourage greater output and more specialised forms
of production. Emphasis was also placed upon the
modernisation of Polish industry, and on increases
in output via the adoption of new technology. Most
of the new techniques were to be imported from the
West, and were to be paid for in part by a
substantial increase in the export of coal. The
supply of consumer goods, of housing, and of
educational and medical services were also to be
increased greatly. Experiments was conducted
between 1972 and 1975 with new machinery for spatial
planning, and in 1975 - just as all the elements
which had been required by the 1961 Spatial Planning
Act were approaching completion, including local
plans for each of about four hundred **powiats** - the
system was radically altered.

The new system, like its predecessor, was set
within the context of the long-term development of
the economy, but it afforded much greater scope to
the role of spatial planning, at least at the level
of central government, for the spatial plan was now
accorded the same status as that for the economic
and social development of the country. The first
element in the hierarchy of spatial plans since 1975
has been the National Spatial Plan, which lays down
the general aims of regional policy and sets out the
course for their implementation over a period of
twenty years. More particularly, it sets out the
future distribution of population, the settlement
structure, the provision of the social and technical
infrastructure, and the distribution of industrial
and agricultural production over the whole country,
and indicates the way in which the natural
resources, and especially minerals and water
supplies, are to be exploited. It contains all
major investment projects, and is presented at a
scale of 1:1,000,000.

The second element is the macro-regional plan.
The introduction of these plans followed the change
in the number and responsibilities of the
voivodships. Under the 1975 reform their number was
raised from twenty-two to forty-nine, and the new
units were supposed to be delimited in such a way as
to enable them to develop as functional regions
centred upon a single medium-sized or large town,
with a clear dominance of, or specialisation in,
industry, agriculture or tourism. It was hoped that

in possessing a clearer and simpler economic and spatial structure than their predecessors the future development of these units could be planned more efficiently. However, it was felt that there were some important matters which would be better handled at a scale which was larger than that of the voivodship, but smaller than that of the whole country, including the provision of water and other infrastructural needs, the control of pollution and the development of the settlement hierarchy and tourism, and so eight macro-regions were recognised (Figure 8.4). Plans for these are drawn up by groups of planners seconded from the State Planning Commission to each macro-region, in consultation with the voivodship authorities, and are presented at the scale of 1:200,000.

Voivodship plans, by contrast, are no longer of a strategic nature, but merely local in form, dealing with the spatial arrangement of land uses, and the coordination of the local provision of housing and transport services with the major developments which have been allocated to the area by central government. Each voivodship must now draw up a long-term development plan, based upon the National and macro-regional strategic plans, at a scale of 1;100,000, and it must also prepare separate plans for any agglomerations in the voivodship, for each of the towns, for areas of special interest, such as those concerned with industry or tourism, and for the gminy (communes) – the lowest level of administrative unit, of which there are about 2,100 – at the scale of 1:10,000. Each plan shows such things as the future arrangement of industry, central and local service areas, green spaces and the transport network, and indicates the densities of development which will be allowed in the residential areas. Thus, voivodship planning is very different from that which existed under the 1961 Spatial Planning Act. In particular, the removal of strategic planning has broken the link between spatial and economic planning at this level, and has re-established the role of the central authorities as the sole arbiters of the distribution of major investments. However, there is now a broader range of local planning activity at voivodship level, and some of the more populous communes have their own planning offices, which draw up the local plan, and also exercise some controls over development.

The National Spatial Plan for the country up to 1990 was based upon a variety of criteria. Some of

Since 1975

.... Voivodships
▬ ▬ Macroregions

0 _____ 150 km

Figure 8.4 The Administrative Divisions of Poland since 1975

these were vague, and contained little indication as to what they might mean in any particular location decision. One such was the desirability of 'the creation of a spatial environment in keeping with the needs of present and future generations'. Others, by contrast, were more informative. They included the acceleration of development through the use of the natural resources available in the various parts of the country, the rational choice of locations for new investments, and the reduction in the inter-regional differences in the levels of industrialisation, urbanisation, infrastructural provision and the standard of living through the faster development of the more backward areas. It was also intended to strengthen the economic links

with other socialist countries, and to protect the
environment and landscape (Komitet 1974, p. 54).
However, it must be noted that these aims are not
complementary, that the pursuit of all would
inevitably lead to conflicts, and that no priority
has been accorded to them to assist in the
resolution of such conflicts.

It was believed that the aims behind the Plan
could be met most satisfactorily by adopting the
idea of a series of 'moderately concentrated
polycentric agglomerations' as the basis for the
Polish space economy of the future. It was
anticipated that the concentrations of industry and
population would create pools of educated and
skilled labour, would allow the provision of
high-order educational and research services, and
thereby could stimulate innovation and new forms of
science-based industry. Several types of
agglomeration were recognised for the purposes of
long-term planning - 'established agglomerations',
such as the Warsaw and Łódź city regions, and Upper
Silesia, 'developing agglomerations' and 'potential
agglomerations' (Figure 8.1b). Several
free-standing towns, whose growth would be of
national significance, were also identified. It was
anticipated that most employment and population
growth would take place within these four types of
area, and that the rural population would fall by
about 3,000,000 from the 1970 figure of 15,600,000,
as agriculture continued to shed labour and to
operate at larger scales and greater productivity.
However, the contributions of each of the four types
of urban area to the future growth of the urban
population were to be very different. Although the
fastest rates of growth were to be in the
free-standing towns and the 'potential
agglomerations' respectively, and the slowest in the
'established agglomerations', the absolute increases
were to be in almost exactly the reverse order.
More than 4,000,000 of the anticipated increase of
7,600,000 in the urban population was expected to
occur in the 'established agglomeration' (Komitet
1974, p. 65). Moreover, it should be noted that,
although the principle of assisting the backward
areas to 'catch up' with the rest of the country was
to be honoured through the intensification of
agriculture and the development of services,
small-scale industry and tourism within them, it was
also believed that these regions would benefit more
from the rapid development of the national economy
as a whole than from a policy aimed directly at

changing the structure of their economies by steering investment to them. In other words, economic development in rural areas was only to be allowed in ways which complemented as fast a rate of growth in the national economy as could be sustained, and were in accord with the preference for siting new industry in existing urban centres.

One form of rural development which was perceived to be complementary to that of the agglomerations was specialisation in agriculture. Areas with high quality soil or other natural conditions which were favourable for agriculture were earmarked for the development of intensive, specialised forms of production. Noxious activities, such as polluting industry, were to be excluded from them, and extra investment was to be made available in an attempt to raise output. Almost a third of the country was designated for this type of development (Panko 1977, p. 22).

The 1970s also saw an increase in official concern about the closely-related matter of rural land, and the strategic implications of the rapid changes which had been occurring in the use of land since the Second World War. Urban expansion, often onto land of high quality, and afforestation of the poorest soils, had reduced the proportion of the country in agricultural use from sixty-six percent in 1946 to sixty-two percent in 1971, notwithstanding the responsibilities of the voivodship authorities to earmark and protect areas which were of significance for agriculture under the 1961 Spatial Planning Act; and it was expected that this would fall to fifty-eight percent by 1990 (Jastrzębski 1976, p. 25). Some action had been taken during the 1960s to prevent the sporadic construction of houses on rural land away from villages, and to set up a forest-belt around the Upper Silesian conurbation, but little else had been done to plan the use of land outside the urban areas. However, in 1971 legislation laid down that agricultural land in the first four categories of quality (out of a six-fold classification) and all forest-land was to be protected from development, and wide powers were given to the voivodship and gmina authorities to zone any rural land around towns and health resorts for rural uses only. All proposals for the transfer of protected land to other uses must be approved by the local planning authority, and where land is released for manufacturing or mining a fee must be paid which is intended to cover the loss of the agricultural output from the land for a period of twenty years. Furthermore, all land which is damaged by the mining industry must be restored. As a result of this legislation, more than half of the rural land in Poland was brought within the scope of land-use planning, and by the late 1970s a marked fall had occurred in the quantity of high-quality farmland which was being transferred to other uses (Glowny Urzad Statystyczny 1983, p. 12). The effect of this legislation upon the form of the village was particularly apparent. Much new housebuilding took place as rural incomes rose, but almost all was kept within or around the edges of existing settlements. However, reclamation did not keep pace with the damage to land by mining (Główny Urząd Statystyczny 1982, p. 65), and Michalak has reported that most of the 4,000 privately-owned holiday houses which were built between 1976 and 1978 in the northern Lake District, the Beskid Mountains and around the major cities had not received planning permission (1979, p. 69).

There was also an increase in official concern over the problem of pollution. Several Acts had been passed by the Polish parliament during the 1960s, but it was not until 1972 that a Ministry for Local Economies and Environmental Protection was established, or until 1975 that statistics of pollution were published on a regular basis. Hefty fines were introduced for damage to forests through atmospheric pollution in 1970, and for the illegal disposal of effluents in 1974, and it was accepted that new industrial plants should no longer be sited immediately adjacent to towns and architectural monuments of cultural or historic importance (Fullenback 1981, pp. 31-33, 62). Some rivers have been set aside in the National Spatial Plan as sites on which no further water-using or waste-creating industry should be placed. However, levels of pollution of the atmosphere and rivers remain high, and the officially permitted levels of atmospheric pollution are grossly exceeded in Upper Silesia, Kraków, Kielce and other industrial areas (Zmuda 1980, pp. 121-123).

Lastly, some comment should be made upon the detailed planning of settlements during the 1970s. In cities such as Kraków and Zamość much effort was expended on the restoration of the historic cores and the exclusion of traffic from them. However, in general Polish towns were notable for a continuing failure to redevelop the areas of nineteenth-century tenements around the centres, some of which had few basic amenities (Frackiewicz 1982, pp. 130-131), and for the construction of huge, slab-like blocks of flats on the outskirts. These blocks, which are of the severest uniformity and functional appearance, rise in some cases to fifteen storeys, and many house more than a thousand people each. Moreover, they are provided with few shops or other services, very limited car-parking space, and usually stand in bare, unattractive surroundings which emphasise the impression that they have been erected in the cheapest possible manner. Conversely, it should be noted that at least as much attention has been paid to the growing number of private cars in the planning of transport as to improvements in the public services, and major new motorways have been built in Warsaw, including new bridges across the Vistula. No further progress, however, has been made with the construction of an underground railway system for the city.

Thus, official interest in regional, local land-use and environmental planning, which had begun to develop in Poland before the Second World War, and had revived immediately after it, but which had been much reduced during the 1950s, was firmly re-established under Gierek's government.

COMPARISON AND DENOUEMENT

It is of interest, in looking back over the post-war period of planning in Poland, to note the considerable changes in the structure of the economy which have occurred, and in the associated distribution of the population, not to mention the growth of both population and production. But it is also of interest to compare those achievements with the targets which have been set at various times in the past by the authorities in their plans. Both the national plan, which was sketched out in the 1940s and the long-term plan which was initiated in the 1960s looked for their achievement in 1980, and in Table 8.4 some of the basic demographic forecasts and economic targets from them are compared with the situation which actually existed in that year. Of course, both plans were overtaken by subsequent events, and when 1980 dawned Poland was mid-way through the perspective plan period which was targeted to 1990. Nevertheless, the comparison in Table 8.4 is revealing for it demonstrates how difficult one of the key elements - demographic forecasting - can be, with the 1980 population

221

falling almost equally between the numbers which were used to draw up the two plans. Secondly, it shows that structural change in the economy has been slower than either plan intended, and that in particular, a much larger proportion of the labour force has remained in agriculture than was planned. Nevertheless, the proportion of the population in towns was higher in 1980 than the 1961-1980 plan had envisaged.

Table 8.4: Poland in 1980 - Plan and Performance

	1947 National Plan	Long-term Plan 1961-80	1980
Population (millions)	32	37.6	35.4
Population in towns (percent)	60	57.4	58.2
Employment (percent)			
Agriculture and Forestry	25	25	31
Industry and Building	30	37	31
Services	45	38	38

Sources: Malisz, B. (1974), pp. 16-23; Secomski, K. (1966), pp. 446-457

Similarly, there have been great changes in the regional pattern of the economy since 1945, but the contrasts of the pre-war period have not yet been eliminated. For example, the dependence of the population upon agriculture (Figure 8.2b), as well as the density of that population per hectare of farmland, at the end of the 1970s, demonstrates that there has been a considerable evening down between one part of the country and another since 1950, although somewhat higher values still persisted in the central and eastern parts. Furthermore, the numbers of people per room in residential accommodation are now much lower over most of the country than in 1950, and also show less variation than they did (Figure 8.3b). (Unfortunately, only the very broadest comparisons are possible in most indices of development as a result of the change in 1975 in the boundaries within which the data are reported.) However, some other measures of the effect of regional planning show a somewhat different picture. For instance, the provision of basic amenities in houses in eastern Poland is still far below that in the rest of the country (Kulesza 1982); the distribution of the thirty largest towns and cities in 1980 shows little change from that in 1950, or indeed that of the 1930s, though all are now much larger; and some other indicators, such as the number of cars and television licences per thousand of the population (Figures 8.5a and 8.5b), reveal not only wide variations between one part of Poland and another, but contrasts with a similar spatial arrangement to those which have traditionally set the poorer south and east against the richer north and west.

A further area of comparison is that between the National Spatial Plan for 1990 and the sketches which were made by the planners during the 1940s. Such a comparison reveals some striking similarities. In particular, the 'node and link' diagrammatic presentations of the pattern of future urban development and transport, which appear in the Plan replete with agglomerations at the intersections of the transport network (Figure 8.1b), bear a close resemblance both in their general conception and detail to those which were published in 1947, but which were subsequently scorned by the Stalinists. Indeed, in the 1947 plan (Figure 8.1a) twenty-three important nodes were identified, and exactly the same number of agglomerations - either 'established', 'developing' or 'potential' - were included in the 1970s plan, though only seventeen were common to both plans.

Thus, the aim of spatial planning in Poland at the national scale passed from an extreme of localised specialisation of production in the 1940s to its opposite in the 1950s, when 'the equal distribution of industry' was espoused. During the 1960s there was a policy of limited deglomeration from the chief industrial areas, and in the 1970s a return to a plan which has many similarities with that of the 1940s. Nevertheless, it is clear that some of the consequences of the capitalist development of the area before 1939 are still apparent, as is the influence upon the distribution of production of the pattern of mineral resources. Furthermore, distinct echoes of the capitalist

Poland

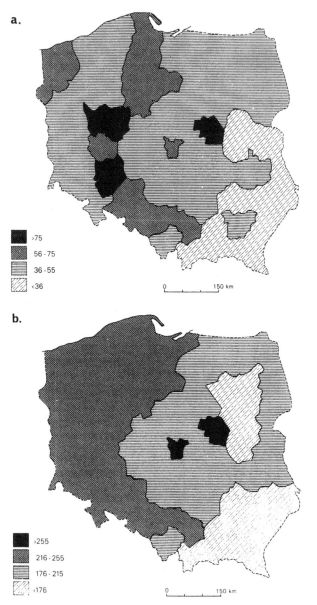

Figure 8.5 Numbers of (a) Private Cars and (b)
Television Licences in Poland per Thousand of the
Population in 1979

pattern are to be discerned in the distribution of some of the most modern talismen of the consumer society. However, responsibility for this cannot be laid at the door of spatial planning. Except at the local level, spatial planning has been either non-existent or extremely weak during most of the post-war period. Even during the 1970s it does not appear that the spatial plan has determined the quantity of investment which has been accorded to each region, or the type of development which has taken place, to such an extent that the aims of the spatial plan have been allowed to determine the rate of accumulation and growth in the economy. Rather, the emphasis has continued to be on the achievement of the fastest rate of growth which has been possible, and the regional pattern of development has been arranged largely to fit that target.

However, in spite of further considerable increases in the output of most goods during the 1970s (Table 8.1) the country was overtaken by yet another crisis – that associated with a further attempt to raise food prices, the establishment of Solidarity, and the 1981 declaration of martial law – just as the drawing up of the national, macro-regional, voivodship and gmina plans was being completed. Production fell sharply – an event which had never happened before in Poland since the Second World War – as imports of spare parts for machinery and other goods declined. Work on major new industrial plants stopped, and the knock-on effects of all this in the taut system of centralised economic planning spread rapidly. The flow of foreign tourists – upon which some of the plans of the 1970s had been based – almost ceased. The 1981-1985 Five Year Plan was abandoned, and the targets for the long-term plans, both economic and spatial – which had been ambitious – became unattainable. Thus, the Polish government failed yet again to achieve sustainable economic growth at a pace and in a way which was consonant with the rising expectations of the Polish people. As a result, it has been obliged to consider afresh how growth is to be achieved. Is it to be by accelerated investment and accumulation, at the expense of consumption and the environment, building upon the advantages offered by the established industrial centres, as has been very largely the case ever since 1950? Or is it to be through economic reforms which will allow the market a greater say in the setting of prices, and allow investment to flow into those activities and

locations in which it will yield the highest
returns? A more market-oriented approach would
probably accelerate the migration of labour from
country to town, and from old to new industries, for
it would almost certainly lead to the development,
not of the heavy and basic industries which are tied
to localised raw materials and which have been at
the heart of so much economic planning in Poland
since 1950, but to lighter forms of manufacturing,
to house building and to services. However, while
the Soviet Union continues to emphasise the
importance of the basic industries and to use the
system of central planning, the possibility of the
adoption of such a radical reform programme - let
alone the acceptance of regional and environmental
aims as overriding determinants of economic
decision-making - in Poland remains remote.

REFERENCES

Christaller, W. (1933), Die zentralen Orte in
Süddeutschland, Jena.
Frackiewicz, L. (1982), Problemy społeczne
górnośląskiego okręgu przemysłowego, KPZK Biuletyn,
118, 128-134.
Fullenbach, J. (1981), European Environmental
Policy: East and West, Butterworths, London.
Główny Urząd Statystyczny (1963), Rocznik
Statystyczny 1963, Warszawa.
Główny Urząd Statystyczny (1964), Rocznik
Statystyczny 1964, Warszawa.
Główny Urząd Statystyczny (1966), Rocznik
Statystyczny 1966, Warszawa.
Główny Urząd Statystyczny (1967a), Rocznik
Statystyczny 1967, Warszawa.
Główny Urząd Statystyczny (1967b), Rozwoj
Gospodarczy Powiatów w latach 1950-1965, Warszawa.
Główny Urząd Statystyczny (1968), Rocznik
Statystyczny 1968, Warszawa.
Główny Urząd Statystyczny (1980), Rocznik
Statystyczny 1980, Warszawa.
Główny Urząd Statystyczny (1982), Ochronna
Środowiska i Gospodarka Wodna 1982, Warszawa.
Główny Urząd Statystyczny (1983), Rocznik
Statystyczny 1983, Warszawa.
Hamilton, F.E.I. (1982), Regional Policy in
Poland: A Search for Equity, Geoforum 13, 121-132.
Jachniak-Ganguly, D. (1978), Administration
and Spatial Planning as Tools of Land Management in
Poland, Centre for Environmental Studies, London.

Jastrzębski, S. (1976), **Kierunki ochronny środowiska przyrodniczego w Polsce**, Polska Akademia Nauk, Warszawa.

Karpiński, A. (1964), **Twenty Years of Poland's Economic Development 1944-1964**, Polonia, Warsaw.

Komitet Przestrzennego Zagospodarowania Kraju (1974), **Plan Przestrzennego Zagospodarowania Kraju do Roku 1990**, Warszawa.

Kotela, C. (1966), Main Urban Planning Problems in the Silesian-Krakow Industrial Region, in **City and Regional Planning in Poland**, ed. J.C.Fisher, Cornell U.P., Ithaca, 111-132.

Kulesza, H. (1982), Geografia nie zaspokojonych potrzeb mieszkaniowych, KPZK **Biuletyn**, 118, 84-127.

Lijewski, T. (1977), **Geografia Transportu Polski**, PWE, Warszawa.

Malisz, B. (1966), Urban Planning Theory: Methods and Results, in **City and Regional Planning in Poland**, ed. J.C.Fisher, Cornell U.P., Ithaca, 57-84.

Malisz, B. (1974), **Problematyka przestrzennego zagospodarowania Kraju**, PWN, Warszawa.

Michalak, J. (1979), Indiwidualne domki rekreacyjne na wsi, **Wieś Współczesna**, 23, 67-74.

Panko, W. (1977), Planowanie przestrzenne, ochronna gruntów rolnych oraz regionalizacja rolnicza jako srodki kształtowania produkcyjnej przestrzeni rolniczej, in **Wpływ Instrumentów Prawnych Na Przestrzenną Strukturę Rolnictwa w Polsce**, Komitet Przestrzennego Zagospodarowania Kraju, Warszawa.

Prezydium Rady Narodowej Miasta Stołecznego Warszawy (1965), **Plan Generalny Warszawy**, Warszawa.

Secomski, K. (1966), The Long-Term Plan for Polish Expansion, in **City and Regional Planning in Poland**, ed. J.C.Fisher, Cornell U.P., Ithaca, 441-460.

Wróbel, A. and Zawadzki, S.M. (1966), Location Policy and Regional Efficiency of Investments, in **City and Regional Planning in Poland**, ed. J.C.Fisher, Cornell U.P., Ithaca, 423-440.

Zaremba, J. (1966), Regional Planning in Poland: Theory, Methods and Results, in **City and Regional Planning in Poland**, ed. J.C.Fisher, Cornell U.P., Ithaca, 271-298.

Zimon, H.A. (1979), Regional Inequalities in Poland: 1960-1975, **Economic Geography**, 55, 242-252.

Zmuda, S. (1980), Environmental development barriers of the territory of the Katowice

Poland

voivodship, _Folia Geographica_, XIII, 115-128.

Chapter 9

ROMANIA

David Turnock

THE CONTEXT OF PLANNING

The long-term modernisation of Romania began in
the nineteenth century, but it has accelerated since
the Second World War, and those in charge of the
country since then have claimed that the system of
central planning which they introduced has been a
sine qua non of this post-war progress. Indeed,
planning in post-war Romania has been a fundamental
element of a state which has been concerned to
modernise within the political context of the
building of socialism, for this context has required
the encouragement of uniformity in the cultural,
economic, political and social fields (Tráistaru and
Tráistaru 1979), and this uniformity is only
possible in the modern state if government is
willing to enforce it. Romanian planning has been
comprehensive, covering all sectors of the economy
in an attempt to achieve both uniformity and the
maximisation of production; it has been long-term,
demanding sacrifices from the present generation so
that their descendants may reap the benefits; and,
more surprising in view of the internationalist
ethic of Marxism, it has concentrated on the nation
state. Over the years the Romanians have been able
to resist unacceptable entanglements with the
Council for Mutual Economic Assistance (COMECON),
and, in view of the lack of any real constraint on
Romanian planning from this source, it will not be
discussed in this chapter. Nor will the general
scenario of the aims and methods of the Romanian
planning system or the long-term programmes that
have been produced (Romanian Communist Party 1974)
be examined here, for all are couched in terms which
are too generalised to permit of meaningful
analysis. It is, rather, with some limited aspects

229

of the comprehensive planning system that this
chapter is concerned, and, in particular, with two
important themes of spatial economic planning - the
allocation of resources to regions - planificare -
and the reorganisation of the settlement pattern -
sistematizare.

PLANIFICARE

Nationalisation of the means of production in
1948 went hand in hand with the establishment of a
state planning commission and the direction of the
economy through medium-term plans. A One Year Plan
was produced for 1949, and this was followed by a
succession of Five Year Plans, which have run
consecutively without interruption from 1951-1955,
except when the Second Plan was abandoned after four
years and followed by a Six Year Plan for 1960-1965.
These plans have consistently placed heavy emphasis
on industry, which has received about half the total
investment in each of them (Table 9.1), and heavy
industry has usually taken between nine and ten
times more investment than light (Dimitru 1955). In
particular, there was an extremely high level of
investment in industry in 1951-1955, which was at
the expense of agriculture and forestry, housing and
construction, and the shares of those sectors have
subsequently always been higher, though agriculture
and forestry slipped back after 1965. In contrast,
the share of investment in transport and
distribution has been fairly constant, but education
and health have both declined. Thus, different
sectors of the economy have received widely
different shares of the investment budget.

In the same way, there have also been wide
contrasts in the allocation of investment between
different parts of the country. The communist
government deplored the spatial contrasts which it
had inherited in the level of development
(Gherasimov et al.1960, vol.2, 73-108), and set as
one of its goals the more equitable distribution of
economic activity (Costache 1961). Indeed, it was
later claimed that
   "an intensive development of the productive
   forces in all parts of the country, in a
   unitary and long-term perspective, is a
   precondition for the creation of the socialist
   society"
(Ceauşescu 1969, vol.12, 414-418) - a principle
which sounds well, but which on closer inspection

Table 9.1: Romanian Investment 1951-1980 by Sector as a Percentage of the Total

Sector	1951–1955	1956–1960	1961–1965	1966–1970	1971–1975	1976–1980
Heavy Industry	48.9	40	41.9	43	43.5	43.4
Light Industry	4.8	4.9	4.6	7	7	5.8
Agriculture and Forestry	11.3	17.3	19.4	16.1	14.4	13.8
Housing and Construction	15	21.2	17.9	16.1	16.9	20
Transport and Distribution	12.8	10.3	11.3	13.1	13.7	13.4
Education and Science	4.2	3.7	3	2.6	2.6	2.1
Health Services	1.8	1.7	1.2	1.2	0.9	0.7
Administration	0.3	0.5	0.6	0.6	0.6	0.8
Total (in billion lei)	61.9	100.2	199.7	330.8	549.0	931.9

Note: Heavy Industry includes fuel and power, metallurgy, engineering, chemicals (including ceramics and glass), building materials and wood processing (including paper). Light Industry includes textiles, clothing, leather and footwear, food processing, cosmetics and printing.

Source: Direcția Centrală de Statistică, Anuarul Statistic, various years.

raises many questions. For instance, what criteria
are to be adopted to measure the economic
performance of each part of the country? What
regional system should be taken as the basis for
comparisons of this sort, and to what extent should
the performance of the nation as a whole be
compromised in order to increase output in the
poorer regions where relatively high levels of
investment may be needed? However, these issues
have not been seriously debated in the Romanian
literature (Moisuc and Tamas 1972).

The early post-war regional development
programme was undertaken in the context of a new
administrative system of twenty-eight regions
(regiuni). These were established in 1950 in place
of the fifty-eight counties (judete) of the earlier
local government structure, and the number was
further reduced to eighteen in 1952 and to sixteen
in 1956 (Cucu 1961a and 1961b, Rădulescu 1950).
(Lower tiers in the system were provided by the
raione and comune, but they cannot be considered in
detail here because of a lack of statistical
material for them.) Most of these already boasted a
substantial urban-industrial core (Biji et al.1964),
and where this did not exist some investment was
made to provide a modest base in cities like Craiova
and Suceava. However, the more advanced regions
attracted shares of investment which were beyond the
levels which would have been expected on demographic
grounds alone (Bugă 1961; Hermansen 1972), and, as a
result, the share of total production contributed by
the eight most highly developed regions fell only
slightly between 1955 and 1965, from 77.6 percent to
76.4 (Turnock 1979). Furthermore, industry was not
built up in towns other than the regional capitals.
It was not until the 1960s that dissatisfaction
arose within the party over the high level of
investment in the more advanced regions and the
regional capitals, nor until then that, with the
establishment of large-scale fertiliser and
wood-processing combines, a significant number of
towns acquired major industries. (The ball-bearing
factory at Bîrlad in Iaşi region might appear to
have been an important exception to this pattern –
reflecting perhaps the Moldavian connections of the
then party leader, Gh. Gheorghui-Dej – but the
Bîrlad area initially enjoyed regional status and
was only later partitioned in favour of the adjacent
Bacău, Galaţi and Iaşi regions.) So, soon after
assuming power in 1965 the new leader, N.
Ceauşescu, called for a better distribution of

industry, and indicated that the less developed regions would make faster progress, though not at the expense of economic efficiency (Ceauşescu 1969, vol.1, 44; Cioponea 1971; Cucu 1980; Ion 1971 and 1972). A new regional system of thirty-nine counties and the city of Bucharest was introduced in 1968 in time for the 1971-1975 Five Year Plan, the raione were abandoned, and the number of communes was reduced from 4260 to 2706 (Helin 1967; Tufescu and Herbst 1969).

Little is known of the reasons behind the new arrangement. However, the Romanians may have thought it necessary to establish a finer spatial focus for the allocation of investment, and one which could both take account of labour catchments which were capable of fuller exploitation and achieve a distribution of energy through the national electricity grid which would enhance the potential of the less developed centres, and especially those with valuable raw materials (Gruescu 1971). Counties were, indeed, identified in terms of their raw material base, and boundaries were drawn so as to respect the hinterlands of the larger towns. A high level of self-sufficiency in agriculture was also thought desirable for them, although it was intended that all counties should deliver some surplus to the central reserves. However, the variations in the level of economic development between the counties were much greater than those amongst the regions which they replaced - an inevitable consequence of using smaller spatial units - for, despite the fact that the poorer regions had been helped in the 1960s, some pockets of backwardness remained, and it was these that the new administrative system highlighted. These included not only underdeveloped areas in generally backward regions, such as Botoşani in Suceava region, Vaslui in Iaşi region and Vrancea in Galaţi region, but also poorer districts in relatively advanced regions, such as Bistriţa and Sălaj in Cluj region. In 1965 per capita industrial output in the most advanced region (Braşov) had been nearly five times higher than that in the most backward (Suceava). But the recalculation of figures to fit the new administrative regions showed that in that year the most advanced county (which was also Braşov) had a per capita industrial output which was no less than twelve times greater than the most backward (Sălaj). Economists recognized several instances of counties with similar levels of development, and proposed groupings of them

(Dobrescu and Blaga 1973; Popovici et al.1976); and we shall examine the progress of Romania's post-war regional development with the help of one such scheme, that proposed by V. Trebici (1971), which is shown in Figure 9.1, by comparing the spatial distribution of investment and job creation within it with that of the population.

Table 9.2 indicates the spatial distribution of investments over the last three decades according to Trebici's regionalisation. Clearly, Bucharest and Groups 1 and 2 were most favoured during much of this period, with shares of the investments in industry and services which exceeded their shares of the population. This may have been a consequence of the fact that all the counties in these two groups were the core areas of the regions that were in use until 1968 (with the exception of Arad in the Banat region, centred on Timişoara, and Brăila, which was part of the Galaţi region). Particular concentrations of investment occurred in the tertiary sector, with Bucharest attracting a share which was 4.6 times greater than that of population in the 1950s and 4.5 times in the 1960s; and the city also registered high values in education (8.0 in the 1950s and 4.4 in the 1960s) and administration (7.8 and 8.3). However, investment in agriculture and forestry has been more evenly spread, and Bucharest and Group 1 have consistently failed to attract what in population terms would be a fair share, though it should be noted that Bucharest has comparatively little agricultural land, and that most of the Group 1 counties include hilly and mountainous terrain which might not have rewarded such investment as well as the lowlands.

However, after the introduction of the new system of counties the distribution of investment appears to have become more even. In the case of industry, which was the most important recipient of funds, Bucharest's share fell much more into line with that of its population, and, although Group 1 continued to receive a disproportionate share, it was only 1.3 times that of population in 1976-1980, instead of 2.6 in the 1950s, 2.0 in the 1960s and 1.7 between 1971 and 1975. As a result, only about half as many new industrial jobs were created in Groups 1 and 2 between 1976 and 1980 as in the early 1970s, whereas in the country as a whole the figure was more than three-quarters. However, some of the Group's counties, and especially Braşov and Prahova, constitute the country's industrial heartland, with excellent infrastructure and a highly skilled work

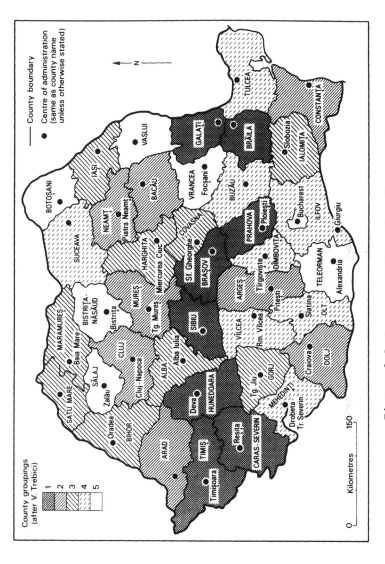

Figure 9.1 Groups of Counties in Romania

Table 9.2: Romanian Investment by Branches of the Economy

(The figures in the table refer to the share of investment received by each group of counties, related to their share of the population. Thus, groups which have received more investment than their proportion of population have values in excess of 1).

County Group	All Investment	Branches of the Economy							
		A	B	C	D	E	F	G	H
1951-1960									
Bucharest	2.2	1.0	0.4	5.0	4.0	8.0	4.6	7.8	4.8
Group 1	2.0	2.6	0.8	1.2	1.2	0.7	1.1	0.8	1.4
Group 2	1.3	1.4	1.3	1.1	1.3	0.6	1.2	0.7	1.1
Group 3	0.6	0.5	1.2	0.5	0.5	0.3	0.5	0.3	0.5
Group 4	0.5	0.5	1.0	0.4	0.5	0.5	0.5	0.4	0.4
Group 5	0.3	0.2	0.8	0.3	0.3	0.5	0.4	0.2	0.3
1961-1970									
Bucharest	2.1	1.3	0.3	4.2	4.5	4.4	1.9	8.3	4.0
Group 1	1.6	2.0	0.8	1.0	0.8	0.9	0.8	0.4	1.2
Group 2	1.2	1.2	1.3	1.1	1.1	0.8	1.6	0.5	1.1
Group 3	0.6	0.6	1.1	0.6	0.6	0.6	0.9	0.3	0.6
Group 4	0.7	0.8	1.0	0.6	0.5	0.8	0.6	0.3	0.5
Group 5	0.4	0.4	1.0	0.3	0.3	0.5	0.4	0.2	0.3

	A	B	C	D	E	F	G	H	Total
1971–1975									
Bucharest	1.8	1.1	0.2	3.4	3.2	3.8	2.2	6.6	3.5
Group 1	1.5	1.7	0.8	0.9	0.9	0.9	0.9	0.2	1.0
Group 2	1.1	1.2	1.2	1.1	1.3	0.8	0.9	0.1	1.0
Group 3	0.7	0.8	1.1	0.6	0.6	0.6	0.9	0.5	0.6
Group 4	0.8	0.9	1.1	0.6	0.6	0.8	0.8	0.7	0.6
Group 5	0.4	0.4	1.1	0.5	0.4	0.6	0.9	1.0	0.5
1976–1980									
Bucharest	1.5	0.9	0.2	2.9	2.6	3.7	1.9	6.4	2.9
Group 1	1.0	1.3	0.8	0.8	0.6	1.0	0.8	0.4	0.9
Group 2	1.2	1.1	1.2	1.4	1.7	0.8	1.1	0.9	1.2
Group 3	0.9	1.1	1.0	0.7	0.6	0.6	1.0	0.3	0.7
Group 4	0.7	0.7	1.2	0.6	0.7	0.7	0.9	0.3	0.5
Group 5	0.7	0.8	1.1	0.5	0.5	0.5	0.7	0.3	0.6

A Industry
B Agriculture and Forestry
C All Services
D Transport and Distribution Services

E Education and Science Services
F Health Services
G Administration
H Other Services, mainly Construction

Source: Direcţia Centrală de Statistică, Anuarul Statistic, various years.

force, and it is difficult to see how such areas can ever lose their claim to some priority in industrial investment. Nevertheless, the counties of Group 3 achieved their 'fair share' of investment for the first time in 1976-1980, and Group 4 and especially Group 5 moved nearer to that position. Indeed, only in Group 5 were there more new jobs in both heavy and light industry during the second half of the decade than there had been in the first. However, this may have been the result of an increasing labour shortage in the more highly industrialised areas (Spornic 1975), for, although investment increased in 1976-1980 in comparison with 1971-1975, the level of new job creation fell. Moreover, it would be rash to expect that the trends in favour of the poorer counties will have necessarily continued into the 1980s, especially during the period of rising energy costs and the world recession. Indeed, it has been suggested that the effort to develop an industrial base there was only intended to relieve some immediate problems of rural underemployment in the short term (Ronnas 1984, p.70) without the need for large-scale long-distance migration. Henceforth, those regions in which the natural conditions for agriculture are favourable may have to find compensation for their inferior status in manufacturing through the intensification of farming.

Thus, there is some evidence to suggest that the Romanian government moved some way towards its goal of a more even pattern of development, at least during the 1970s. However, it should not be assumed that that development was of the same type in all parts of the country. For example, Table 9.3 indicates that, in all three periods for which statistics are available, the number of new jobs created has shown a bias to heavy industry in Bucharest and in Groups 1 and 2 of the counties, and a bias to light industry in Groups 3, 4 and 5. Indeed, employment in light industry in Bucharest actually fell between 1976 and 1980. Furthermore, although the overall share of the more advanced areas has fallen in both types of industry, the ratio between them has altered, with 1.24 new jobs in heavy industry for each one in light industry in 1966-1970, 1.25 in 1971-1975 and 1.84 in 1976-1980. The figures for the poorer regions, in contrast, have been 0.72, 0.75 and 0.68. Bucharest's disproportionately high share of investment in the tertiary sector has also continued, though at a lower level, with 3.4 times that of its population in 1971-1975 and 2.9 times in 1976-1980. High levels of investment in administration and education have also persisted, as might have been expected in view of Romania's highly centralised form of government, the national importance of the city's university and the relatively large number of special schools and research institutes there. The poorer counties gained some ground in the tertiary sector, although 'fair shares' were only achieved in the case of Group 3 for health services in 1976-1980 and Group 5 for administration in 1971-1975, but Group 2 stands out clearly as the main beneficiary of investment in transport as a result of harbour extensions at Constanta and the construction of the Danube-Black Sea Canal. However, the table gives only a very generalised impression of the contrasts, and it may be helpful to consider the profiles of the individual counties that comprise each group.

Table 9.4 deals with the gains in employment in the economy during the 1960s and 1970s in relation to 1960. Figures are given for the whole economy, for industry, and for heavy industry alone. Comparability is possible because all the figures are adjusted to the size of the population, but some problems arise because the official statistics of regular wage earners exclude those working on cooperative and private farms. However, workers in state farms and forests are fully enumerated. The table provides abundant evidence to show that central planning does not produce a pattern of uniform progress. The gains in employment in industry were greater in the more advanced areas during the 1960s - a point which applies in the case of heavy industry also. This is especially true of Braşov, which recorded an increase which was 69.2 percent higher than that for Group 1 as a whole for industry and 88.1 percent higher than that for heavy industry. This underlines both the great importance of the engineering industry in the area and the central location of Braşov in the country with regard to the movement of raw materials, components, finished products and labour. Similarly, Argeş stands out in Group 2, with a gain in employment which was 36 percent above the average, and one in heavy industry which was 39.4 percent above, in the 1960s as a result of the very high level of investment in the engineering, petrochemical and wood-processing industries in the Pitesti area. However, it should be noted that the level of employment in this county in 1960 was only 86.1 percent of the average for Group 2, and that there

Table 9.3: Employment and Investment in Heavy and Light Industry in Romania 1966-1980

County Group	Growth of Employment Heavy		Light		Investment Heavy		Light		Investment[1] per job Heavy	Light
	a.	b.	a.	b.	a.	b.	a.	b.	Heavy	Light
1966-1970										
Bucharest	43.8	18.2	7.4	4.9	13.3	9.7	3.4	12.0	3.0	4.6
Group 1	63.9	26.5	22.4	14.7	43.4	31.6	5.7	20.1	6.8	2.5
Group 2	53.4	22.1	52.9	34.7	35.4	25.8	7.2	25.5	6.6	1.4
Group 3	38.4	15.9	34.1	22.4	17.9	13.0	4.6	16.2	4.7	1.3
Group 4	32.7	13.6	24.0	15.7	21.4	15.6	6.2	22.0	6.6	2.6
Group 5	8.9	3.7	11.7	7.6	5.8	4.2	1.2	4.2	6.5	1.0
Romania	241.1	100.0	152.4	100.0	137.2	100.0	28.3	100.0	5.7	1.9
1971-1975										
Bucharest	82.6	16.9	13.9	5.6	19.1	8.2	4.0	8.9	2.3	2.9
Group 1	121.4	24.8	45.9	18.5	66.6	28.6	8.6	19.2	5.5	1.9
Group 2	100.7	20.6	63.5	25.6	58.9	25.3	10.0	22.4	5.8	1.6
Group 3	72.8	14.9	52.6	21.2	37.5	16.1	7.2	16.1	5.2	1.4
Group 4	75.2	15.4	48.6	19.6	39.4	16.9	11.7	26.2	5.2	2.4
Group 5	35.8	7.3	23.2	9.4	11.0	4.7	3.2	7.2	3.1	1.4
Romania	488.6	100.0	247.6	100.0	232.6	100.0	44.7	100.0	4.8	1.9

1976-1980										
Bucharest	24.0	6.3	-0.5	-0.3	32.3	8.0	5.6	9.9	13.5	–
Group 1	83.1	21.9	17.8	12.1	86.2	21.4	8.5	15.0	10.4	4.8
Group 2	86.9	22.9	23.7	16.1	100.6	25.0	10.5	18.6	11.6	4.4
Group 3	93.2	24.5	36.8	25.0	99.7	24.8	7.6	13.4	10.7	2.1
Group 4	53.7	14.1	38.7	26.3	46.8	11.6	14.0	24.7	8.7	3.6
Group 5	39.0	10.3	30.7	20.9	36.3	9.0	10.4	18.4	9.3	3.4
Romania	379.9	100.0	147.2	100.0	401.9	100.0	56.6	100.0	10.6	3.8

a. Actual employment (thousands) and investment (thousand million lei)
b. Share of the total national employment and investment

1 Hundred thousand lei per job

Source: Direcţia Centrală de Statistică, Anuarul Statistic, various years.

Table 9.4: Employment in Romania 1960-1980 per Thousand of the Population

County	All Sectors			Industry			Heavy Industry		
	a.	b.	c.	a.	b.	c.	a.	b.	c.
Bucharest	364.6	192.4	125.2	160.0	60.0	44.5	82.4	56.4	55.1
Group 1	225.1	100.1	187.7	126.9	54.3	68.4	90.3	39.6	52.7
Braşov	308.3	167.4	146.7	173.5	91.9	105.0	134.4	74.5	96.6
Caraş Severin	216.1	79.4	98.3	115.4	36.3	48.0	108.7	32.1	37.6
Hunedoara	280.7	71.8	75.8	147.3	39.4	35.8	135.3	30.5	21.2
Prahova	242.2	89.4	98.8	117.1	47.4	69.9	90.3	34.2	55.5
Sibiu	233.4	118.3	104.1	124.2	72.8	71.9	49.9	43.6	48.1
Timiş	249.2	84.9	116.1	96.8	44.7	68.0	40.0	28.6	47.0
Group 2	176.0	113.7	104.1	63.3	47.8	56.2	37.5	29.7	39.2
Arad	186.0	83.3	85.6	84.3	32.9	43.5	42.2	24.1	31.1
Argeş	135.0	145.1	112.3	54.5	65.0	73.6	38.3	41.4	54.7
Bacău	173.8	60.2	92.7	65.2	38.9	51.5	37.1	26.4	31.3
Brăila	173.8	105.6	106.6	57.9	42.7	49.5	35.9	25.9	30.1
Cluj	209.9	106.9	97.3	87.3	54.5	60.2	50.8	27.7	32.0
Constanţa	215.8	177.9	147.7	39.1	42.1	47.0	25.3	20.4	36.3
Galaţi	148.0	148.0	96.8	46.2	49.9	60.5	27.2	38.2	51.4
Mureş	162.7	96.9	90.2	62.5	52.0	58.5	37.7	32.8	43.8

Group 3									
Alba	137.5	95.2	107.4	52.1	42.1	63.9	36.6	28.0	42.8
Bihor	141.6	102.1	109.6	63.2	50.7	67.7	49.9	38.7	49.3
Covasna	160.1	97.0	91.9	59.8	49.0	52.9	30.6	30.4	30.4
Dîmbovița	149.8	85.4	144.8	74.1	28.2	87.9	46.9	14.2	66.8
Dolj	138.8	75.1	135.3	70.0	31.0	93.6	51.7	22.8	81.5
Gorj	107.4	106.8	89.7	26.2	41.4	49.2	13.5	26.9	35.4
Harghita	122.7	110.2	136.3	42.5	57.7	74.6	35.2	49.3	53.1
Ialomița	150.1	116.2	119.2	76.1	50.3	76.3	55.9	25.5	40.7
Maramureș	114.8	130.3	70.0	6.9	30.0	31.9	2.2	8.8	12.6
Neamț	139.8	100.4	104.0	67.1	44.2	62.1	58.0	33.0	33.1
	162.1	38.0	111.5	60.2	34.9	67.3	46.2	26.1	42.5
Group 4									
Buzău	113.7	81.0	87.8	34.2	30.4	48.9	21.5	16.1	26.7
Iași	100.8	59.1	117.6	28.5	19.7	80.1	20.4	10.2	48.6
Ilfov	118.9	97.4	105.2	29.2	38.8	61.1	14.1	21.1	42.8
Mehedinți	86.7	73.2	55.9	17.4	21.5	23.9	8.7	10.2	6.0
Satu Mare	104.2	98.1	64.8	33.9	21.3	44.4	23.5	11.7	23.3
Suceava	133.0	77.9	97.5	54.3	39.5	58.6	32.6	21.4	31.5
Tulcea	137.4	78.9	73.9	52.9	42.4	36.2	40.3	25.5	6.1
Vîlcea	150.0	72.2	131.6	41.8	32.6	48.7	16.9	9.7	27.5
	105.7	96.0	84.5	31.5	27.1	50.3	23.3	15.5	39.6

Table 9.4 (cont'd)

Romania

County	All Sectors			Industry			Heavy Industry		
	a.	b.	c.	a.	b.	c.	a.	b.	c.
Group 5	79.8	56.4	98.9	15.7	18.5	53.7	9.0	9.9	32.4
Bistriţa-Năsăud	88.9	58.5	120.3	30.0	8.9	57.6	24.4	4.5	36.7
Botoşani	74.0	33.4	95.8	13.0	13.1	50.5	3.8	2.2	21.9
Olt	73.0	75.6	107.9	9.4	20.4	65.1	4.9	12.4	44.9
Sălaj	74.9	55.8	111.9	19.8	21.2	51.8	13.7	17.8	35.5
Teleorman	67.7	62.9	92.2	9.2	20.7	52.2	2.9	14.2	37.1
Vaslui	87.1	43.3	100.2	17.6	18.1	59.7	11.1	7.2	28.8
Vrancea	101.9	65.8	72.2	20.5	26.2	35.4	13.4	12.2	19.5
Romania	170.1	97.3	100.5	65.7	42.5	58.6	41.8	27.4	40.3

a. 1960
b. Increase 1960-1970
c. Increase 1970-1980

Source: Direcţia Centrală de Statistică, Anuarul Statistic, various years.

were substantial labour reserves in the rural districts close to the industrial centres, all of which suggests that the planners had no hesitation in placing large projects in relatively unindustrialised locations as long as there were sound economic reasons for doing so.

Increases in industrial employment in the more backward areas, however, were smaller, though variations abounded. Gorj, in Group 3, more than doubled its employment in both industry and heavy industry in the 1960s thanks to large-scale lignite mining and cement production, while in Group 4 Suceava benefited from a major expansion of wood processing. Similarly, in Group 5 Olt and Teleorman made great progress, especially in heavy industry, following the decision to build an aluminium smelter at Slatina and a fertiliser factory at Turnu Măgurele. However, all these investments were planned and largely implemented before the new structure of counties came into existence, which suggests that some dispersal was in fact being achieved before the 1968 reform and that locations were being looked at on their merits. For instance, Gorj offered suitable raw materials and, in the case of cement, a convenient location for distribution throughout southwestern Romania; Slatina lay on the high voltage electricity grid close to a complex of power stations; and Turnu Măgurele, as a river port, could import raw materials by the Danube waterway and distribute its fertiliser to the surrounding lowlands. But, in no case was any division of the investments countenanced in the interest of spreading the employment benefits. Efficiency came first.

In the 1970s, with the counties fully active as administrative and planning units, the rates of new job creation have been much more uniform at the group level. Whereas Group 1 rates exceeded the national average by 27.8 percent for industry and 44.5 percent for heavy industry in the 1960s, those excesses fell to 16.7 percent and 30.8 percent respectively in the 1970s. At the other extreme, Group 5's deficits against the national average were only 8.4 percent and 19.6 percent respectively in the 1970s, compared with figures of 56.5 and 73.9 in the previous decade. Nevertheless, variations within groups continued. Braşov was still outstanding in Group 1, with 105 new jobs in industry per thousand of the population, of which 96.6 were in heavy industry, and Argeş maintained its ascendancy in Group 2. In the lower groups it is interesting to see that the greatest gains were made in Covasna and Dimboviţa in Group 3, in Buzău in Group 4 and Olt in Group 5, all of which are close to existing complexes of heavy industry and generally in the most economically dynamic part of the country, the southeast. Although all other counties expanded their role in heavy industry, the bias to light industry in some remoter districts, such as Botoşani in Group 5, remained very evident.

One further test of the effectiveness or otherwise of planificare may be provided by the changing distribution of population across the country. Table 9.5 shows the populations of all the groups of counties and indicates that, although the population in every group has increased, there have been wide variations in the rates of growth between them. For instance, the population of Bucharest grew at 1.33 times the rate for the whole country between 1948 and 1977, while in Groups 1 and 2 the growth was 1.07 times the national rate. Growth in Groups 3 to 5, however, was only 0.92 times that rate. An effective regional development policy might be considered to be one which reduced such discrepancies, but, during the inter-censal period 1966-1977 there were net outflows of 300,000 people from Group 5, 190,000 from Group 4 and 90,000 from Group 3, which were balanced by net inflows of 390,000 to Bucharest, 180,000 to Group 1 and 10,000 to Group 2. The scale of these migrations can be gauged by comparing them with the natural increase (Baranovsky and Rusenescu 1970; Ştefănescu 1975; Ştefănescu and Baranovsky 1978; Tufescu and Ştefănescu 1974). For instance, emigration from Group 5 accounted for nearly nine-tenths of the natural increase in those counties, while the immigration to Bucharest was 4.3 times the city's natural increase. In short, the demographic evidence indicates that Romania's regional development policy has been slow to take effect (Modoran et al.1971), but that there seems little doubt that a significant shift is now occurring. Thus, although industry has been distributed more widely during the post-war period in pursuit of the creation of uniformity between the different parts of the country, significant contrasts still remain. What is more, these have been exacerbated, for there has been some concentration of the lighter industries in the less developed counties, of heavy industry in the traditional manufacturing and mining centres, and of services in the capital. Of course, this may make good economic sense, for there is no

Table 9.5: The Changing Distribution of Romania's Population 1948-1977

County Group	Population (millions) 1948	1977	Share of Population (percent) 1948	1977	Population change (millions) 1966-1977 A	B	C	D
Bucharest	1.07	1.93	6.72	8.97	+0.48	+0.48	+0.09	+0.39
Group 1	2.39	3.47	15.07	16.09	+0.62	+0.70	+0.44	+0.18
Group 2	3.25	4.70	20.45	21.80	+0.59	+0.69	+0.58	+0.01
Group 3	3.56	4.56	22.46	21.15	+0.41	+0.47	+0.50	-0.09
Group 4	3.15	4.04	19.86	18.74	+0.30	+0.33	+0.49	-0.19
Group 5	2.45	2.85	15.44	13.22	+0.04	+0.18	+0.34	-0.30
Romania	15.87	21.56	100.00	100.00	+2.44	+2.85	+2.44	0.00

A: Total change   B: Urban Change   C: Natural Increase   D: Net Migration

Source: Direcţia Centrală de Statistică, Anuarul Statistic, various years.

evidence to suggest that the Romanians have compromised economic rationality in their location decisions for investments. Indeed, they have never invoked any intrinsically 'socialist' location principles to guide their programme of regional development (Hamilton 1971; Herbst et al.1972 and 1975; Herbst and Letea 1976; Seers 1972; Thomas 1974; Velcea 1970).

SISTEMATIZARE

In the past, village settlement in Romania was distinct from urban, for its association with peasant agriculture made individual settlements small, of low density as a result of the vegetable gardens and vineyards surrounding the farmhouses, and of homogeneous culture and occupation (Chayanov 1966; Marica 1948; Sorokin et al.1930-1). Planning for the villages in the inter-war period was approached through the rhythms of agricultural activity in the different parts of the country, and there were many publications by contemporary sociologists, led by Gusti, about it (Golopentia and Chibulenteanu 1941). However, since the war agricultural work has been transformed by the formation of cooperatives in all but the most mountainous areas and by irrigation, mechanisation and the introduction of new enterprises. Thus, agriculture has become less of a distinctive way of life, even for the people who still work on the land (Ştefánescu 1982). At the same time, alternative sources of employment in industry and services have been developed in rural areas, commuting to jobs in the towns has become very important (Bejenaru 1946; Ianoş and Olaru 1980; Iordan 1973 and 1975; Raboaca and Pert 1976), and 'bus services into town are now widespread and cheap, if rather uncomfortable. Indeed, commuting from the villages has allowed industrial growth to occur in urban areas without the need to provide housing for all those who have been employed, and as a result the incomes of rural dwellers, who produce much of their own food from their gardens or obtain it from the private plots on cooperative farms in cases in which at least one member of the family is still active, have risen markedly (Blaga 1972; Rusenescu 1974; Trebici 1976; Tufescu 1980; Velcea 1972). However, in rural settlements which are remote from the towns these conditions do not apply, and depopulation has reached an advanced stage in many of them

(Apǎvǎloaie 1976; Apǎvǎloaie and Lupu-Bratiloveanu 1980; Bǎcǎnaru 1964; Giosu 1979; Marica and Aluaş 1972; Urucu 1983).

The distinction between town and country is, therefore, becoming less profound, and it is realistic to think of a unified settlement system within which urbanisation is the fundamental force in the creation of a homogenous society in the image of the 'new socialist man' (Deica et al.1976). Marx and Engels had little time for the rural way of life, which was already coming under pressure from the forces of capitalism when they were writing. They considered that it was necessary to pluck the agricultural population away from the "isolation and dullness in which it had vegetated for thousands of years", and so overcome urban-rural contrasts (Khodzhaev and Khorev 1973), and in this the Romanian Communist Party has followed them. Nevertheless, little thought was given to an overall strategy for the villages until the mid-1960s.

Thinking about the modernisation of villages during the last two decades has focussed on two types of special case. Firstly, notions of economic efficiency have led to the designation of about 5,000 small rural settlements as 'irrational'. Some of these are too small for cost-effective servicing, some too remote for daily commuting, and some are even inappropriate as residences for agricultural workers as a result of the formation of large cooperative farms. Some of these unwanted settlements have already disappeared from the landscape, and others may go during the remainder of the century. Secondly, the irregular distribution of towns, which leaves many rural areas more than fifteen kilometres from an urban centre, and the need to provide a range of services and employment for every group of communes, have suggested that between 300 and 400 villages should be promoted to urban status by 1990. (In 1945 there were only 153 towns in Romania, and eight of these lost urban status between 1950 and 1952.) Thirty-eight settlements were in fact promoted to town status in the period up to 1968, and fifty-three more new towns were created in that year, but promotion seems to have been governed largely by industrial status, and as a result the irregularity of the network was accentuated during the 1950s and 60s.

The Romanian policy of sistematizare is remarkable for, while some precedent exists in Russia (Pallot 1979), there has been relatively little interest in radical schemes for reshaping the settlement network in Eastern Europe. New growth points have been identified in other countries, but there has been little enthusiasm for the abolition of small settlements. It may be true, as Johnson has argued (1970, p.375), that "the village of four or five hundred people is an archaic extravagance that a developing country cannot afford". However, other than in Romania, massive reorganisation has been seen as counterproductive (Mihailovic 1972), perhaps because the detailed specification of the settlement pattern which will allow the maximisation of economic growth is very difficult, not least because settlements that have limited economic potential at one point in time may subsequently gain new functions in the future as a consequence of changing fashions or technology. Interest in sistematizare in Romania seems to date from the appointment of Ceaușescu as party leader in 1965, and, in view of the simultaneous revamping of regional development policies, it may have been part of the determination to reduce the inequalities in living standards and employment opportunities between one part of the country and another. It may also have reflected a concern over losses of agricultural land, for, since the 1960s, Romania has sought to modernise with minimal losses of agricultural land, and high density urban development has resulted. In the rural case this has been expressed in a keen desire to consolidate settlements and to accommodate expanding communities within restrictive perimeters, and during a party meeting in 1965 the leader made a strong plea for rural development, with tight control of new building so that the settlement pattern could be restructured and further losses of agricultural land avoided. It may also be relevant to point out that, with the completion of the collectivisation programme in 1963, the Romanians were able to adopt a more autonomous political stance on a number of issues within the communist world (Ionescu 1964; Jowitt 1971).

A central commission for village rationalisation was established in 1965 (Bold 1965), and Romanian academics produced a steady flow of publications dealing with the urbanisation process (Bogdan et al.1970; Brescan et al.1973; Cazacu et al 1970). Various studies were undertaken to show the wide range of rural settlement patterns that would have to be dealt with (Băcănaru 1967; Herbst-Rădoi 1968), and the geographer I. Băcănaru made some particularly effective assessments of rural settlement which showed how physical constraints would inhibit the consolidation process (Băcănaru et al.1963; Băcănaru 1969 and 1974). This work was followed by a useful collection of case studies (Băcănaru and Stănescu 1976; Savu and Ionescu 1978; Schram et al.1978; Tanescu and Băcănaru 1979). The reform of local administration in 1968 also had important consequences for rural planning because, as a consequence of the reduction in the number of the basic units, the communes, from 4259 to 2706, more viable settlement groupings were created, in so far as this was possible in relation to traditional ties and the then current socio-economic linkages. As a result of these changes all communes were supposed to include the full range of primary education services, such basic facilities as a cultural centre, dispensary, library and maternity ward, and a number of shops, including a bakery, grocery, non-food store and various repair and service units. At the same time, the optimum population for a commune was considered to be between 4,500 and 5,000, though many in hilly and mountainous districts are below this because of the low density of settlement.

The Tenth Congress of the Party in 1969 approved a programme for planning the development of both the counties and individual settlements, and, over the following three years, a great many studies were carried out to assess the population, labour force and raw material potential of each settlement (Cardaş 1970 and 1977). By 1972 a fairly clear plan had emerged, and a conference on rural planning produced directives which called for the restructuring of the settlement system with strict land-use controls (Bold et al.1974; Ciobotaru 1974; Gusti 1974). Most of the 13,150 rural settlements were to be retained and gradually provided with better facilities. There was to be some provision for apartment blocks within them, and all new building was to be confined within a building perimeter (perimetrul construibil). House plots were to be restricted to 250 square metres, with any excess liable to expropriation. Thus, agricultural land was to be protected. However, forty percent of the villages had populations of below 500, and many of these were considered to be economically irrational. Those which were so designated were not to be provided with building perimeters, and thus, they would automatically lie outside the areas permitted for building. After a period of great uncertainty it transpired that people in such 'dis-affected' (dezafectat) settlements would not be forced to leave their homes and that structural repairs would be allowed on old property, but the lack of any state investment will inevitably lead to further depopulation. There would in effect be a process of self-destruction (autodezfiinţare). At the other extreme, however, it was declared that upwards of 300 communes would acquire urban status over a twenty-year period, with the first batch of between 120 and 130 due for promotion in 1980.

The essential features of the strategy were considered by the Eleventh Congress of the Party in 1974, and gained legal status in the same year. The media gave the programme very wide coverage, and during the late 1970s sistematizare was one of the nation's principal preoccupations. Under this strategy plans are produced by the planning office (Institut de Proiectare) in each county. They consist of a series of documents for each commune – a background profile outlining the potential of the area (studiu de sistematizare); schiţe de sistematizare, which outlines the proposed spatial pattern for development, with alternatives; and studiu de amplasament, which is a detailed plan for each building. After scrutiny by the communal People's Council (Consiliul Popular) the plans go to Bucharest for consideration by a Committee for the Problems of People's Councils, supervised by a committee of the party. In the event, many of the plans have been quite radical and have given rise to much concern and questioning in the villages. For instance, can a home be maintained in a village categorised as dezafectat? How can the means be found to build a two-storey house within a building perimeter? Will private property be expropriated to make way for such new public facilities as a civic centre or gas distribution system? It is fair to say that over the years reasonable compromises have been achieved on many issues, but it is very much in the nature of things for draconian laws to be passed before procedures have been clarified. Citizens are called upon to participate in the implementation of plans, yet they can only negotiate with difficulty, for even a local plan carries great authority as part of a National Plan which is supported by the party and government acting in the general interest (interes general), and reflects national policy. Any accommodation of individual interests (interes particular) within local plans is strongly resisted by local activists who seek to 'educate' recalcitrant individuals to subordinate their aspirations to the general good. In particular, the concept of economic rationality, which has been fundamental in the selection of villages to be endowed with building perimeters, and the party's notion of equality in the context of urbanisation, namely, that everyone should live in high density settlements with a standard range of services, make it particularly difficult for people living in economically irrational settlements to make an effective plea for their survival. Some foreign writers have argued for a more pragmatic approach, discarding the notion of <u>interes general</u> and allowing each community to plan its own future, but, given the party's insistence on leadership (which is so fundamental to all regimes which are based on the Soviet model), there is no possibility of reform (Sampson 1976 and 1982).

These conflicts have some interesting academic expressions. In particular, it would appear that the flow of professional advice into the government machine tends to be somewhat biased. Architects and economists, who are broadly sympathetic to a radical restructuring of settlements, enjoy a higher status than geographers and sociologists, who also approve of the programme but would prefer that it be approached more cautiously. This latter group argues that the rapid urbanisation of villages runs the risk of transforming rural dwellers from producers of food into consumers. Given the intensive cultivation of garden ground at present, the restriction of the size of building plots could result in the loss of more produce than would be gained by cropping the land which would eventually be made available through the shrinkage of the villages into their perimeters. Urbanisation will triumph in the end, but arguably a country that depends heavily on the production of foodstuffs and agricultural raw materials should, for the time being at least, place a premium on agrarian self-reliance. The same line of argument has been advanced in the case of allegedly irrational settlements, for production from the land adjacent to such settlements might well decline sharply if the labour base is removed to a central settlement in the commune, making it uneconomic for the cooperative to send workers out daily to tend the orchards or vineyards at the <u>dezafectat</u> settlements. These problems are particularly significant in the mountain districts, where even the grouping of the remaining private farms into micro-cooperatives will require some perpetuation of dispersed settlement

(Dimitru 1972; Leonovici and Lungu 1972;˙Morariu et al. 1968; Rey 1979; Ştefănescu 1972). Reservations have also been expressed over the adequacy of certain of the sites which have been earmarked for resettlement, and this underlines the need for local plans to have a sound ecological base (Matei and Matei 1978 and 1979). Lastly, respect for traditional architectural styles has slowed the advance towards uniformity in housing.

Much thought went into the selection of the communes which were to be upgraded to towns by 1980 (Miftode 1978), and various survey methods were devised to compare the potential and performance of each commune on a scientific basis (Baranovsky and Rusenescu 1967; Chiriac 1978; Molnar 1967 and 1970; Socorovsci et al. 1978; Ştefănescu and Baranovsky 1980). Many choices were straightforward, for there are some communes with a long-standing administrative and commercial role, and especially those places which had been the centres of administrative districts in the 1930s and 1950s, but which had lost that status (Deica and Karteva 1967; Herbay 1946; Tufescu 1942). Where these places were more than fifteen kilometres from an existing town they had good prospects of becoming effective growth points for their localities; and this was all the more so where the population was large, there was some industry already in existence, and there were satisfactory sites for further development. Secondly, there were settlements which had become important because of the discovery of mineral resources nearby, the construction of power stations or the development of manufacturing related to local timber or agricultural products, all of which strengthened their claims to town status (Apavaloaie et al.1974; Onisor and Susan 1966). But it has also been evident that the ideological factor has been at work, for some of the communes that were involved in the 1907 peasant revolt have also been promoted. However, in many of the areas in which a new town was considered to be necessary several communes advanced competing claims. It would seem that some of these have been resolved by granting urban status to communes whose local officials have been particularly diligent in attracting small industries, such as engineering or textiles, but it also appears that other decisions have owed something to close connections between members of the administrative hierarchies at the county and commune levels. In the end, 129 communes were selected, and investments were made in them to allow for their declaration as towns in 1980. However, only one town has so far been recognized - Rovinari in Gorj County in 1982 - and it is not clear whether the delay has been caused by a lack of resources for the provision of a large number of new industrial projects in the chosen settlements, or from a fundamental rethinking arising out of the decision to give greater priority to agriculture (Jackson 1983-4), or both. Certainly, agricultural self-sufficiency was an important element of the 1981-1985 Five Year Plan, with revised state purchase prices in 1981 to provide progressive bonuses for extra deliveries; and much attention was also given to small-scale industry of the type which which can be developed very satisfactorily in the villages (Gruescu 1980 and 1982; Petö 1981; Popovici and Foscolo 1982).

Had the proposed new towns been officially designated in 1980 they would have provided a network of agro-industrial centres which would have been the lowest tier in the urban hierarchy. Above them would have come the larger sub-regional and regional centres, such as the administrative centres for the counties and a number of other towns with particularly well developed commercial and industrial functions, and finally the state capital, Bucharest (Cucu and Bugǎ 1980). In the past it has been these larger towns that have shown the highest rates of growth, for there has been a concentration of investment in the regional centres and, to a large extent since 1968, those of the counties (Caloianu et al.1976; Deica 1972; Molnar et al.1975; Panaite et al. 1978). Although Marxist-inspired notions of urban utopia have focussed on small towns, as a reaction to bad living conditions in large cities, the efficiency of investment has been greater in the principal towns, and it has been those which have been favoured by the Romanian planners. Thus, by 1977 Bucharest had a population of 1,800,000, there were eight cities with populations exceeding 200,000, and nine others of between 100,000 and 200,000; and it was in these places that the new suburbs, consisting of very high density developments using apartment blocks, had become most prominent (Cucu 1970 and 1972; Stan 1969). However, much attention has been given to controlling the further growth of these larger urban settlements in recent years. In particular, migration controls were introduced in 1976 to limit growth to that of natural increase, and the only immigration which was permitted was of certain people with essential skills. Furthermore, since 1980 new investments have been diverted, wherever possible, to the smaller towns (Enache 1973). Dragomirescu estimates that the long-term effect of these controls will be that cities with populations of below 100,000 will account for 55.8 percent of the total urban population in the year 2000, compared with 46.3 in 1977, and that much of that change will involve towns with less than 20,000 inhabitants. At the same time the number of towns is destined to grow from 236 to 638, and the proportion of the population living in towns should advance from fifty percent to as much as seventy-five (Table 9.6).

Some assessment of these changing emphases in the development of the urban settlement net can be made by relating urban growth rates to population size. Six size groups have been chosen, and the top four, with populations exceeding 25,000, are defined as large towns. These accounted for 74 of the 236 towns in 1977, or 31.4 percent, and had a combined population of 7,770,000, or 83 percent of the total urban population. During the period from 1966 to 1977 the large towns grew by 42.4 percent, while the small towns increased by only 23.7, and the growth of towns with populations exceeding 50,000 was particularly brisk. Indeed, the government has consistently underestimated the growth of the largest cities, and in both 1965 and 1976 the population estimates were well below the census figures that were returned one year later. However, one major exception was Bucharest, which grew at less than the national average.

But these trends appear to have altered since the late 1970s (Table 9.7). Since 1977 twenty-four large towns in Groups 1 and 2 grew more slowly than the national average, only twelve more rapidly, and only one registered more than twice the national rate, whereas in Groups 4 and 5 only four towns grew more slowly, while sixteen grew more rapidly, and six grew at more than double the national rate. In all except fifteen cases the county centre was the fastest growing town in the county, and this was particularly evident in Groups 4 and 5, where on average the growth rate of the most dynamic town, other than the county centre, was only 81.3 percent of that for the centres, Iaşi being the only major exception (table 9.8). Group 5 county centres grew particularly rapidly. For example, if the national urban growth rate between 1977 and 1982 is taken to be 100, Alexandria achieved a value of 146, Focşani

Table 9.6: Romania's Urban Population 1977-2000

Size Group	1977 Census			2000 Estimate		
	a.	b.	c.	a.	b.	c.
Below 20,000	143	1.46	15.5	434	5.20	23.1
20,000 - 50,000	57	1.69	18.0	122	3.78	16.8
50,000 - 100,000	18	1.20	12.8	46	3.58	15.9
100,000 - 200,000	9	1.28	13.6	21	3.08	13.7
200,000 - 400,000	8	1.97	21.0	14	4.54	20.2
Over 400,000	1	1.80	19.1	1	2.32	10.3
Romania	236	9.40	100.0	638	22.50	100.0

a. Number of Towns
b. Total Population (The estimate for the year 2000 has been calculated on the basis of a population of 30 million of which 75 percent would be resident in towns)
c. Share of Total Population

Source: R. Dragomirescu quoted by P. Ronnas (1983), p. 75.

Table 9.7: Urban Growth in Romania 1977-1982

County Group	Number of towns showing : [in relation to the national average (= 100)] Growth					Total Number of Towns
	Over 200	100 - 200	50 - 99	Below 50	Decline	
			Large Towns			
Bucharest	–	1	–	–	–	1
Group 1	–	4	10	3	–	17
Group 2	1	7	9	2	–	19
Group 3	4	8	4	1	–	17
Group 4	–	8	1	–	–	9
Group 5	6	2	2	1	–	11
Romania	11	30	26	7	–	74

Small Towns

Bucharest	—	—	—	—	—	—
Group 1	1	7	17	12	2	39
Group 2	1	3	11	10	2	27
Group 3	1	12	17	10	5	45
Group 4	—	5	15	9	2	31
Group 5	—	6	6	6	2	20
Romania	3	33	66	47	13	162

All Towns

Bucharest	—	—	—	—	—	1
Group 1	1	11	27	15	2	56
Group 2	2	10	20	12	2	46
Group 3	5	20	21	11	5	62
Group 4	—	13	16	9	2	40
Group 5	6	8	8	7	2	31
Romania	14	63	92	54	13	236

Source: Directia Centrală de Statistică, Anuarul Statistic, various years.

Romania

Table 9.8: The Fastest-Growing Towns in Romania 1977-1982 by County

County		A. County Town Rate of Growth (percent)	B. Fastest-Growing Town (apart from County Town) Rate of Growth		B as a percentage of A
Group 1					
Braşov	Braşov	28.2	Făgăraş	14.6	52
Caraş-Severin	Reşiţa	14.6	*Băile Herculane	35.4	242
Hunedoara	Deva	19.6	*Haţeg	19.8	101
Prahova	Ploieşti	13.1	*Văleni de Munte	17.1	131
Sibiu	Sibiu	10.9	*Agnita	12.5	115
Timiş	Timişoara	10.9	Lugoj	12.7	117
Group 2					
Arad	Arad	6.9	*Sebiş	11.8	171
Argeş	Piteşti	15.4	Cîmpulung	22.5	146
Bacău	Bacău	25.6	Gh.Gheorghui-Dej	14.1	55
Brăila	Brăila	14.2	*Faurei	7.3	51
Cluj	Cluj-Napoca	12.8	*Gherla	20.5	160
Constanţa	Constanţa	17.9	*Năvodari	81.6	456
Galaţi	Galaţi	14.2	Tecuci	14.2	100
Mureş	Tîrgu Mureş	13.5	Reghin	13.9	103

Group 3

County	City		*Second		
Alba	Alba Iulia	31.6	*Abrud	18.0	57
Bihor	Oradea	16.0	*Dr.P.Groza	23.7	148
Covasna	Sfîntu Gheorghe	43.7	*Tîrgu Secuiesc	24.1	55
Dîmbovița	Tirgoviște	26.2	*Titu	19.1	73
Dolj	Craiova	11.8	*Filiași	13.4	114
Gorj	Tîrgu Jiu	22.3	*Motru	16.5	74
Harghita	Miercurea Ciuc	31.3	*Cristuru Secuiesc	31.6	101
Ialomița	Slobozia	34.0	Călărași	20.9	61
Maramureș	Baia Mare	23.0	*Boraș	9.9	43
Neamț	Piatra Neamț	24.3	Roman	25.2	104

Group 4

County	City		*Second		
Buzău	Buzău	23.8	Rîmnicu Sărat	18.6	78
Iași	Iași	9.4	*Pașcani	27.5	293
Ilfov	Guirgiu	18.4	*Urziceni	18.4	100
Mehedinți	Drobeta-T.Severin	16.2	*Baia de Arama	11.7	72
Satu Mare	Satu Mare	17.0	*Carei	9.4	55
Suceava	Suceava	26.6	*Fălticeni	21.9	82
Tulcea	Tulcea	22.0	*Sulina	11.5	52
Vîlcea	Rîmnicu Vîlcea	23.7	*Drăgășani	14.0	99

Table 9.8 (cont'd)

County	A. County Town Rate of Growth (percent)		B. Fastest-Growing Town (apart from County Town) Rate of Growth		B as a percentage of A
Group 5					
Bistriţa-Nasaud	Bistriţa	39.7	*Beclean	25.4	64
Botoşani	Botoşani	39.4	*Dorohoi	25.6	65
Olt	Slatina-Olt	39.8	Caracal	12.2	31
Sălaj	Zalău	42.8	*Jibou	16.6	39
Teleorman	Alexandria	20.7	*Zimnicea	20.4	99
Vaslui	Vaslui	33.7	Bîrlad	14.2	42
Vrancea	Focşani	29.7	*Adjud	26.4	89

* indicates small towns

Note: Slight distortion arises through the boundary changes in the Southeast as a result of which Calarasi is now a county town. However the 1968 arrangement is used here and Giurgiu (rather than Bucharest) is taken as the county town of Ilfov.

Source: Direcţia Centrală de Statistică, Anuarul Statistic, various years.

209, Vaslui 237, Bistriţa 280, Slatina 280 and Zalău 301. Some county centres from Groups 3 and 4 also registered high growth rates. Miercurea Ciuc achieved 220, Alba Iulia 222, Slobozia 239 and Sf.Gheorghe 308, and all the others except Craiova and Iaşi were above the average. Conversely, in Groups 1 and 2 only half the county centres were above the average, with the best performances being at Bacău, with 180, and Braşov, with 199. However, above-average growth was not restricted to county centres, and in only ten counties was there no other town that was growing faster than the national average. Looking at the matter from the point of town size, on the other hand, it must be noted that small towns in general did not perform well, with only thirty-five showing above average rates, as against 127 below.

All this does suggest that there has been some emphasis on the small towns in the recent past, but the fact remains that from 1977 to 1982 the total population of the seventy-four large towns grew by 1,144,029, or by 15,460 each, while the 162 small towns grew by 203.623, or by only 1,257 each. Thus, the former continued to increase their share of the urban population, which had been 80.1 percent in 1966, to 83.2 percent in 1982, and, even in those cities which have been subject to immigration controls since 1976 (Arad, Brăila, Braşov, Bucharest, Cluj-Napoca, Constanţa, Craiova, Galaţi, Iaşi, Piteşti, Sibiu, Timişoara and Tîrgu Mureş) above-average rates of growth have been maintained. However, that rate of growth has fallen relative to the average, from 1.36 between 1966 and 1977 to 1.18 between 1977 and 1980 and 1.07 for the 1980 to 1982 period. In other words, the achievements of sistematizare in the period up to the early 1980s were limited but were becoming increasingly important in shaping the form of the settlement pattern.

PLANNING AND GOVERNMENT IN ROMANIA

Looking back over the post-war period in Romania we can see that the programmes of planificare and sistematizare have taken some while to evolve, even though the problems which they are intended to solve were recognised at an early stage, and have taken even longer to begin to establish those conditions of equality and uniformity in the space economy which are desired by the builders of socialism. Nevertheless, it is now clear that much work has gone into the planning of both the distribution of economic activity, and especially industry, and the design of the network of towns. As we have seen, many opportunities for industrial development in the more backward regions have been taken, though the ideal of equality, which has been much emphasised in public statements, has not been allowed to interfere with the maximisation of economic growth rates, and therefore the main industrial concentrations have continued to expand. Moreover, during the 1970s, as planning became more sophisticated, the ambitious restructuring programme for the settlement network was launched, and there has been an attempt to slow down the rate of growth of the largest cities and to divert resources to the smaller towns and those villages which have the potential to become towns.

However, misgivings of both a particular and a general nature exist about both these policies. In particular, any excessive dispersal of projects may restrict the economies of scale which would otherwise be available. Secondly, as towns are developed differences in standards of living may emerge between them and those outlying villages where a substantial agricultural workforce must be retained; and thirdly, there have been many conflicts between planners and villagers, with individuals frequently seeking to defend their personal interests. The search for compromise between the two groups in a context of media campaigns which seek to develop a higher level of 'socialist consciousness', on the one hand, and discreet modifications of top-level directives by local government and other supposedly subordinate agencies, on the other, has produced a spatial pattern of economic and settlement development which is as fascinating as it is complex. Furthermore, there are general problems surrounding all such attempts at planning the Romanian space economy. Plans which have been drawn up at the centre, and which may not have taken proper account of local characteristics, cannot be seriously scrutinised at more local levels of government because of the ideological objection to tampering with any proposal which is an essential part of the National Plan. Some outside commentators have responded to these problems by suggesting that economic reforms are necessary, that the high level of centralisation should be reduced, and that some limited flexibility must be introduced into the economy if it is to

function more efficiently, but tne party has not
been prepared to grant these greater freedoms so
far. It is unfortunate that Romanian literature has
very little to say on this matter. But it is not
surprising, for, because the planning system is so
fundamental to the nature of the Romanian state, it
is not really open to serious discussion, and
Romanian scholars have been involved much more with
details of plan implementation. They regard
difficulties not as faults of the plan or of the
planning system, but merely indications of a lack of
'education' on the part of those involved. It would
be unfortunate if the further improvement of the
standard of living of the Romanian people and the
provision of facilities and services for them were
to be hindered by the system of government amongst
whose chief aims these improvements are.

REFERENCES

Apăvăloaie, M. (1976), Mobilitatea populatiei
din judeţul Vaslui, Analel stiinţifice ale Univ.
A.I. Cuza din Iaşi II, 22, 100-104.
Apăvăloaie, M, et al. (1974), Asezările rurale
cu industrie din Moldova, Analele stiinţifice ale
Univ. A.I. Cuza din Iaşi IIc, 20, 101-108.
Apăvăloaie, M. and Lupu-Bratiloveanu, N.
(1980), Changements dans la structure de la
population active des agglomérations rurales du
départment de Iaşi, Analele stiinţifice ale Univ.
A.I. Cuza din Iaşi II, 26, 115-120.
Băcănaru, I. et al. (1964), Deplasări de
populatiei şi asezări rurale în Vrancea, Studii şi
Cercetări: Geografie, 11, 117-134.
Băcănaru, I. (1967), Quelques aspects
géographiques de la systématisation des localités du
delta danubien, Revue Roumaine: Géographie, 11,
79-90.
Băcănaru, I. (1969), La systématisation des
localités rurales en Roumanie considerée au point de
vue géographique, Revue Roumaine: Géographie, 13,
73-82.
Băcănaru, I. (1974), Principes et méthodes
concernant la typologie des établissements ruraux en
Roumanie, Revue Roumaine: Géographie, 18, 71-77.
Băcănaru, I. et al. (1963), Contribuţii la
studiul clasificării funcţionale a asezărilor rurale
din R.P.R., Probleme de Geografie, 10, 29-53.
Băcănaru, I. and Cândea, M. (1977), Aspecte
geografice în alimentarea cu apă a localitaţilor

rurale şi urbane din Romanîa, Studii şi Cercetări:
Geografie, 24, 249-258.

Băcăuaru, V. and Stănescu, I. (1976), Cîteva
aspecte geomorfologice care intereseaza
sistematizarea comunei Belceşti, Analele stiinţifice
ale Univ. A.I. Cuza din Iaşi II, 22, 82-86.

Baranovsky, N. and Rusenescu, C. (1967),
Indicatori demografici în sistematizarea rurală,
Studia Univ. Babeş-Boyai: Geologie-Geografie,
12(2), 265-270.

Barbat, A. (1978), Cu privire la conceptul de
urbanizare, Viitorul social, 7(2),

Bejenaru, Z. (1946), Deplasări pentru lucru la
uzinele Reşiţei, in Lucrările seminarului de
geografie economică, ed. N.A. Rădulescu, Academia
de Inalte Studii Comerciale şi Industriale,
Bucharest, 105-107.

Biji, M. et al. (1964), Dezvoltarea economică
a României 1944-1964, Ed. Academiei R.P.R.,
Bucharest.

Blaga, I. (1972), Romania's population,
Meridiane, Bucharest.

Bogdan, T. et al. (1970), Procesul de
urbanizare în România: Zona Braşov, Ed. Politică,
Bucharest.

Bold, I. (1965), Probleme ale sistematizarii
teritoriului agricol, Probleme economice, 18(11),
84-95.

Bold, I. et al. (1974), Sistematizarea
rurală, Ed. Tehnică, Bucharest.

Brescan, M. et al. (1973), Procesul de
urbanizare în R.S.R.: Zona Vaslui, Ed. Academiei
R.S.R., Bucharest.

Bugă, D. (1961), Noi ramuri industriale
aparute în regiunea Oltenia în anii regimului
democrat-popular, Studii şi Cercetari: Geografie,
8, 385-398.

Caloianu, N. et al. (1976), Les grandes
villes de la Roumanie et leurs zones d'attraction,
Revue Roumaine: Géographie, 21, 51-62.

Cardaş, M. (1970), Sistematizarea teritoriului
rurale, Arhitectura, 18(1), 27-29.

Cardaş, M. (1977), Sistematizarea
localitaţiilor rurale, in Sistematizarea, ed. A.
Miu, Academia Ştefan Gheorghiu, Bucharest, 136-143.

Cazacu, A. et al. (1970), Procesul de
urbanizare in R.S.R.: Zona Slatina-Olt, Ed.
Academiei R.S.R., Bucharest.

Ceauşescu, N. (1969-), Romania on the way of
building up the multilaterally developed socialist
society, Meridiane, Bucharest.

Chiriac, D. (1978), Cîteva observaţii geografice privind centrele locale de polarizare din Moldova cu posibilitati de evoluţie spre urbanizare, Analele ştiintifice ale Univ. A.I. Cuza din Iaşi IIb, 24, 121-126.

Ciobotaru, I. (1974), Sistematizarea şi urbanizarea: probleme de eficienţa economică, Ed. Tehnică, Bucharest.

Cioponea, M. (1971), Repartizarea raţională a forţelor de producţie pe teritoriu, Viaţa economică, 9(32), 10-11.

Costache, M. (1961), Politica P.M.R. de repartizare raţională a forţelor de producţie pe teritoriul R.P.R., Natura: Geografie-Geologie, 13(2), 32-40.

Cucu, V. (1961a), Imbunataţirea imparţirii administrative-economice a teritoriului R.P.R., Studii şi Cercetări: geografie, 8, 29-40.

Cucu, V. (1961b), Imparţirea politico-administrativa a R.P.R. in anul 1960, Natura: Geografie-Geologie, 13(2), 52-56.

Cucu, V. (1970), Oraşele Romaniei, Ed. Ştiinţifică, Bucharest.

Cucu, V. (1972), Economical and demogeographical premises in the urbanization of the S.R.R., Revue Roumaine: Géographie, 16, 103-109.

Cucu, V. (1980), Politica P.C.R. de dezvoltare echilibrata a judeţelor R.S.R., Terra, 12(4), 3-10.

Cucu, V. et al. (1975), Bevölkerung und Erwerbsquellen in Rumänien, Geoforum, 6, 39-48.

Cucu, V. and Buga, D. (1980), Hierarchisation des centres urbains de Roumanie, Revue Roumaine: Géographie, 24, 127-132.

Deica, P. (1972), Les grandes villes dans la système des établissements urbains de Roumanie, Revue Roumaine: Géographie, 20, 163-168.

Deica, P. et al. (1976), The interdependence between the territorial structure of the national economy and the unitary system of settlements in Roumania, Revue Roumaine: Géographie, 20, 203-211.

Deica, P. and Karteva, V. (1967), Geografia residinţelor raionale din R.S.R., Studii şi Cercetări: Geografie, 14, 41-49.

Deica, P. and Ştefănescu, I. (1972), Forms of the territorial grouping of the settlement network in the S.R.R., Revue Roumaine: Géographie, 16, 215-216.

Dimitru, V. (1955), Rolul industriei grele în construirea bazei materiale de producţie a socialismului in R.P.R., Probleme economice, 8(4),

31-47.

Dobrescu, E. and Blaga, I. (1973), Structural patterns of Romanian economy, Meridiane, Bucharest.

Dimitru, N.S. (1972), Ponderea şi implicaţiile factorului natural-geografic in optimizarea sistemului socio-economic al unei zone depresionare, in Sociologia Mititans: Sociologie geografică, ed. T. Herseni et al., Ed. Ştiinţifică, Bucharest, 115-200.

Enache, M. (1973), Towards a methodology for comprehensive planning in Romania, Johns Hopkins University Center for Metropolitan Planning and Research, Baltimore.

Gherasimov, I.P. et al. (eds) (1960), Monografia geografică a R.P.R., Ed. Academiei R.P.R., Bucharest.

Giosu, V. (1979), Mutaţii geodemografici în jud. Iaşi în perioada 1966-1977, Analele ştiinţifice ale Univ. A.I. Cuza din Iaşi IIb, 25, 105-113.

Golopentia, A. and Chibulenteanu, I. (1941), 60 sate romaneşti: populaţie, Institutul de Ştiinţe Sociale al României, Bucharest.

Gruescu, I.S. (1971), Dezvoltarea şi repartiţia geografică a industriei electro-energetice a României, Terra, 3(6), 3-14.

Gruescu, I.S. (1980), Industria mică şi artizanală, Terra, 12(2), 43-45.

Gruescu, I.S. (1982), Posibilitaţi şi perspective de dezvoltare a industriei mici şi artizanale in R.S.R., Terra, 14(1), 41-44.

Gusti, G. (1974), Sistematizarea şi urbanism: forme noi de asezăre, Ed. Tehnică, Bucharest.

Hamilton, F.E.I. (1971), Decision making and industrial location in Eastern Europe, Transactions Institute of British Geographers, 52, 77-97.

Helin, R. (1967), The volatile administrative map of Romania, Annals Association of American Geographers, 57, 481-502.

Herbay, A. (1946), Târgurile din bazinul Arieşului, Revista Geografica I.C.G.R., 3, 108-133.

Herbst, C. et al. (1972), Industrializarea socialistă în R.S.R., Terra, 4(3), 41-50.

Herbst, C. et al. (1975), The structure and territorial distribution of industry in Romania, Geoforum, 6, 49-55.

Herbst, C. and Letea, I. (1976), Regional modification in the industry of Romania, Revue Roumaine: Géographie, 20, 211-215.

Herbst-Rădoi, A. (1968), Problèmes géographiques concernant la systématisation des vilages de la Dobrogea, Revue Roumaine: Géographie, 12, 167-170.

Hermansen, T. (1972), Development poles and development centres in national and regional development: elements of a theoretical framework, in Growth poles and growth centres in regional planning, ed. A. Kuklinski, Mouton, The Hague, 1-68.

Ianoş, I. and Olaru, M. (1980), Contributions to the study of daily commutation in Caras-Severin county, Revue Roumaine: Géographie, 24, 161-166.

Ion, I.S. (1971), Raţionalitate în repartizarea teritorială a forţelor de producţie, Probleme economice, 24(4), 85-97.

Ion, I.S. (1972), Repartizarea judicioasă per teritoriu a fortelor de producţie, in Probleme fundamentale ale faururii societaţii socialiste multilateral dezvoltate, ed. C. Moisuc and S. Tamas, Ed. Politică, Bucharest, 203-277.

Ionescu, G. (1964), Communism in Rumania 1944-1964, Oxford University Press, London.

Iordan, I. (1973), Zona periurbană a Bucureştilor, Ed. Academiei R.S.R., Bucharest.

Iordan, I. (1975), Commutation in the peri-urban zone of Bucharest, Revue Roumaine: Géographie, 19, 87-94.

Jackson, M.R. (1983-4), Romania's debt crisis: its causes and consequences, Arizona State University Bureau of Business and Economic Research College of Business Administration Faculty Working Papers.

Johnson, E.A. (1970), The organization of space in developing countries, Harvard University Press, Cambridge (Mass).

Jowitt, K. (1971), Revolutionary breakthroughs and national development, University of California Press, Berkeley.

Khodzhaev, D. and Khorev, B. (1973), The concept of a unified settlement system and the planned control of the growth of towns in the U.S.S.R., Geographia Polonica, 27, 43-51.

Leonovici, M. and Lungu, M. (1972), O varianţa posibilă de construire a tipologiei actuale a satelor din zona pastorală, in Sociologia Militans: Sociologie geografică, ed. T. Herseni et al., Ed. Ştiinţifică, Bucharest, 201-208.

Marica, G. (1948), Satul ca structura psihică si socială, Uniunea Naţionala a Studentilor din România, Cluj.

Marica, G. and Aluaş, I. (1972), Fenomenul migraţional şi efectele lui în satul românesc

Romania

contemporan, Viitorul social, 1, 146-153.
Matei, I. and Matei, M. (1978), Le
développement integré du territoire et des localités
dans la R.S.R., Revue Roumaine: Sociologie, 23,
77-84.
Matei, I. and Matei, M. (1979), Le
développement proportionnel de tous les départements
et régions du pays, Revue Roumaine: Sociologie, 23,
77-84.
Mellor, R.E.H. (1971), Comecon: challenge to
the West, Van Nostrand, New York.
Mellor, R.E.H. (1975), Eastern Europe: a
geography of the Comecon countries, Methuen, London.
Miftode, V. (1978), Migratiile si dezvoltarea
urbană, Ed. Junimea, Iasi.
Mihailovic, K. (1972), Regional development:
experience and prospects in Eastern Europe, Mouton,
The Hague.
Modoran, V. et al. (1971), Dezvoltarea
economiei românesti 1966-1970, Ed. Politica,
Bucharest.
Moisuc, C. and Tamas, S. (ed) (1972),
Probleme fundamentale ale fauririi societatii
socialiste multilateral dezvoltate, Ed. Politică,
Bucharest.
Molnar, E. (1967), Importanta potentialului
economic al asezărilor rurale si metoda stabilirii
lui, Studia Univ. Babes-Bolyai:
Geologie-Geografie, 13(2), 131-138.
Molnar, E. et al. (1975), Centre si aria de
convergenta în R.S.R., Studia Univ. Babes-Bolyai:
Geologie-Geografie, 20, 61-71.
Montias, J.M. (1964-5), Background and origins
of the Romanian dispute with Comecon, Soviet
Studies, 16, 125-151.
Morariu, T. et al. (1968), High zone
settlements in the Romanian Carpathians, Revue
Roumaine: Géographie, 12, 155-162.
Murgescu, C. (1964), Problemele ale relatiilor
economice dintre tările socialiste, Bib. viata
Economică, Bucharest.
Onisor, T. and Susan, A. (1966), Asezări
asimilate urbanului, Studia Univ. Babes-Bolyai:
Geologie-Geografie, 11(1), 115-125.
Pallot, J. (1979), Rural settlement planning
in the U.S.S.R., Soviet Studies, 31, 214-230.
Panaite, L. et al. (1978), First rank
polarizing centres in Romania's urban settlement
network, Revue Roumaine: Géographie, 22, 251-256.
Petö, L.A. (1981), Industria mică si
artizanală din depresiunile Ciuc si Casin, Terra,

13(1), 23-25.

Popovici, I. et al. (1976), Realisări şi perspective privind dezvoltarea şi repartizarea geografia a industriei româneşti, Terra, 8(1), 7-12.

Popovici, R. and Foscolo, E. (1982), Rolul industriei mici şi artizanale în dezvoltarea economico-socială a jud. Constanţa, Terra, 14(3), 34-36.

Raboaca, G. and Pert, S. (1976), Mobilitatea forţei de munca, Ed. Academiei R.S.R., Bucharest.

Rădulescu, I. (1950), Raionarea administrativă-economica a teritoriului R.P.R. şi rolulsau in opera mareata de construire a socialismului, Natura: Geografie-Geologie, 2(5), 24-34.

Rey, R. (1979), Viitor în Carpaţi, Ed. Scrisul Românesc, Craiova.

Rodwin, L. (1970), Nations and cities: a comparison of strategies for urban growth, Houghton-Mifflin, Boston (Mass).

Romanian Communist Party (1974), Programme of the R.C.P. for the building of the multilaterally developed socialist society, Meridiane, Bucharest.

Ronnås, P. (1984), Urbanization in Romania: a geography of social and economic change since independence, School of Economics, Stockholm.

Rusenescu, C. (1974), L'influence de l'urbanisation sur la vie rurale de la R.S.R., Revue Roumaine: Géographie, 18, 239-247.

Sampson, S. (1976), Feldioara: the city comes to the peasant, Dialectical Anthropology, 1, 321-347.

Sampson, S. (1982), The planners and the peasants: an anthropological study of urban development in Romania, University Centre of South Jutland Institute of East-West Studies, Esbjerg.

Savu, A. and Ionescu, A. (1978), Factorii geografici in sistematizarea comunei Scorniceşti-Olt, Studia Univ. Babeş-Bolyai: Geologie-Geografie, 23(2), 45-50.

Schaefer, H.W. (1972), Comecon and the politics of integration, Praeger, New York.

Schram, M. et al. (1978), Contribuţii la studiul geohidromórfologic al teritoriului comunei Sipote în sprijinul sistematizarii, Analele ştiinţifice ale Univ. A.I. Cuza din Iaşi IIb, 24, 87-96.

Seers, D. (1972), What are we trying to measure?, Journal of Development Studies, 8, 21-36.

Socorovsci, V. et al. (1978), Optiminazarea in procesul urbanizarii comunelor din jud. Cluj,

Studia Univ. Babeş-Bolyai: Geologie-Geografie, 23(2), 66-77.

Sorokin, P. et al. (1930-1), A systematic source book in rural sociology, University of Minnesota Press, Minneapolis.

Spornic, A. (1975), Utilizarea eficienţă a resurselor de munca feminine în României, Ed. Academiei R.S.R., Bucharest.

Stan, C. (1969), Industrialisation et urbanisation en Roumanie, Revue Roumaine: Géographie, 13,

Ştefănescu, I. (1972), Subcărpatii dintre Suşita-Zabraut şi Buzău, Ed. Academiei R.S.R., Bucharest.

Ştefănescu, I. (1975), The migratory movement in Roumania, Revue Roumaine: Géographie, 18, 227-238.

Ştefănescu, I. (1982), La repartition géographique de la population active dans l'agriculture de la Roumaine', Revue Roumaine: Géographie, 26, 81-88.

Ştefănescu, I. and Baranovsky, N. (1978), Romania's population dynamics over the 1966-1977 period, Revue Roumaine: Géographie, 23, 265-274.

Ştefănescu, I. and Baranovsky, N. (1980), Marimea medie a asezărilor rurale din R.S.R.,Studii şi Cercetări: Geografie, 27, 91-98.

Tanescu, I. and Băcăuaru, V. (1979), Cîteva consideraţii de geomorfologie aplicată privind comunei Strunga, Analele ştiinţifice ale Univ. A.I. Cuza din Iaşi IIb, 25, 129-130.

Thomas, C. (1974), Dependence and transformation: the economics of transition to socialism, Monthly Review Press, New York.

Trăistaru, E. and Trăistaru, I. (1979), Omogenizarea societatii româneşti, Scrisul Românesc, Craiova.

Trebici, V. (1971), Populaţia României şi cresterea economică, Ed. Ştiinţifica, Bucharest.

Trebici, V. (1976), Romania's population and demographic trends, Meridiane, Bucharest.

Tufescu, V. (1942), Târguşoarele din Moldova şi importanţa lor economică, Buletinul S.R.G., 60, 91-142.

Tufescu, V. (1980), Sur l'urbanisation des villages de Roumaine, Revue Roumaine: Géographie, 24, 139-146.

Tufescu, V. and Herbst, C. (1969), The new administrative territorial organisation of Romania, Revue Roumaine: Géographie, 13, 25-37.

Tufescu, V. and Ştefǎnescu, I. (1974), Les déplacements de la force de travail dans l'industrie de la roumaine, Revue Roumaine: Géographie, 18, 227-238.

Turnock, D. (1979), Spatial aspects of modernisation in Eastern Europe: the Romanian case', Contact: Journal of Urban and Environmental Affairs, 11(2), 113-142.

Urucu, V. (1983), Piemontul Olteţului: aspecte ale dezvoltarii economice, Revue Roumaine: Géographie, 30, 61-66.

Velcea, I. (1970), Cu privire la raspindirea şi concentrarea industriei in R.S.R., Terra, 2(2), 2-19.

Velcea, I. (1972), The urbanization process of rural settlement in Romania, Revue Roumaine: Géographie, 16, 93-101.

Chapter 10

YUGOSLAVIA

Andrew H.Dawson

THE CONTEXT OF PLANNING

Of all the countries of Eastern Europe, Yugoslavia is one of the most intriguing subjects for a study of the post-war attempt to plan the space economy. It is a country of marked topographical contrasts, though in this it differs little from, say, Bulgaria or Romania. It is populated by a wider range of peoples than any of the other countries of the area, not excluding Czechoslovakia. Like Albania, it has enjoyed a very significant degree of independence in organising its own affairs since the Second World War. It has retained a large private sector in its economy, especially in agriculture, which is proportionally larger than that of Poland; and, with Hungary, it has moved further along the road of market socialism than the rest of Eastern Europe or the USSR. However, in so far as Yugoslavia combines all this natural, cultural and economic variety within its borders it differs markedly from the other countries of the area.

The landforms of Yugoslavia may be divided into two regions, though each of these is by no means internally homogeneous (Figure 10.1). Only about a third of the country lies below 200 metres above sea level, and most of this is in the southward extension of the Danube Basin which forms the Pannonian Plain and the wide lower valleys of the Drava and Sava rivers in the north of the country. Much of this is covered with chernozem and brown forest soils developed from loess deposits, and, although the area suffers from frequent summer droughts, it offers by far the richest agricultural base in Yugoslavia. For the rest, the country is mountainous. Indeed, a further third lies above 900

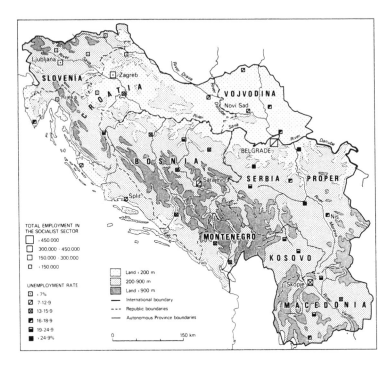

Figure 10.1 Yugoslavia: Relief and Unemployment in Towns in 1984

metres, and the topography of the west, centre and south is complex. Alpine ranges parallel the coast, separating the limited lowlands along the Adriatic from interior karstic basins and narrow valleys, and from the lowlands of the north. Massifs and high-level plateaux cover much of the centre and east of the country in the western section of the Rhodope Mountains; and, everywhere the land is characterised by the contrast between limited lowlands and steep slopes. This is a problematic environment, and areas which combine suitable topographic, climatic, pedological and hydrologic conditions for agriculture are scanty and small. Much of the sloping land, and almost all of that above 900 metres, is forested; and, where it is not, soil erosion is a long-standing, widespread and serious problem. The south of the country, around Skopje, is tectonically unstable, with frequent earth tremors and occasional severe earthquakes;

and, in the centre and south travellers must follow
slow and tortuous routes through the mountains.
However, high precipitation in the mountains and
steep, narrow valleys have created a very large
potential for hydro-electricity; and there are a
large number of small deposits of coals of various
types and other minerals.

One further consequence of this physical
environment is that there are substantial parts of
the country which have either been isolated from the
rest of it, or more accessible to areas beyond its
borders, or both. It should not be surprising,
therefore, that a wide range of peoples of different
culture and language have survived within the
relatively small area of Yugoslavia. Of these, the
most important are the Serbs, a slavonic people with
a cyrillic alphabet, who account for about two
fifths of the total population and live
predominantly in the northeast of the country, in
the Morava valley and Belgrade. Croats, who account
for almost a quarter of the total, are also
slavonic, but use the roman alphabet and live
chiefly in the Drava and Sava valleys and in Zagreb.
The Macedonians and Slovenes are smaller slavonic
groups, with languages which are different from
Serbo-Croat, and there are also small groups of
Albanians and Hungarians. In addition, the
population is divided along religious lines. The
alphabetic division reflects traditional allegiance
to the Orthodox and Roman Catholic churches, but
there is also a large Muslim community in the south.
All this has made for a highly developed sense of
individuality within each of the groups, and for
much rivalry and strife between them, even in the
very recent past. It has also restricted migration
and obliged those in the mountainous areas to remain
there, even when the number of people was greater
than the physical environment could sustain
permanently, to the detriment of their economic
development. The union of such a diverse range of
peoples into a single state has been greatly
assisted by the adoption of a federal structure and
the devolution of a considerable amount of power to
each of the constituent republics and autonomous
areas. Thus, the Croatian, Macedonian and Slovenian
republics are inhabited very largely by the peoples
of those names, as is Serbia proper - one of three
divisions of the Serbian Republic - but the others -
the Autonomous District of Kosovo-Metohija (Kosmet),
in the south, and the Autonomous Province of
Vojvodina, in the north - contain respectively the

large Albanian and Hungarian minorities as well as Serbs and small numbers of some other peoples. Each republic and autonomous region was accorded substantial rights under the 1946 Constitution to plan, invest in and intervene in its own economy, and these have been strengthened, by later revisions, so that the rivalry between the country's constituent peoples has been institutionalised within the planning system.

The economic problems facing the country in 1945 were very large. Not only had it been one of the poorest in Eastern Europe before the war, but it had also suffered much wartime damage. One of the most serious problems was the surplus of rural population. During the 1930s this had been estimated to be not less than 4,000,000, including at least 1,000,000 economically active people; and, although many people had been killed or expelled during and after the war, the surplus was probably still in excess of 3,000,000 in the early post-war years (Čobeljić and Mihailović 1953; Moore 1954, pp.64, 72, 206, 208). Population pressure was especially great in the more backward, rural areas. Moreover, it looked certain to increase. Although birth rates were lower than they had been between the wars, so were death rates, natural increase in the country as a whole was still running at about sixteen per thousand in the late 1940s in the country as a whole, and it was much higher among the Muslims in the rural areas of the centre and south (Yugoslavia 1964, pp.82-83). Thus, there was a need to undertake those types of economic and educational development which would encourage a fall in the birth rate, create jobs for a growing workforce and shift the huge inherited surplus of labour out of agriculture.

Moreover, these problems displayed a strong regional incidence. For example, the Vojvodina, which had had the most developed farming industry before the war, had lost much of its population through the expulsion of the Germans, and required to be resettled. However, the physical and infrastructural environment of the area is very different from those of the mountainous centre and south of the country, where the surplus of rural labour was greatest and from where settlers might, most obviously, have been recruited. Conversely, the centre and south, including Bosnia-Herzegovina, Kosmet, Macedonia and Montenegro, are characterised by difficult natural environments, and suffered from acute overpopulation, rapid population increase, illiteracy and under-development of all forms, with the result that they had a standard of living which was only about half that of the country as a whole (Hamilton 1968, p.104). Because the population there was almost entirely rural, and was living in small settlements, there were few urban centres which were of sufficient size to provide a suitable location for new industries of medium or large scale, which might provide alternative employment, and it was apparent from an early stage that the economic development of these areas would require much expenditure on infrastructure. Nevertheless, these areas were not without resources, and it was recognised that much development could be achieved if they could be exploited. However, it was also clear that it would be necessary to improve the transport network if a national market for their products was to become a reality. Thirdly, there were the republics of Croatia and, in particular, Slovenia, both of which had benefited from a long association with the Austro-Hungarian Empire before 1918; had much more developed economies than the rest of the country; and, with Vojvodina, enjoyed by far the highest standards of living. These areas were, perhaps, the obvious ones in terms of existing expertise and infrastructure to accommodate economic growth, but, if such growth were to be on a scale sufficient to draw the surplus labour out of the south, it would require much extra expenditure on housing and social facilities. However, if a more even distribution of investment was to be undertaken across the country, the relative prosperity of these republics indicated that it would be them which would be called upon to subsidise the development of other regions, and thus other ethnic groups.

The response of the Yugoslavian authorities to these problems, once the immediate work of post-war reconstruction had been completed, was two-fold. Firstly, it seemed clear that very rapid economic growth was required in order to take up the labour surplus from agriculture, and that this could only be achieved through major structural changes in the economy. In particular, labour could be transferred at once to maximise the exploitation of the country's existing resources by reclaiming land for agriculture, and by making full use of existing industrial plant and the introduction of two- and three-shift working. Moreover, a very large part of the mineral output of the country before the war had been exported, and therefore there were considerable opportunities for the development of processing industries and for import-substitution of other manufactured goods, all of which could absorb surplus farm workers; and priority was given to electricity generation, metallurgy, chemicals, engineering and cement production. Secondly, the government emphasised the need to reduce the wide regional contrasts in the standard of living.

It is of some interest to note that, in attempting these tasks, Yugoslavia has been able to win for itself much greater flexibility in policy making than any of the other countries of Eastern Europe, with the possible exception of Albania. Because its ruler, Tito, was able to survive the break with the Soviet Union in 1948, he was able to adapt the Soviet model of economic development to the particular needs of the country. Furthermore, because he exerted strong control over the general direction of policy throughout almost all the post-war period, his system of planning became well established, and seems to have survived his death in 1980.

He was able to vary the Soviet model in three important ways. Firstly, although it was decided that the route to development lay chiefly through the expansion of manufacturing, and although almost all mining, manufacturing and service industry was nationalised in the 1940s, that development has been managed in a very different, devolved manner than in any of the other countries of Eastern Europe, with the exception of Hungary. To begin with, in the late 1940s, a highly-centralised command economy of the Soviet type was set up, in which all major decisions, and most of the details, concerning investment and production were decided by the federal government and incorporated within a Five Year Plan. However, the First Plan was far too ambitious and was jeopardised by severe droughts and the expulsion of Yugoslavia from the Cominform, which severed the economic links with the other Eastern European countries and caused dislocations in production and trade. This system was replaced in the early 1950s by the introduction of the 'self-management' of enterprises by their employees. However, the state continued to lay down general economic guidelines, and it retained control over investment, set minima for production from each enterprise and controlled foreign trade, so that the scope for 'worker-management' was rather small. Nevertheless, the Constitutional Law of 1953 incorporated the idea of self-management, and so established a fundamentally new form of economic management in Eastern Europe.

Rapid economic growth followed these changes, but difficulties in the early 1960s led to a further set of reforms in 1965, which are generally considered to have ushered in the period of 'market socialism'. Most prices were freed, and were set thereafter by enterprises according to the state of the market; the banking system was decentralised; most financing of investment was transferred to communal and republican banks, which were controlled by their local communities; and emphasis on the 'rentability' or likely return from investments was increased in deciding which projects should receive funds. However, major infrastructural projects remained the responsibility of central government. Production targets were abandoned, and output and wages were determined, to some extent, by supply and demand, though there were limits to the range over which they were allowed to vary. Similarly, local communities were made responsible for providing social services and for raising their own funds to do this. Thus, the Yugoslav system became highly devolved and polycentric, with decision-making by central, republican and communal branches of government, and by individual enterprises. The economy was guided by a largely free market, and prices and profitability determined much of the allocation of resources within it. Government funds covered less than a fifth of fixed capital investment in the late 1960s, and the chief sources were the banks, followed by the enterprises, using their own funds. Ownership of the means of production outwith agriculture remained communal, but otherwise the economy had more in common with those of the market, rather than the centrally-planned, countries.

However, 'market socialism' failed to solve the problems with which it had been designed to deal, and further changes were made in the early 1970s which devolved power still further. These introduced a system of 'self-management agreements' between all decision-makers, subject to 'social compacts' between them about the priorities for development, and gave the League of Communists (the Communist Party) an integrating role in all these negotiations. The effect was to weaken market mechanisms and to substitute for them, at least in part, agreements between officially-recognised groups of workers. Government at all levels and enterprises were now represented by 'basic organisations of associated labour' or OOURs, and all investment and production decisions became the responsibility of the groups of workers involved. However, the economy has continued to suffer from very serious problems, and in the early 1980s the increase in oil prices and the world recession led to an acceleration of inflation to very high levels, a sudden fall in the rate of economic growth, and a continuation in the rise of unemployment. Standards of living fell as a stringent Stabilization Programme was adopted in 1983.

Thus, Yugoslavia has experimented with a variety of planning mechanisms for its economy, but since the early 1950s, and especially since 1965, it has been characterised by a polycentric system of decision making in which there have been many hundreds of organisations within the social sector, of which the central government has been an important, but by no means the dominant, one. At the same time, decisions have been subject to market forces, though these have been constrained to varying degrees over the period, and have never been allowed free rein. For example, most prices in agriculture and heavy industry have continued to be set centrally, as have interest rates. Nevertheless, the economy has been much closer in many of its workings to those of the 'market economies' than the command economies in other parts of Eastern Europe, with their legally-enforceable plans and fixed prices. Central and local government still draw up Five Year Plans, but these are very general statements which are designed to provide advice to OOURs about future growth in the economy as a whole. Indeed, they may be more important from a political, than an economic, point of view in so far as they demonstrate that it is possible to reach agreement among the republics, and thus bind the nation together, even if those agreements prove subsequently to be unenforceable (Singleton and Carter 1982, p.165).

The second of Tito's major departures from the Soviet model of development was that he allowed, and later encouraged, the survival of a significant privately-owned sector within the economy. The first stage in this was the abandonment of the forced collectivisation of agriculture in 1953, since when more than four fifths of the farmland has been in the hands of the peasants, and of compulsory deliveries of farm products to the state. However, the maximum size of holdings of ten hectares (or fifteen where the soil is poor) means that, in the absence of very considerable investment and associated intensification, holdings are inadequate to support large families, and a very large proportion of peasant households have at least one member in full-time employment elsewhere (Bergmann 1975, pp.140-141). Thus, it would not be appropriate to consider that the agricultural sector was capitalist in any developed sense, though it is no longer predominantly self-sufficient, as it was over much of the country before the war. Later, in the 1970s, private cooperatives (CNOALs) were encouraged in the non-agricultural sectors of the economy, using private capital. There are also many small, often family, concerns, especially in craft industry, retailing, catering and tourism, and the repair and maintenance of cars, refrigerators and other durable-use consumer goods (Singleton and Carter 1982, pp.200-202). Thus, in 1952, the private sector accounted for 30.5 percent of the economy, and, although this declined as the share of agriculture in general did, to 12.5 percent in 1979, it had risen again to 15.4 percent in 1983 (OECD 1984, p.44).

The third modification of the Soviet model has been in the area of foreign economic relations, and in particular, in that of links with the market economies of the West. UNRRA aid after the war helped to re-establish the rail system; American help was received after the abandonment of collectivisation; the IMF and World Bank, amongst others, have assisted the country; and joint ventures have been undertaken with foreign firms since the late 1960s. Thus, foreign capital has been available for investment even though the dinar has not been made fully convertible. Moreover, some of the labour surplus has been exported. Unlike any of the other countries of Eastern Europe, Yugoslavia has allowed its people to emigrate temporarily to work in Western Europe. In the early 1970s over a million workers and their dependents, or about a tenth of the workforce, took advantage of that opportunity, many of whom remitted earnings; and, even in the 1980s, there were still about 750,000 abroad, many of whom were in West Germany (OECD 1984, p.73). Moreover, a third of those who had returned during the previous ten years, or about 200,000, had opened private businesses with their savings or invested them in the public sector, so ensuring themselves of a job (Trevissan 1985). It is clear that the tasks of raising the standard of living inside Yugoslavia and of solving the problem of surplus rural labour would have been much more difficult in the absence of this openness of the economy to outside assistance.

Partly as a consequence of these innovations in the system of economic management much development has occurred since the end of the war. The output of manufacturing has soared; mineral extraction, which was relatively well developed between the wars, has also been much increased; service industries have been built up; and the structure of the economy has been brought into a much better balance. Between 1951 and 1983 employment in manufacturing and mining rose from 590,000 to 2,370,000; there was a similar rise in the number of service jobs; and the agricultural population fell from about 10,500,000 to 4,000,000 (Yugoslavia 1984, pp.81, 88). National income has risen much faster than even the rapid increase in population - averaging about six percent each year, though fluctuating widely during the period - while population grew from 15,700,000 in 1947 to 22,800,000 in 1983. However, a large surplus of labour still existed in the mid-1980s. Registered unemployment of more than one million accounted for almost fifteen percent of the labour force in 1985; low productivity in industry indicated that there may be much hidden unemployment in enterprises in the social sector of the economy; and Tyson (1980, p.53) has reported that between twenty and thirty percent of the workforce in agriculture was unemployed or underemployed in the late 1970s. In other words, the basic problems of underdevelopment had not been solved by the mid-1980s, though much progress had been made in that direction.

REGIONAL PLANNING

The regional problem has been approached in a variety of ways since the war. Firstly, funds have been made available for the development of backward areas on an increasing scale during the post-war period. Until the mid-1950s these funds were controlled by the federal government, but in 1954 a General Investment Fund was set up, though this allocated money, at least in part, on the basis of the highest rate of return. This was followed in 1961 by a specific fund for the development of backward areas, subsequently entitled the Federal Fund for Crediting Accelerated Development in Under-Developed Republics and Provinces; and, since 1976, a separate allocation of federal money has been made to improve the social services in the poorer regions. Much of the money which has been invested in Bosnia-Herzegovina, Kosovo, Macedonia and Montenegro has been collected through levies on enterprises in the socialist sector, and has involved the subsidy of the less-developed south by the richer north of the country. Kosovo, the poorest of the regions, has received an increasing proportion of its investment – more than seventy percent during the early 1970s – from these transfers (Singleton and Carter 1982, p.224). Financial assistance for the regions has also been received from a variety of foreign, Western sources. Secondly, the allocation of these funds within each republic has been subject to the plans which have been drawn up by the republican governments; but thirdly, the initiative for development has been placed increasingly, in the devolved system of control in Yugoslavia, in the hands of individual enterprises and communal authorities and their employees. Thus, the spatial arrangement of investment has not been plan based, and there has never been a detailed regional development plan in which the needs and resources of all parts of the country have been evaluated against each other, even during the first few years of the post-war period. Rather, it has become the product of a complex system of bargaining between federal, republican and communal authorities, enterprises and workers.

The results of these initiatives have included a marked broadening of the economic base of the poorer regions and an improvement in their standards of living. Mineral resources have been exploited, with marked increases in the output of brown coal and lignite in Bosnia, eastern Serbia and Kosovo, and the development of the hydro-electric potential of these areas. Iron and steel works have been set up in Bosnia, Macedonia and Montenegro, and now exist in all the republics, and by the 1980s Bosnia was producing two-fifths of Yugoslavia's steel, using local raw materials. Bauxite, copper, lead, zinc and several other non-ferrous ores are extracted in large quantities and processed locally in the south of the country; chemical, engineering and other forms of manufacturing have been established in many parts of the country which had been almost entirely dependent on peasant agriculture before the war; and the range and number of jobs in administration, education, health and social services have been greatly increased. Many rural people have moved into the towns to take

285

advantage of these new opportunities, and many more commute, sometimes over very long distances, from their villages. Sarajevo and Zenica in Bosnia, Skopje in Macedonia, and Niksic in Montenegro have all become important industrial towns.

Nevertheless, marked regional disparities continue, and the contrast between the most-developed republics and the least has actually widened since the late 1940s. In 1983 Slovenia enjoyed a level of national income per capita which was seven times that of Kosovo and about three times those of Bosnia, Macedonia and Montenegro; and, while Croatia and Slovenia had increased their level of national income per capita in relation to the national average since 1947, those of Bosnia and Kosovo had declined markedly, though the rank order of the republics and provinces changed little (Table 10.1). Other indicators tell a similar story. For instance, unemployment is highest in the south and east, lowest in Slovenia, and varied in the principal towns in 1983 from one or two percent in Slovenia to between a fifth and a third of the workforce in parts of Bosnia, Kosovo and Serbia proper (Figure 10.1). The net income of workers in Kosovo in 1983 was only seventy percent of that in Slovenia (Table 10.1); and the number of private cars in Kosovo, at thirty-four per thousand of the population, was only a third of that in Serbia as a whole, a quarter of that in Croatia and a seventh of that in Slovenia (Yugoslavia 1984, pp.419, 424). Thus, although the standard of living has risen substantially in all parts of the country, the regional contrasts have remained, and this has provoked tension between both the richer areas, which resent the extent to which they are required to assist the south (Sirc 1979, pp.224-225), and Kosovo, where unrest has occurred among the Albanian minority on several occasions since the late 1960s, and the rest of the country, so emphasizing the diverse and potentially disunited nature of Yugoslavia.

The question arises, therefore, as to why the considerable measures which have been taken since the war to equalise the level of development have not been more successful. The answers to this question have been many (Moore 1980, pp.148-150), but some have been identified by most writers and appear to be of particular importance. Firstly, much, and perhaps too much, of the available investment has been put into the more-developed regions. However, there is a limit to which

Table 10.1: Some Regional Development Indicators for Yugoslavia

Region	National Income per Capita (Yugoslavia = 100) 1947	National Income per Capita (Yugoslavia = 100) 1983	Agricultural Population 1981 as a Percentage of Total Population	Cars per Thousand of Population in 1983	Live Births per Hundred of Population in 1983
Bosnia-Herzegovina	82	69	16.5	82	17.1
Croatia	105	125	14.4	141	14.3
Macedonia	69	65	20.5	111	20.2
Montenegro	79	77	13.0	90	18.3
Slovenia	153	197	9.2	243	15.2
Serbia proper	99	99	26.5	125	14.2
Kosovo	50	28	23.8	34	31.8
Vojvodina	122	120	19.2	126	13.1

Source: Yugoslavia, Statistička Godišnjak SFRJ, various years.

investment can be transferred from more- to less-developed areas if existing industries and settlements in the north are not to stagnate (Hamilton 1968, p.141). Moreover, it has been shown that the returns from investment in some key industries have been very much greater in the more-developed regions than elsewhere (Bombelles 1968, pp.100, 220; Tyson 1980, p.48), and therefore it is hardly surprising if the funds which have been generated for further investment by enterprises and communes in those regions have been growing more rapidly, even after they have been taxed by the federal government to finance development elsewhere, than those in other parts of the country. Thirdly, because the population has been growing very much faster in the south, and especially in Kosovo, than in the richer regions, the problems of overpopulation there have not been eliminated and have continued to hold down the level of development.

But these are not the only reasons for the persistence of the regional contrasts, and there are others which reflect the peculiarly difficult nature of the problem of holding together such a diverse society as that of Yugoslavia, let alone reducing that diversity. At the most obvious and basic of levels much effort has been expended in attempting to link the different parts of the country together through improvements to the transport network, and thus encourage the internal migration and integration of the population and also the movement of goods and the integration of the economy. Much new railway track has been installed, replacing almost all of the previous narrow-gauge lines, and the route between the northwestern frontier and Zagreb, Belgade, Skopje and Greece has been upgraded. Similarly, the main roads across the country from western Europe to Greece and along the Adriatic have been greatly improved. Rail and road links between Belgrade, and Serbia in general, and the Adriatic coast, across Bosnia and Montenegro, have also been extended and upgraded. All republics and provinces have been connected to both the standard-gauge and main road systems, and most of the larger towns are now served by both electrified rail services and the motorway network. Nevertheless, the service on the railways has been hampered by the decentralisation of the system; some key stretches of the road network have not been completed; and the OECD has reported that transport costs are "significantly higher than in other

European countries with similar transport and geographical conditions" (1984, p.46).

Moreover, this physical integration of the federation has not been accompanied by the growth of the economic and social links which it has made possible. The internal market within the country continues to be fragmented, and the mobility of factors and products which is necessary for the development of regional specialisation according to notions of comparative advantage has not occurred. For instance, Tomic (1984) has noted that in mountainous areas local surpluses of agricultural products have often accumulated and been wasted because of the localised nature of the marketing arrangements and limited capacity of the local markets, thus depressing farm incomes (Tomic 1984); while, more generally, the OECD has reported that the level of inter-regional trade in the country has been falling as a proportion of total trade, and that by the early 1980s it was even below that between many countries in Europe (1984, p.48). This fragmentation is, in large measure, a result of the devolution of power to the regional authorities, including decentralisation of much responsibility for banking and foreign exchange control. Each republic and province has had its own 'national' bank since the early 1970s, and before that many local banks had been established as a result of the reforms of the mid-1960s. Federal investment funds are channelled through the republics' national banks; and banks, enterprises and local authorities - as represented by their workers - in any area are closely linked and have a common interest in supporting their own localities, so that investment funds are often both generated and spent locally. This has led to the duplication of productive capacity in different regions and communes; enterprises are often operating at small scales; and an overall excess of capacity has been developed in some industries. In short, investment often goes to the wrong projects in the wrong places and on the wrong scale, thus reducing the country's potential for development. Nor is the alternative to the movement of capital - internal migration of labour - any greater (Singleton and Carter 1982, pp.228-229). Indeed, in view of the apparent willingness of the workforce to settle abroad, if only temporarily, and the relative absence of internal administrative constraints on movement within the country, the small scale of migration at the inter-regional level is all the more indicative of the barriers and tensions between the ethnic groups.

CONCLUSION

This essay has described something of the regional diversity which characterises Yugoslavia and the attempt which has been made since the war to reduce the wide variations in the standard of living among those regions. The decentralisation of economic management, which has made Yugoslavia so different from the other countries of Eastern Europe, has been part of that attempt. But this decentralisation has placed powerful machinery in local hands, and has increased the opportunities for those forces in the economy which would make for wider, and not narrower, regional contrasts. Thus, the Yugoslav federal authorities face a dilemma. Such are the differences between the resources, both natural and human, in, for instance, Kosovo and Slovenia that any further reduction of the degree of economic control, that is, any further movement towards a market economy, might well have the effect of encouraging greater mobility of capital within the country, but would almost certainly increase its concentration in the more-developed areas of the country and provoke further trouble in the south. However, the alternative of re-centralisation and increased direction of the location of investment by the federal government might slow economic growth still further, as well as antagonise the Croats and Slovenes. In other words, the fundamental problem of the Yugoslav state and economy - the balancing of economic growth against the demands of regional equality - which has characterised the country since the Second World War, has yet to be solved.

REFERENCES

Bergmann, T. (1975), _Farm Policies in Socialist Countries_, Saxon House, Farnborough.

Bombelles, J.T. (1968), _The Economic Development of Communist Yugoslavia_, Stanford

Čobeljić, N. and Mihailović, K. (1953), Agrarna Prenaseljenost, _Ekonomist_, 1, 16-17.

Hamilton, F.E.I. (1968), _Yugoslavia: Patterns of Economic Activity_, Bell, London.

Moore, J.H. (1980), _Growth with Self-Management_, Hoover Institution Press, Stanford.

Moore, W.E. (1954), _Economic Demography of Eastern and South-Eastern Europe_, League of Nations, Geneva.

OECD (1984), _Yugoslavia_, Paris.

Singleton, F. and Carter, B. (1982), _The Economy of Yugoslavia_, Croom Helm, London.

Sirc, L. (1979), _The Yugoslav Economy under Self-Management_, Macmillan, London.

Tomic, D. (1984), Development Problems of the Market for Agricultural Products in Yugoslavia, in _Price and Market Policies in European Agriculture_, ed. K.J.Thomson and R.M.Warren, Department of Agricultural Economics, University of Newcastle-upon-Tyne, pp.407-424.

Trevissan, D. (1985), Economy upsets homecoming, _The Times_, London 27th. June, p.6.

Tyson, L.D. (1980), _The Yugoslav Economic System and Its Performance in the 1970s_, Institute of International Studies, Berkeley.

Yugoslavia (1964), _Statistički Godišnjak SFRJ 1964_, Belgrade.

Yugoslavia (1984), _Statistički Godišnjak SFRJ 1984_, Belgrade.

Chapter 11

COMECON

R.E.H.Mellor

THE ORIGINS OF COMECON

Other contributors to this volume have dealt
almost exclusively with the issues which have faced
the various countries of Eastern Europe individually
since the Second World War, and have examined the
policies which have been adopted by each for their
space economies; and frequent reference has been
made to the influence of the Soviet Union and of its
own model of development. However, it must not be
forgotten that the aims of the Soviet Union in
extending its influence into Eastern Europe were not
only political, but also economic, and that it has
attempted both to ensure that the Soviet model of
development has been followed in each of the
countries, and also that the whole economy of the
region has been integrated in a manner which is
beneficial to the USSR. These latter efforts have
had clear effects upon the structure of, and links
between, the economies of the individual countries.
In short, there has been an attempt to plan the
pattern of the space economy not only at the
national, but also at the international, scale, and
the chief vehicle of this has been the Council for
Mutual Economic Assistance, COMECON. From a Soviet
point of view, the potential economic gain through
control of Eastern European was probably as valuable
as the political gain, for, behind Soviet strategic
and political strength, lay an economy which hardly
measured up to its new, post-war status as one of
the two super-powers. Some observers believed that
Stalin's real intention was to integrate the Eastern
European countries into the Soviet system as fully
as the Ukraine or Byelorussia, and that he would
even have been prepared to see some measure of
territorial reorganisation as a way of maximising

the economic potential of the area.

Despite disruption and weakness in the wake of war Stalin quickly found subtle opposition to his plans. In his view the new satellites wanted to follow all-too-independent national lines of development, whereas he expected complete orthodoxy in accepting Soviet models and precepts. As early as 1947 the Bulgarians made it clear they had no wish for integration to go too fast or too far. Poland made equally plain that it did not regard its own form of democracy as the same as that of the Soviet Union, and that the structure of Polish society was different and would remain so. Particularly disfavoured by Stalin were indications of a tentative move by Bulgaria and Yugoslavia towards some form of union, even though neither gave any sign of abandoning the basic philosophy and content of Marxism.

Stalin brought pressure to bear on the satellites to come into line with the orthodoxy he prescribed. Their leaderships were purged of all uncertain elements, particularly those with nationalistic tendencies, and new constitutions were drawn up which made clear their links with and dependence on the USSR, as well as confirming the unchallengeable leadership of the Communist Party. Soviet practice became the norm for all economic, political and social developments, however unsuitable it might be for the geographical, economic or social conditions in the satellite states. Moreover, in 1948 an example was made when Yugoslavia was expelled from the 'family of fraternal Communist parties', though instead of falling from power as a consequence, the dissident Tito seemed to flourish all the more.

This strengthening of Soviet control began to concern Western Europe, where it was feared that the hardships after the war might lead to repeats of the coup d'état in Czechoslovakia. This fear was given substance by Communist efforts to take control of Greece and to strengthen their already important position in Italy. Realising the urgent need to stabilise the situation in Europe by accelerating reconstruction, the United States offered all the European nations which had been affected by the war generous material aid. Not surprisingly, the offer was willingly accepted in Western Europe, and Poland and Czechoslovakia were also anxious to join, while Hungary made tentative enquiries. Sensing the prestige won by the American offer and its longer term implications, the Soviet Union set out to sabotage its success. Moscow abstained from participation, and forced Poland and Czechoslovakia - which had already accepted membership - to withdraw. No Soviet bloc country participated in the Organisation for European Economic Co-operation - the body constituted in 1948 to administer the aid programme - and they withheld realistic co-operation from the United Nations' agency, the Economic Commission for Europe, from 1949 until 1953.

Despite the strength of its position in Eastern Europe, the Soviet Union felt the need to make some compensatory gesture of aid to offset the American offer, even if only as a propaganda measure. It also saw the desirability of framing the gesture in terms of the reconstruction of Eastern Europe, thus suggesting that the Soviet Union was sacrificing some of the momentum of its own recovery to help its client states. The outcome was a surprise announcement in 1949 that the Council for Mutual Economic Assistance had been set up. The founding members were the USSR, Bulgaria, Czechoslovakia, Hungary, Poland and Romania. Albania joined within a month, though by 1961 it was to let its membership slip as it drifted into the Chinese camp, and within a year the German Democratic Republic had also joined. As Soviet relations with China soured, membership was amended in 1962 to allow Asian countries to join. The first was the Mongolian People's Republic and later Vietnam (1978), and this amendment made membership possible for Cuba in 1972. Since 1962 dissident Yugoslavia has been an associate, and membership has become possible for any state which is willing to abide by the COMECON charter, which really means accepting the Soviet interpretation of Marxism.

The speed and secrecy with which COMECON was created, and the absence of any publicity beyond the initial high-sounding, but vague, communique for several years made Western observers seek reasons for its creation other than those in that communique. One suggestion was that it pandered to the intensifying xenophobia of the ageing Stalin by providing a means of depriving the satellites of outside contacts, and thus enabling him to isolate the Soviet imperium from the world as completely as possible. It was also seen, variously, as Soviet retaliation against Western actions following the blockade of Berlin, a means to make more effective the ostracism of Yugoslavia, and as a way of strengthening centripetal tendencies - drawing the satellites closer to the Soviet Union - after the centrifugalism of 1947 and 1948. It was further suggested that Stalin's belief that the 'all-embracing world market' of pre-war times had collapsed into 'capitalist' and 'socialist' markets underlay the idea that COMECON might be appropriately used to organise the latter.

ORGANISATION AND AIMS

Whatever the objective, COMECON is faced with significant geographical, economic and social differences between its members, though in every dimension of geography, economics, natural resources, population and political influence the Council is dominated by the Soviet Union. The other members fall into several groups - one containing the more advanced economies with a considerable industrial component - Czechoslovakia, the GDR, Poland, and perhaps Hungary - and a second including the countries with strong agrarian elements - Bulgaria, Romania, Yugoslavia and, for a short period, Albania. A third, more recently admitted group includes the backward economies of the non-European members - Cuba, Mongolia and Vietnam.

COMECON is a rigid, hierarchical bureaucracy, typical of the management patterns of the socialist bloc, and decisions and directives tend to filter slowly through its cumbersome administration. The key to the development of policy is the annual meeting of the Council, attended by the premiers of member countries, their chief planners and any necessary ministerial heads, which meets in a different capital city on each occasion, and is chaired by that country. As the highest organ within the structure it makes the key decisions (Figure 11.1). Deputy premiers and their advisers attend the meetings of the Executive Committee, which usually meets quarterly and supervises all the other organisations within the Council's competence. The Executive has over twenty commissions which are subordinate to it, some of which are responsible for individual branches of industry and some for more general activities, such as foreign trade. The commissions are made up of representatives from member countries under an appropriate minister from the country in which a commission has its seat. They are all charged with promoting cooperation between members in their own field. Moscow is the seat of nine commissions, three sit in East Berlin, two each in Budapest, Prague, Sofia and Warsaw, and

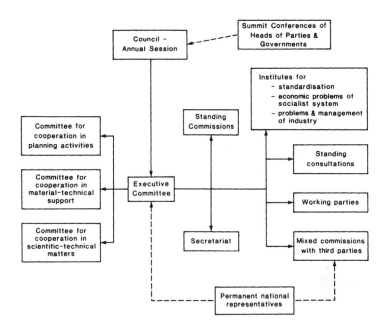

Figure 11.1 The Organisation of COMECON

one each in Bucharest and Ulan Bator. Three committees are of special importance to the work of the Executive - for Co-operation in Planning Activities, for Co-operation in Material and Technical Supplies, and for Scientific and Technical Co-operation. Their members are all of ministerial or equivalent rank, one from each member country. Finally, day-to-day work is handled by the Secretariat in Moscow. It has no executive power but is a liaison office, responsible for co-ordinating activities, including those of the Institutes of Standards, of Industrial Management Problems and of Economic Problems of the Socialist World System, as well as six or so standing conferences, various working parties and mixed commissions for cooperation with some overseas countries.

On paper each member country has equal voting rights and an equal status. Again, on paper the powers of the COMECON organs are narrowly circumscribed, for they are not allowed to make binding decisions but only recommendations, which may be accepted or rejected by a unanimous vote by

297

countries expressing an interest in them. Countries declaring their disinterest need take no further action, but may not in any way hinder or impede the others. When such recommendations are accepted, they acquire the character of mutual economic agreements.

Thus, COMECON is a large and, indeed, unwieldy structure, presenting a 'highly institutionalised dissipation of effort', and its management is further complicated by the consultations which are carried on by party leaders of the member countries outside its formal machinery. Though these in no way substitute for the annual Council meetings, they are in some instances equally significant in the decisions made.

In making comparisons between COMECON and the European Economic Community it should be recalled that COMECON was established considerably earlier and for quite different reasons. The original communique noted that the aim was to "accelerate the restoration and development of the national economies of the members", and the Leninist respect for national sovereignty has constantly been reiterated. Thus, the approach makes no allowance for several of the fundamental aims, policies and mechanisms of the European Economic Community. In particular, COMECON had no intention of creating one 'common market', as in the EEC, but rather of facilitating the participation of national economies in a socialist world market with its own pricing system. Again, unlike EEC participation in the international division of labour, with competition identifying the most advantageous locations in which to produce, COMECON has agreed to national specialisation among its members as part of a 'socialist division of labour', with agreements and planned co-ordination between its members as the keys to this process. Furthermore, whereas the members of the EEC have accepted adjustments to national economic policies in order to achieve fairer competition in such sectors as farming, energy and transport, and equalisation in social policies, the emphasis in COMECON has been on the co-ordinated planning of investment, trade and transport. Initially, COMECON made no provision for eventual monetary union, though it has been working towards more sophisticated financial accounting in trade, and even vaguely mentioning a 'collective currency' with ready transferability. On the other hand, both COMECON and the EEC have encouraged international cooperation in technical and research matters. One very important difference between the two organisations has been their attitudes towards supranational policies. COMECON has never considered such policies and has given no place to such EEC programmes as that for regional aid, which is financed by levies on the member countries but distributed by the central bodies of the EEC. Nor has it adopted such aims as the freedom for the citizens of its members to move in search of work or residence from one country to another. However, COMECON has stressed the need to remove the differences in the level of development among its members at both the national and intra-national (regional) scales.

PHASES OF DEVELOPMENT

Five stages may be discerned in the development of COMECON. In the first after its establishment in 1949 members had little opportunity other than to imitate Russia slavishly. In particular, efforts were made to create autarky on the model of the inter-war USSR, and thus the seeds of later difficulties were sown, for even the more fortunate members had relatively poor endowments of natural resources, and all had domestic markets which were too small and poor to permit significant economies of scale in most industries. Investment which could be ill spared was squandered. The more sophisticated and advanced the economy, the more unreal was the objective of autarky. However, at the same time and despite the fact that trade had been of little importance to the Soviet Union before the war, the Eastern European countries became heavily dependent on the Soviet Union as their new heavy industries were tied to Soviet supplies of coal, coke and ore, while the USSR helped to reconstruct their war-devastated economies.

Stalin's death in 1953 opened a second phase in which the new Soviet collective leadership made significant changes. The pursuit of autarky was largely abandoned, and there was a shift towards the 'socialist division of labour', in which countries were to specialise in what they could do best and trade their surpluses to meet other member's deficits; and the Soviet Union openly recognised the significance of trade by widening the basis of its own. Under Khrushchev greater recognition was given to the long-neglected agricultural sector, an emphasis which was copied in Eastern Europe; a

rigorous effort was made to refine planning
concepts; and attention was given to the search for
optimal locations for new developments.

A third phase may be recognised from 1956 when,
under pressure from Khrushchev, intensive
exploration began into ways to co-ordinate and
synchronise planning among the members. At its 1956
meeting COMECON chose to publicise itself as an
effective organisation, making progress towards
international cooperation in a manner comparable to
that in Western Europe, and by 1959 a proper Charter
had been formulated, laying out its principles and
methods of working. COMECON began to show itself to
be an operational body, with technical commissions
to oversee various sectors of its work, and there
were moves towards the creation of an international
electricity grid and arrangements for the
'rationalisation' of production between members. By
1962, after considerable pressure from the Eastern
Europeans, a final programme for the socialist
division of labour was ratified.

In 1964 COMECON entered a long fourth phase,
when national aspirations surfaced, showing that
some members were concerned lest the strenuous
efforts at overall planning and co-ordination might
fail to take full account of their special national
problems. Romania was particularly dissatisfied
with what it saw as its relatively subordinate role
in the perspective plans for the period up to 1980,
which did not, in its view, properly acknowledge its
programme of rapid industrialisation. In
particular, the Russians suggested that, in order to
gain the maximum benefit, some Romanian planning
should be on an international scale, and that some
of its proposed developments might even be moved to
the Ukraine or to Bulgaria. Romania showed its
dissent from this by agreeing to the Iron Gates
hydro-electric barrage project with Yugoslavia, and
by doing so through the medium of the Danube
Commission rather than through COMECON.
Furthermore, it expressed the view, which was also
held by some other members, that such developments
might "make sovereignty a notion without content"
and open the gates to "great power chauvinism".
Considerable unhappiness also arose from a belief
that such overall planning might limit countries'
ability to trade outside the bloc, where the most
favourable opportunities for several, and
particularly those with large agricultural sectors,
lay. Thus, COMECON passed through a major and
probably irreversible change, in which the dominance

of the USSR gave way to a measure of hegemony, though with the pace being set increasingly by the Eastern Europeans.

This change was clearly seen in the efforts which were made to improve COMECON's financial arrangements, as the crudities of the Stalinist period were slowly removed. The Eastern European countries' interest in trade encouraged them to seek more refined and sophisticated longer-term debt management and to improve ways of raising capital for major projects. However, progress towards true convertibility and effective multilateral clearing has been painfully slow, falling far behind the target dates. Furthermore, difficulties have subsequently arisen because COMECON is not beyond the influence of world events, and its monetary system has shown considerable strain as the capitalist economies have gone into recession.

This phase also coincided with what turned out to be largely abortive efforts at economic reform, though there were further shifts away from the earlier slavish imitation of Soviet practice. Considerable pressures were exerted by the Czechoslovaks and the Hungarians, both of whom were anxious to create a form of market economy, for wide-ranging reforms, and they were supported by the Romanians (who were conservatively minded in planning) and the Bulgarians (who were radical in economic reform despite giving staunch support to the Soviet Union). This group urged the transformation of COMECON into a tariff preference area. On the other hand, the USSR and Poland, with support from the GDR and Mongolia, strongly recommended planned co-ordination of the type which had been thwarted since the early 1960s by Romanian insistence on respect for national sovereignty. In the end, the Hungarians managed to introduce a measure of competitiveness into their economy, but the Czechoslovaks moved too rashly. Fearing that they wished to diverge from Marxist orthodoxy the Soviet Union occupied the country in 1968 and imposed a rigid return to former policies. The collapse of the Czechoslovak reformers gave the supporters of planned co-ordination renewed influence and credibility, and COMECON moved slowly towards wider integration.

The publication of a "Complex Programme" of development for the next fifteen to twenty years heralded the fifth phase in 1971. It was claimed that the Programme would generate a high level of economic growth, improve technical achievement and industrial and production structures, achieve an adequate output of fuels, raw materials, machinery, foodstuffs and consumer goods, and strengthen COMECON in the world economic system. These objectives were to be attained by consultation between members on basic questions of economic policy and through the co-ordination of planning activities in several key branches of industry. Cooperative specialisation was to be a significant stimulus to research and the development of new sources of raw materials, and trade was to be vigorously encouraged. Improved organisation, notably among the various technical commissions, and clarification and codification of the legal basis of COMECON, were also to be undertaken. The Complex Programme set the tempo up to the early 1980s, though progress was increasingly influenced, and slowed, by happenings in the world at large. Nevertheless, it has been claimed that this has been the decisive phase in the integration of the organisation, though some observers believe that it was superseded by a sixth phase, starting as early as 1973, which was marked by the limitation of the aim of integration to major projects only and by the toning down (either through the modification of the objectives or the lengthening of the time span) of the less readily realisable parts of the programme.

COMECON'S INFLUENCE ON THE ECONOMIC GEOGRAPHY OF EASTERN EUROPE

In view of all these changes it is relevant to ask what influence, if any, COMECON has had upon the the changing economic geography of Eastern Europe (Figure 11.2)? We shall attempt to answer this question by looking, in turn, at the development of some basic industries, at specialisation in manufacturing between the member countries, at regional development within some of them, and at transport and trade.

(1) Basic Industries

The Stalinist emphasis on autarky led to the establishment of several large iron and steel works in areas which were backward in the 1950s but which had large reserves of labour, notably Nowa Huta in Poland, Eisenhuttenstadt in the GDR, Kosice in Czechoslovakia, Dunaujvaros in Hungary and Kremikovsti in Bulgaria. A plant was even projected in Albania at Elbasan. (In contrast, the Galati

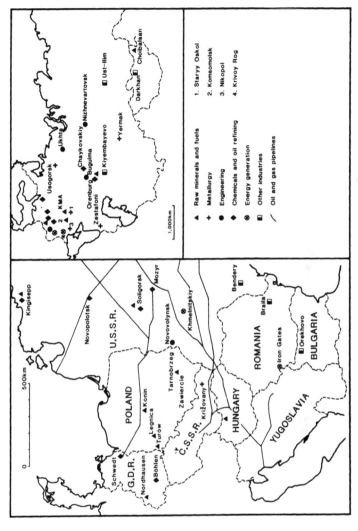

Figure 11.2
Some Joint
Projects within
COMECON.
Projects
developed
jointly between
the Soviet
Union and any
one other
member, the Mir
electricity
grid and links
involving Cuba
and the Asian
members are
omitted.
Source:
Sotrudnichestvo
Stran-Chlesnov
SEV, Map 204,
Geograficheskiy
Atlas, 4th.
ed., Moscow
1980.

plant in Romania was begun quite late, and as a 'native' project which was much criticised by the Soviet Union.) These plants were all dependent to a varying, but substantial, degree on Soviet raw materials, but with the passing of autarkic policies Intermetal was set up to rationalise the production and consumption of iron and steel in 1964. All the Eastern European countries and the Soviet Union are members, though Romania and Yugoslavia cooperate rather than participate.

COMECON has also played a significant role in the changing spatial pattern of energy supplies in Eastern Europe. Considerable emphasis was given to electricity, and as early as 1954 a decision was taken to create an international grid. Links were built between the member countries between 1955 and 1962, when the Balkans were effectively joined to the rest, and a central switching station and administration was set up in Prague. Major power stations, of which the hydro-electric barrage at the Iron Gates on the Danube has been one of the largest, were built in association with this 'united energy system', the Mir grid. However, it has been the Soviet Union which has been the major partner in the construction of nuclear power stations, as a consequence of its development work at the United Institute for Nuclear Research (set up in 1956 at Dubna, south of Moscow) and its manufacturing capacity at the Volgodonsk plant. The GDR, in particular, has benefited from this, and now has at least three nuclear stations, but Bulgaria, Czechoslovakia and Hungary have also received aid. (A Czechoslovak project for a heavy-water reactor plant of their own design was a failure.) Work has been co-ordinated through the international industrial association Interatomenergo, which was set up in 1973. According to a 1975 plan it was intended to have sixty nuclear reactors of 60,000 MW capacity by 1980 and 175, with a capacity of 175,000 MW, by 1990, but this will not be achieved.

The Eastern European countries are joined to the energy system of the western Ukraine. For instance, Hungary imports about twenty-five percent of its energy requirements and has built a special high voltage link of 750 kV (compared to the 220 kV of the basic system) in co-operation with the Russians from Vinnitsa in the Ukraine to Albertissa. A similar line is now projected from a nuclear plant at Khmelnitskiy in the Ukraine to Rzeszów in Poland; and in the early 1970s COMECON was involved in tentative talks about an 'energy bridge' from

Eastern European or Soviet power plants across the GDR to West Germany. All the installations in these networks remain national property, and the operating and maintenance costs of the links are paid for by the state across whose territory they run, but administrative costs are shared. The system is said to enhance the ability to level out peak usage internationally through the wide areal spread of the grid and the time differences between its members, and this will be further strengthened as other Soviet regional grids are linked to it. It is also claimed that the **Mir** grid promotes a rational location policy for thermal power stations, allowing them to be sited near to cheap, low-grade or otherwise untransportable fuel. Thus, it has made possible the rationalisation of energy generation and consumption on an international basis and allowed considerable economies in installed generating capacity compared to what would otherwise have been needed by the individual national systems.

The shift away from coal as a primary source of energy has been slower in Eastern than in Western Europe, but COMECON has had only a marginal interest in this branch of the fuel industry. In 1959 Poland and Hungary set up a joint company, **Haldex**, to rationalise the use of coal, to develop briquetting of low-grade fuel and to find ways of turning coal waste into building materials. Otherwise, trade has been on a pattern not dissimilar to pre-war, though the flow of coal from Upper Silesia to Central Germany, which was an internal German movement before 1945, has become an item in international trade. Poland has become a major exporter again to Eastern and Western Europe and to the Scandinavian countries from its large Upper Silesian coalfield; and Czechoslovakia has also supplied coal from its part of the Silesian field. However, a new element has been introduced with substantial shipments of coking coal from the Soviet Union, mostly from the Donbass. Moreover, the GDR and Czechoslovakia have both been sending lignite to West Germany, while the GDR, as a major lignite producer, has helped its neighbours to develop their own resources, notably Poland at Konin and Turoszów.

In contrast to coal COMECON has played a considerable part in the rising use of oil and natural gas in Eastern Europe. Several countries are producers, but their consumption has generally far outstripped their own output, and they have become dependent on supplies from the USSR. Romania, which was once a major European producer

305

and in the world league, has suffered particularly badly through being unable to increase its output and proven reserves, but it has nevertheless managed without large oil imports by rigorous economy measures.

Eastern Europe is supplied in large part through the Friendship Pipeline, which was begun in 1959, from the Ural-Volga oilfields to Poland and the GDR in the north, and to Hungary and Czechoslovakia in the south. This pipeline has provided the basis for the substantial growth of petrochemical production in all the countries which it serves, and its construction appears to have been related in part to the 'chemicals offensive', in which petrochemicals were particularly important, which was launched by Khrushchev. The large refinery and petrochemical complexes at Mozyr in Byelorussia, Płock in Poland, Schwedt in the GDR, Hrdlo-Bratislava in Czechoslovakia and Szóny in Hungary have been directly related to the pipeline. The growing demand for petroleum from Eastern Europe raised Soviet misgivings, especially after the energy crisis in 1973, and Moscow has attempted to contain that growth by pointing out that these countries cannot expect their 'favoured nation' status to continue indefinitely. This threat has made these countries more willing, if unenthusiastically so, to cooperate in joint projects with Russia. Although the Russians do not want to lose the dominant position which they hold in supplying Eastern Europe, with all its political advantages, they have wished to sell more of their surplus at enhanced prices in world markets, for, as Soviet trade has become more indebted to the West, raw materials, and particularly energy sources, have become increasingly important commodities. At the same time, the Eastern European countries have been less enthusiastic to trade for energy in markets outside COMECON because of the higher cost of doing so and their preference for spending what foreign currency they have on technical know-how and equipment. Even so, such trade has grown, and this has been reflected in the building of an oil terminal at Rostock in the GDR, which is joined by pipeline to the refinery at Schwedt, and in a more recent agreement between Czechoslovakia, Hungary and Yugoslavia to construct the <u>Adria</u> Pipeline from Omisalj (Krk) inland. The capacity of this latter line will be 34,000,000 tonnes of crude annually, of which 24,000,000 will be taken by Yugoslavia and 5,000,000 by each of the other two countries. This

compares with the 100,000,000 tonnes annual capacity
of the Friendship Pipeline.
  The Soviet Union has one of the world's richest
endowments of natural gas, and further resources
exist among the other members of COMECON. The first
COMECON gas venture was the Northern Lights pipeline
from northeast European Russia, which linked
Bulgaria, Czechoslovakia, the GDR, Hungary and
Poland between 1966 and 1975. Eastern Europe has
also drawn gas from deposits in the Ukraine by the
more modest Brotherhood Pipeline. A 2,700 kilometre
gas pipeline is being built from the southern Urals,
and under a 1974 agreement construction is being
shared between Bulgaria, Czechoslovakia, the GDR,
Hungary and Poland, with considerable Soviet aid in
planning and in gas preparation installations. The
signatories are also responsible for twenty-two
compressor stations along the route, while Romania
is paying for some special equipment which has been
bought in the West. The pipe is planned to handle
28,000 million cubic metres of gas annually, and its
capacity can be doubled if required. The COMECON
International Investment Bank took out a loan of
$600,000,000 on the Euro-Dollar market in order to
buy equipment for the project in the West, and gas
will be pumped to Western Europe via Czechoslovakia
and the GDR in return for these purchases.
  The overall energy picture in COMECON is good,
comprising about sixty percent of world reserves of
coal, forty percent of oil, almost limitless water
power and a rich endowment of natural gas. The main
difficulties arise from the exceedingly uneven
spatial distribution of these resources, with the
bulk lying in the Soviet Union and especially in its
eastern districts, in harsh and inaccessible
environments. As a result, COMECON's members
display widely varying degrees of dependence on
energy imports. Bulgaria relies for about
three-quarters of its energy requirements on outside
sources, Hungary for over forty percent,
Czechoslovakia and the GDR for about thirty percent,
while since 1970 Romania has become a small net
importer (2.5 percent). Poland, through its coal
shipments, is still a net exporter (seven percent),
and the USSR is also a net exporter, selling more
than fifteen percent of its coal, gas and petroleum
abroad.

(2) Specialisation in Manufacturing
  Specialisation agreements have also had a
substantial effect upon the pattern of manufacturing

within COMECON, and many important examples can be cited. Budapest's long association with the construction of railway equipment has led to Hungary being entrusted with the manufacture of diesel railway locomotives and railcars, besides the making of 'buses; Czechoslovakia, apart from its historic armaments industry (Škoda), specialises in machine tools and electric railway locomotives; Poland has the task of making railway goods wagons to agreed standard designs; and the GDR has been a major supplier of railway passenger coaches and refrigerated wagons. The manufacture of some machinery is even divided among COMECON members according to its type. For instance, turbines of up to fifty megawatts are made by Czechoslovakia, the GDR, Hungary, Poland and the USSR, while those of between fifty and one hundred are allocated to Czechoslovakia, the GDR and the USSR, and those of larger capacities are produced only in the Soviet Union. Similarly, whereas the Soviet Union and Poland concentrate on machinery for the mining and processing of hard coals, the GDR is the principal producer of machinery for the mining and processing of lignite. Poland and the GDR make small rolling mills, the Soviet Union produces heavy mills along with Czechoslovakia, and the Soviet Union is the only member to construct complete steel plants, though others produce individual items of equipment for them. Furthermore, after the fiasco of the self-sufficiency episode, which involved building large steelworks on greenfield sites, COMECON encouraged members with large capacities during the 1960s to become the chief suppliers to those with small industries, rather than allowing the latter to develop sufficient capacity of their own. Nevertheless, in spite of much specialisation between the members supplies of some goods are inadequate within COMECON, and this has been shown by the inability to meet the demand for large diameter pipes, and the need to seek supplies in Western markets.

Specialisation agreements are designed to obviate the difficulties posed by a series of small and relatively poor markets, in none of which can the necessary economies of scale in manufacturing be attained. Thus, in 1956-1957 the Engineering Commission drew up a plan for Eastern Europe which foresaw that the GDR would specialise in cars of up to 1,000 cc with two-stroke engines, Czechoslovakia in those of between 1,000 and 2,000 cc, and Poland in those of over 2,000 cc. The GDR was also to build lorries of up to four tonnes, while those of between four and seven tonnes were to come from Hungary and Czechoslovakia, and the latter was also to make lorries of more than seven tonnes. 'Buses with less than eighteen seats were to be built in the GDR, and larger ones in Czechoslovakia and Hungary. However, the car industry was already established in Eastern Europe before the plan was drawn up, and, perhaps for this reason, the plan has not been without difficulties. Before 1945 both Czechoslovakia and the GDR had had their own motor vehicle industries, and there was also capacity in the Soviet Union, mostly purchased in the 1930s from the USA. Moreover, after the war it also produced the pre-war Opel Olympia for a time as the Moskvich, with equipment taken as reparations from Germany, while Poland had begun producing a version of the Soviet Pobeda car. Later, Poland bought the rights in a discontinued Fiat model, and has since designed its own car, the Polonetz, all of which have been well below the engine size of the 1956 agreement. As envisaged in the plan, the GDR concentrated on two-stroke engines for its Wartburg and Trabant, and supplied them to Poland for its small Syrena. Similarly, Czechoslovakia began well with its Škoda and Tatra models, but it has fallen far behind in technology and design. Romania, in contrast, in its rush for modernisation, bought the right to produce a discontinued Renault model, renamed the Dacia; while the Russians make the discontinued Fiat 125 as the Zhiguli for the home market and as the Lada for export, and several other cars, ranging from the small Zaporozhets to the large Chayka and Volga. In general, experience in the Western world suggests that most COMECON motor vehicle plants remain sub-optimal in their scales of production; and it is, therefore, not surprising that discussion took place in the early 1970s between Czechoslovakia, the GDR and Poland about collaboration in a multi-national venture, which might also open up possibilities for the sale of components to the Western world. One major project has been carried out. This is the construction of the Kama lorry works at Naberezhnye Chelny in the Soviet Union, which was begun in 1976 and is a joint project between the USSR, Czechoslovakia, the GDR and Poland, with a planned annual capacity is of 150,000 vehicles and 200,000 diesel engines, forty percent of which are intended for COMECON members other than the USSR.

The pattern of economic geography has also been influenced by various, more limited, agreements between COMECON members (Table 11.1). These have included close cooperation between Czechoslovakia and the GDR in processing chemicals, and components have been manufactured in the GDR for assembly into electrical equipment in the Puszta village-towns of Hungary. Hungary is also involved in agreements with Poland, the GDR and the Soviet Union over aluminium production, sending its raw materials to plants as far away as the Volga and Siberia, but also to Upper Silesia and the Elbe-Saale basin – all locations where plentiful electric power is available to process bauxite and alumina in contrast to Hungary's own limited sources. There has also been a joint Soviet-Romanian project to produce alloys at Nikopol in the Ukraine and at Yermak in Kazakhstan. The GDR has a major interest in the large cotton yarn plant at Zawiercie in Poland, which was established because labour was available there. Although COMECON has discouraged the international movement of labour, Polish workers cross into the GDR to work in assembly plants in Frankfurt-on-Oder, and into the USSR to the engineering works at Novovolynsk.

One important reason behind the cooperative ventures within COMECON has been the Soviet Union's need for outside investors to help to develop its resources, but the Eastern European states have been too poor to contribute much, and encouragement has also been given to Western powers, of which the Japanese have been the most responsive. One joint COMECON project has been the development of the ores of the Kursk Magnetic Anomaly and the building of the Staryy Oskol steelworks at a site which reflects the intention of the 1971 Complex Programme to locate industries near to their raw materials. When complete, the plant will have a capacity of between 10,000,000 and 12,000,000 tonnes per annum, and a variety of related industries, using both its products and waste, will be developed around it. This classic type of territorial production complex will stimulate the economy of the southern Russian black earth belt, where industry has been relatively poorly developed. Another joint project is associated with the Kiyembayevo asbestos deposit in the southern Urals, which should cover Eastern Europe's requirements for this material. Two processing units will eventually each produce 250,000 tonnes annually, of which 180,000 will go each year to COMECON members in Eastern Europe for

twelve years, when the complex will pass to Soviet
ownership. However, the large Siberian cellulose
combine at Ust-Ilim, part of the Bratsk territorial
production complex, which also reflects the aim of
bringing industry to its raw materials, is the first
real investment project as defined in the 1971
Complex Programme, in which all the Eastern European
countries except Czechoslovakia have participated.
The total cost of the project is said to be
800,000,000 rubles, of which 330,000,000 have been
invested by the East Europeans. Each will receive
50,000 tonnes of sulphate cellulose annually for
twelve years, but at the end of the period the
installation will become Soviet property.

(3) Regional Development within Member Countries

Geographical change in Eastern Europe has come
about both from the activities of COMECON and from
the national application of long-standing Soviet
planning concepts, but it is sometimes difficult to
separate one from the other. The most readily
identifiable of the Soviet concepts is the aim of
equalising regional economic development, which has
happened at two levels - that of trying to bring the
more backward national economies up to the level of
the more advanced through COMECON's activities, and
that applied to regions within individual countries
by the different national governments. At the first
level, the more backward economies have received
considerable amounts of know-how and equipment from
their more advanced partners, particularly the
Soviet Union, but Soviet trade and aid deals have
generally increased dependence upon Moscow, and some
observers have seen this as reflecting a Soviet wish
to tie Eastern Europe to the USSR in the manner in
which its non-Slav makrorayony were made dependent
on the politically more reliable Slavonic ones in
the 1930s and 1940s. On the other hand, regional
development must be seen in the light of the
constant reiteration of the principle of national
sovereignty. It is said that
    'each socialist country maps out its own
    economic development plans based on the
    concrete conditions in the given country',
though such plans are nevertheless influenced by
'the needs and potentialities of all the socialist
countries'. These countries
    'consider it their internationalist duty to
    direct their efforts to securing a high rate of
    development in industry and agriculture in each
    country commensurate with available

Table 11.1: Forms of International Mobility within COMECON

	Type	Example
1.	Investment of funds in energy and raw materials sources	International distribution of investment to develop raw materials – iron ore, Kursk, USSR – phosphorite, Kingisepp, USSR – potash salts, Soligorsk, USSR – sulphur, Sandomierz, Poland – copper, Lower Silesia, Poland – asbestos, Kiyembayevo, USSR – nickel-cobalt, Cuba
2.	Movement of labour to raw materials	Development of timber potential in the Komi ASSR (USSR) by investment and labour from Bulgaria
3.	Movement of raw materials to particularly advantageous energy sources	Working of Hungarian bauxite at Volvograd (USSR) near to hydro-electric power

4.	Movement of investment to labour sources	Joint GDR-Polish spinning mills at Zawiercie, Poland. Development of the Ust-Ilimsk (USSR) cellulose combine.
5.	Movement of labour to investment sources	Use of labour in joint projects – specialist workers from Hungary, Poland, USSR and GDR in building the power station at Hagenwerder, GDR
6.	Movement of investment to augment other investment	Credits of the International Investment Bank (Comecon) for construction of modern industrial plants of mutual interest to partners

Adapted from Kohlmey, G. (1973), p. 166.

potentialities, progressively equalising economic development levels'.
Wherever the balance of influence lies, it is clear that, unlike the European Community, there are no investment funds available for regional aid, and that in COMECON finance comes indirectly through individual projects which have been agreed jointly between partners, almost all of which have been related to industry, and have usually involved the Soviet Union to some degree of other.

Nevertheless, COMECON projects have greatly assisted the removal of regional inequalities in several of the countries of Eastern Europe and influenced the changing pattern of their economic geography. For instance, in the GDR major new industrial projects on greenfield sites and developments like the port of Rostock and the 'investment complexes' at Schwerin and Neubrandenburg have stimulated the economies of the largely agricultural north and centre of the country, and between 1965 and 1976 industrial production in the northern regions grew by 220 percent compared to 188 percent in the south. However, by the end of the 1970s, perhaps under the influence of the sixth phase of COMECON, emphasis had shifted to the consolidation of efforts to 'rationalise and intensify' existing capacity before embarking on any new spatial shifts.

Hungary has also made great progress in industrialisation, and after 1956 new industrial locations developed. Between 1956 and 1970 over fifty percent of all investment went into industry, and consequently as much as four-fifths of all industrial capacity belongs to the years since 1945. More than 150 new industrial locations include major greenfield developments undertaken with help from COMECON, and the northern part of the central uplands and the lands west of the Danube (Dunantúl) have profited, but much the larger part of the country, especially the Great Plain, still remains poorly provided with industry.

Bulgaria, in contrast, was one of the economically weaker members of COMECON at its foundation, but it has had the highest rate of economic growth after Romania. Development was concentrated first on a few centres of basic industry and mining, and particular emphasis was given to increasing energy production as a motor for the economy and as a locational factor for subsequent development. Soviet aid has been given principally for heavy industry and engineering, and the GDR has assisted in the development of chemical production. Because of the importance of establishing a basic framework of heavy industry, the older industrial centres continued to be very important, and the bulk of industrial production was concentrated in three agglomerations. That around Sofia and Pernik alone accounts for half of all coal production, forty percent of ore output, all pig iron, forty percent of the engineering industry and thirty percent of textile production. However, completely new industrial centres have also been built upon the chemical industry and heavy metallurgy in other areas. Nevertheless, agriculture remains a major sector of the economy over much of the country.

(4) Transport

COMECON has also proved to be successful in integrating the transport systems of Eastern Europe. In the case of the railways most attention has been given to freight; major super-trunk routes have been developed between Berlin, Warsaw and Moscow and between the Baltic and Black Seas; and key lines, such as those between Moscow and Prague, Warsaw and Prague, Prague and Budapest, and between the Donbass, Lvov and Budapest, among others, have been electrified. A common wagon pool and standard designs for freight wagons have helped speed freight turnround, and German technology has developed means of rapidly changing the bogies on coaches and wagons to allow easy passage between Russian broad-gauge and European standard-gauge tracks. Soviet influence is evident in the use of the 'dispatcher system' on several railways. Railway matters are co-ordinated through the COMECON equivalent of the Union Internationale des Chemins de Fer, the OSSHD or Organisatsiya Sotrudnichestvo Zheleznykh Dorog.

Soviet influence was also reflected until recently in the backward position of road haulage throughout Eastern Europe, but the Complex Programme of 1971 has given some impetus to road development. Most countries now have plans to transfer the bulk of movement of under eighty kilometres from rail to road, and road haulage has developed with the greatest vigour in the Balkans and Danubia for the carriage of perishables to Western European markets and for transit traffic between Western Europe and the Middle East. In 1976 COMECON members agreed to the construction of four arterial motorways linking Marienborn, Berlin and Warsaw with Moscow; Rostock, Berlin, Prague, Budapest and Bucharest with

Constanţa; Gdańsk, Warsaw and Bratislava with Budapest; and Moscow and Bucharest with Sofia.

In Stalin's day there was talk of creating a 'waterway ring' by joining the Dnepr via the Vistula to the Elbe, and thus along the Oder to the Danube. However, the recently completed Romanian Danube-Black Sea Canal, which was agreed by the International Danube, Commission, has not met with Soviet approval, even though the Commission has been firmly under Russian influence since 1945. Nevertheless, interest in inland waterways may revive with the completion of the Rhine-Main-Danube Canal in West Germany, which will give a new lease of life to Danube shipping.

COMECON has aimed to carry at least fifty percent of all its seaborne trade in its own ships, and has set up several international agencies to co-ordinate shipping. State shipping lines cooperate in particular traffics - for example, the GDR and Poland co-ordinate shipping from the Baltic to East and West Africa and to South America - and a Standing Conference of all members reviews questions of maritime policy. The COMECON mercantile marine is composed of modern ships under the flags of member countries and mostly built in the Eastern bloc, and agreements were reached in the early 1960s on standard designs for series production.

Air transport throughout COMECON is principally provided by Aeroflot, the Soviet airline, which is claimed to be the world's largest carrier. Nevertheless, each country has its own small national airline - a matter of prestige in the modern world - usually flying on domestic and a few international routes. Similarly, although light aircraft are built in Czechoslovakia and Poland, aircraft construction is dominated by the Soviet Union.

Thus, much has been done to improve and integrate the transport networks of Eastern Europe through COMECON, but in all this much more interest has been shown in easing the international movement of goods than of people. Indeed, visa and other regulations in Eastern Europe are usually cumbersome and bureaucratic, even for travel by citizens of one COMECON member to another. Individual non-official travellers appear to be discouraged, and tourists are preferred in organised groups. In some countries, most notably the Soviet Union, some areas are closed to the nationals of other countries, and COMECON has done little to promote tourism. However, most countries have developed facilities both for their own citizens and for visitors from other countries; visitors from the West have been encouraged in organised tours as a source of hard currencies; and some package holidays including more than one country have been provided by the official East European tourist agencies.

(5) Trade

Despite Stalin's disregard for trade, it has become a significant element in COMECON relationships, both within the bloc and with the West. Indeed, the extent to which such trade occurs could be taken as a measure of the degree to which the countries of Eastern Europe and the USSR have been able to benefit from closer economic integration. Immediately after the war Eastern European trade was sharply reoriented, and the area became heavily dependent on the Soviet Union, but during the 1960s the relaxation of tensions with the West introduced a new element. Countries sought to increase their economic efficiency by purchasing Western equipment and know-how, and this was facilitated by the readiness of Western countries to give generous credits. More recently, however, COMECON trade has been influenced by the general stagnation in the world economy and the strong inflationary tendencies, and the organisation and pricing of intra-bloc trade still require considerable adjustment to bring them closer to general world practice.

Because Stalin was afraid of a schism in his new imperium, the economic relations and trade of Eastern Europe after the war took on a 'radial' pattern, in which Moscow was the focal point and links were established separately with each satellite country. Links between the satellites were given little encouragement unless they were of direct benefit to the Soviet economy, and even now trade between them and the Soviet Union is still more important. In a way, this is to be expected both because of the relatively greater economic power and resource endowment of the Soviet Union and because of its political and military strength. Of course, there have been fluctuations in the share of each member's trade with the Soviet Union over time, as economic and political conditions have varied, but in general the level has remained within fairly close limits. Sharp falls were recorded after Stalin's death, and some distortions occurred when socialist bloc prices failed to respond as quickly as world prices to the oil crisis in 1973-1974, but

these have been rectified and more frequent price
reviews have been undertaken in order to improve
co-ordination with changes in world markets.
However, the future pace of integration of the
members' economies will depend in large part upon
the balance which is struck between this centipetal
trend towards the Soviet Union and the centifugal
tendency for individual members to trade with
Western countries – a tendency which depends in part
upon the willingness, or otherwise, of Western
countries to grant credits and participate in joint
projects. However, the importance of COMECON in
world trade should not be overestimated. With about
forty percent of world industrial output, it has
only about fourteen percent of world trade.

Certain common elements appear in the
composition of the trade between COMECON countries.
Among the Eastern European members manufactured
goods commonly account for a greater share of
exports than they do of imports, whereas fuels and
raw materials contribute a much larger share of the
imports, except in the cases of Poland and Romania,
which were energy exporters until the 1960s, and the
Soviet Union, whose exports of fuels and raw
materials are specially large. The Eastern European
countries have also been increasing the share of
consumer goods in their exports, but such goods have
been poorly represented amongst imports – a
situation which again is almost the reverse of the
pattern for Soviet trade. Bulgaria, Hungary and
Romania have been important exporters of foodstufts,
and food has also been a significant element in
Polish exports. The Soviet Union has exported basic
foodstuffs, particularly grains and beet sugar, but
these exports have been erratic, and bad harvests
have frequently forced it to seek grain imports from
the Western world, and especially from North
America. Most COMECON countries have sought a high
level of self-sufficiency in foodstuffs, but this is
under strain from rising living standards.
Moreover, trade with Cuba has created a difficulty,
for its major export to other members – cane sugar –
has upset their domestic production of beet sugar,
and the re-export of Cuban sugar has provoked
criticism from the Third World.

Soviet exports dominate COMECON's trade in
fuels and minerals, but Czechoslovakia and Poland
are also important exporters of bituminous coal and
coke. These two countries also export modest
amounts of lignite, but the GDR is the main lignite
exporter, though its once large exports to West

Germany have declined as the fuel base there has changed. Bauxite and alumina move from Hungary for processing in Poland, the GDR and the Soviet Union. Romania, in contrast, has always resented COMECON plans for it to remain chiefly as a supplier of raw materials, and it has ceased to be the major source of petroleum that it was in pre-war times, though it does send natural gas to Hungary. The Eastern European countries are, as noted, all dependent on Soviet oil and gas supplies, though these have also been of increasing importance in their trade with countries outside the bloc.

A large part of COMECON trade is in machinery and industrial equipment, and the specialisation agreements have become important, not only in colouring the pattern of movement of specific commodities, but also in increasing the share of machinery and industrial equipment in total trade from around sixty-five to over seventy-five percent. In the later 1970s the Soviet Union was tending to replace imports of these commodities from Eastern Europe by buying in Western markets, though it offset the decline by enhanced purchases of consumer goods. However, because of rising indebtedness during the 1980s problems of financing imports from the West may encourage a rejuvenation of the trade in machinery between COMECON countries. Such a trend will probably favour items designed to Western standards and manufactured either on licence or in cooperation with Western firms. However, trade has been hampered as a result of the Stalinist autarky phase by the tendency of Eastern European countries to produce the same items, thus restricting the openings for exchange, and so, despite the specialisation and other agreements, offers for machinery and industrial equipment are more often competitive than complementary. (In the case of consumer goods the reverse is generally true, therefore tending to encourage trade.) However, it is worth noting that the shares in trade of chemicals, synthetic materials, rubber goods, fertilisers and even building materials have generally grown.

Nevertheless, trade relations between COMECON members have not always been cordial. After Stalin's death it was openly admitted that the Soviet Union had overcharged some countries, notably Poland, for exports and underpaid for imports, and other countries have complained of unfair Soviet trade practices. Pricing has apparently often been 'political' and on the basis of what the trade would bear, sometimes discriminating in favour of COMECON members, but sometimes in favour of Western trading partners. On the other hand, the Soviet Union has complained about the quality, design, poor delivery and servicing of equipment from Eastern Europe - the same shortcomings as those voiced by Western traders about imports from COMECON. Because of the difficulty of trading with the West in machinery and manufactured equipment both the Eastern European members and the Soviet Union have sought to expand the intra-bloc market for these products. However, COMECON members have been anxious to buy Western equipment and technology in order to modernise their industries and solve the problems of poor quality and design. Moreover, major deals can usually be completed with a Western firm inside nine months compared to up to three years with another COMECON member.

THE PROBLEMS OF COMECON

Common difficulties face the members of COMECON in stimulating the overall economy of the bloc. The need for economic reform is generally recognised, but there is a fear that reforms of the type and scale which would truly improve productivity and efficiency, and allow rapid modernisation, would dangerously upset the political balance. For instance, it might no longer be possible to conceal unemployment, which is now achieved quite successfully, and reforms might generate demands of the type voiced by Solidarity in Poland. Underlying the interest in purchasing Western technology is the hope that it will enable necessary economic objectives to be attained without radical reforms. However, the hectic and unco-ordinated rush to buy such technology, backed by generous Western credits, has placed some members in the dangerous situation of owing vast sums to Western bankers, which they cannot now repay on the agreed terms. But this potential insolvency is also a danger to the West, for, if that debt becomes so huge that COMECON members cannot honour their obligations, Western creditor nations may be powerless to enforce repayment. Nevertheless, feverish trading with the West has been a potent factor in slowing down the pursuit of integration. On the other hand, Western inflation has made most members more dependent on each other and especially on the Soviet Union, for the COMECON pricing system still makes such trade cheaper than that with Western countries, and a wider ranging integration of member economies could be beneficial, particularly for the more advanced countries. However, there is always the fear that such a trend would erode still further the remaining political freedoms, and mistrust that integration, specialisation and standardisation are all covert means by which the Soviet Union can consolidate its imperialist hold.

A common dilemma is how to keep the population content. Living standards have risen, but there are expectations of still better things to come - a belief which is constantly emphasised by party propaganda - and appreciable pressure for rapid and substantial improvements, perhaps generated by a growing knowledge of the material quality of life in the West. These aspirations may be dashed as members shift scarce resources to the industrial sector and to exports to pay off their vast foreign debts, and this could create an unhappy, disillusioned population, with many dangerous political consequences. In countries such as Czechoslovakia the government would no doubt like to allow more consumer goods, but they are afraid to do this for, in an environment in which there are still marked variations in living standards between member countries, gains in one country may not always be viewed sympathetically in the others.

SELECT BIBLIOGRAPHY

Bethkenhagen, J. and Machowski, H. (1976), Integration im Rat für Gegenseitige Wirtschaftshilfe, 2nd ed., Berlin.
Billy, J. et al.(1978), Comecon - Progress and Prospects, Colloquium, 1977, NATO Directorate of Economic Affairs, Brussels.
Blažek, M., Demek, J. et al. (1972), Sozialistische Staaten Europa, Teil VI, Thematische Karten zur Welt von Heute, Kiel.
CMEA Secretariat (1969), A Survey of 20 years of the Council of Mutual Economic Assistance, Moscow.
Dawisha, K. and Hanson, P. (1981), Soviet-East European Dilemmas, London.
Dienes, L. and Shabad, T. (1979), The Soviet Energy System, New York.
Dubrowsky, H-J. (1975), Die Zusammenarbeit der RGW-Länder im Transportwesen, Berlin.

Dyakin, B.G. and Pankov, B.G. (1978), _SEV i problemy integratsii_, Moscow.

Ellis, J. (ed.) (1979), _Regional Development in the USSR_, NATO Economics and Information Directorate, Brussels.

Ellis, J. (ed.) (1980), _Economic Reforms in Eastern Europe and Prospects for the 1980s_, NATO Economics and Information Directorate, Brussels.

Ellis, J. (ed.) (1981), _CMEA i Energy 1980-1990_, NATO Economics and Information Directorate, Brussels.

Ellis, J. (ed.) (1982), _The CMEA Five-Year Plans (1981-1985) in a new Perspective_, NATO Economics and Information Directorate, Brussels.

Feigin, J.G. (1956), _Standortverteilung der Produktion im Kapitalismus und Sozialismus_, Berlin.

Forster, H. (1980), _Zur Raumwirksamkeit der Integration in Osteuropa_, Fragenkreise 23546, Paderborn.

Gai, C. (ed.) (1974), _The Politics of Modernization in Eastern Europe - Testing the Soviet Model_, New York.

Harke, H. and Dischereit, M. (1980), _Geographische Aspekte der Sozialistischen ökonomischen Integration_, Gotha.

Hoffmann, E. (1961), _COMECON - der gemeinsame Markt in Osteuropa_, Opladen.

Kaser, M. (1967), _COMECON - Integration Problems of the Planned Economies_, RIIA, London.

Kaser, M. and Radice, E.A. (eds.) (1984), _The Economic History of Eastern Europe 1919-1975_, 2 vols., Oxford.

Kohlmey, G. (1973), _Vergesellschaftung und Integration im Sozialismus_, Berlin.

Lascelles, D. (1976), _COMECON to 1980_, London.

Ledovskiy, S.I. (1975), _Ekonomicheskaya Geografiya Sotsialisticheskikh Stran Evropy_, Moscow.

Levinson, C. (1980), _Vodka-Cola_, Horsham.

Lorenz, P. (1978), _Multinationale Unternehmen sozialistischer Länder - die internationalen Wirtschaftsorganisationen im RGW_, Baden-Baden.

Marer, P. and Montias, J.M. (eds.) (1980), _East European Integration and East-West Trade_, Bloomington.

Marczewksi, J. (1974), _Crisis in Socialist Planning - Eastern Europe and the USSR_, London.

Mellor, R.E.H. (1975), _Eastern Europe - A Geography of the Comecon Countries_, London.

Mellor, R.E.H. (1976), Merchants from the new Near East, _New Society_, 17 June 1976, 628-629.

Meshcheryakov, V. et al. (1975), _SEV = Printsipy, Problemy, Perspektivy_, Moscow.

Morgenstern, K. (1984), _Spezialisierung und Kooperation zwischen den RGW-Ländern_, Berlin.

Okey, R. (1982), _Eastern Europe, 1970-1980_, London.

Oleynik, I.P. et al. (1977), _Ekonomicheskaya Integratsiya i materialnotekhnicheskaya Baza Stran SEV_, Moscow.

Popov, I.V. (1969), _Osnovnyye Napravleniya tekhnicheskogo Progressa v Stranakh SEV_, Moscow.

Potzsch, H. et al.(1977), _COMECON - der Rat für Gegenseitige Wirtschaftshilfe (RGW), Informationen zur Politischen Bildung_ 197, Bonn.

Schaefer, H.W. (1972), _Comecon and the Politics of Integration_, London.

Shchetinin, V.P. (1977), _Ekonomicheskaya Integratsiya Stran-chlenov SEV_, Moscow.

Straszewicz, L. (1974), _Geografia Ekonomiczna Europejskich Krajów Socjalistycznych_, Warsaw.

Vikentev, A.I. and Miroshnichenko, B.P. (1969), _Proizvodstvo i Potrebleniye v Stranakh SEV_, Moscow.

Wilczynski, J. (1974), _Technology in COMECON_, London.

Yevstigneyev, R.N. (ed.) (1977), _Kompleksnye Programmy Razvitiya v Stranakh SEV_ Moscow.

Zimm, A. (1975), Zu einigen Phänomenen der Herausbildung einer internationalen sozialistischen Standortverteilung, _Petermanns Mitteilungen_, 119, 1-6.

Chapter 12

THE ROLE OF PLANNING

Andrew H. Dawson

INTRODUCTION

This book has been concerned with a group of
countries whose economic and social development
since the Second World War has been bound up with
planning. Chapter 2 described, amongst other
things, the revolutionary nature of this system of
economic management as it was adopted in the Soviet
Union under Stalin before the war and extended to
Eastern Europe after 1945; and Chapters 3 to 10 have
shown how it has been used since then to tackle a
variety of problems by the governments of those
countries. Economic planning at the international
level has also been considered, as it has affected
the countries through COMECON, in Chapter 11.
   The approach of the book has been to examine
each of the countries in turn for, as should now be
apparent, their circumstances have varied very
widely, and the policies and procedures which they
have employed have also been far from uniform.
Nevertheless, a more general, comparative assessment
of the role of planning in their development should
be made, and this will be attempted here, using two
approaches. Firstly, a brief account will be given
of the type and extent of the changes which have
occurred in their economies, by way of showing what
was achieved in the first forty years after the war;
and secondly, an attempt will be made to show what
role planning may have played within those changes.

CHANGE IN EASTERN EUROPE SINCE 1945

   There is no doubt that great economic and
social improvements have been made in all the
countries of Eastern Europe since the war. War-time

damage has been repaired, and poverty and backwardness much reduced. These improvements have taken place in conjunction with, and in part as a result of, great structural shifts in their economies and in the associated spatial arrangement of production and settlement (Table 12.1). The surplus of rural labour, which restricted the possibilities for development between the two world wars, has been largely removed; and everywhere, except in Albania, agriculture has declined in absolute terms as a source of employment, in spite of large increases in population which have come largely from the rural communities. Only in East Germany has the population not grown, and even there a considerable shift has occurred out of farming. Great extensions of mining and manufacturing have been achieved, thus raising to record levels the output of goods of many types. The proportion of the labour force in manufacturing, mining and construction has increased substantially, even in those countries - East Germany and Czechoslovakia - in which it was already high at the start of the period; and, in contrast to the position before 1939, industry, rather than agriculture, has become the dominant sector in terms of employment in all except the Albanian economy. Nor should the growth of service employment be ignored, for it too has risen sharply in all parts of Eastern Europe. In short, the economies of Bulgaria, Hungary, Poland and Yugoslavia probably changed more in the forty years after the end of the war than in any comparable period in their history, and passed through something akin to the "take-off" and "drive-to-maturity" stages of Rostow's model of economic growth (Rostow 1960). Moreover, it is apparent that there have been great social changes, some of which have followed from this economic restructuring. Urban standards of education and health care and mains services have been extended into the countryside; illiteracy, which was rife in many rural areas before the war, has almost entirely disappeared; and fertility rates are now much reduced and show a much narrower range of values across Eastern Europe than previously.

This development has been accompanied by a significant restructuring of the space economies of Eastern Europe. For instance, local economies have been diversified by the exploitation and processing of natural resources and agricultural products in what were formerly rural areas, by the location of footloose industries in small towns, and by the

development of tourism. Public transport and tnat
provided by enterprises for their employees, which
have been greatly extended, linking villages to
towns as never before, have enabled large numbers of
people living in the countryside to transfer from
farm to tactory or office work, even though this has
often involved long-distance commuting; and the
number of people moving to the towns has been so
great that the proportion of the population living
there has grown substantially in all the countries,
while that in the rural areas has been stationary or
falling, except in Albania.

Nevertheless, problems persist. At the
national level it would appear that there are still
marked differences between the average standards of
living in the various countries, and their rank
order according to the level of development has been
little changed. East Germany and Czechoslovakia
still appear to enjoy higher standards than the
others, as measured by Gross National Product per
capita, followed by Hungary and Bulgaria, while
Romania and especially Albania remain the 'poor men'
of Eastern Europe.

Contrasts have also survived within the
countries - a fact to which attention has been drawn
in a number of the chapters. International
comparisons of such contrasts are not easy to make,
chiefly because regional data about, say, levels of
income or household amenities are not available on
comparable bases for many of the countries, and in
some cases not at all. However, Table 12.2
indicates something of what has been achieved in one
area in which comparisons are possible, namely, the
restructuring of the urban hierarchy. In
particular, the dominance of the capital cities, as
measured by their proportions of the urban
population, has been weakened in all except Albania,
although in some cases the decline has been very
small; and secondly, the proportion of the urban
population in the largest settlements has also
tended to fall, except in East Germany, thus
indicating that in general urban growth has been
successfully dispersed to the smaller and
middle-sized towns.

These trends are also displayed in Figure 12.1,
where the chief settlements in each country are
compared with the rank-size rule over the period
since the end of the war. The rule states that
there is a tendency for the population of a
settlement to be related to that of the largest in
the country, and to be equal to the population of

327

Table 12.1: Some Indicators of Post-War Development in Eastern Europe

| Country | Population (thousands) | | Percentage of Workforce in | | | | | |
| | | | Agriculture[10] | | Industry[10] | | Services | |
	1946	1983	Late 1940s	1982	Late 1940s	1982	Late 1940s	1982
Albania	1,132	2,840	71[5]	61[7]	18[5]	25[7]	11[5]	14[7]
Bulgaria	7,003	8,940	56[5]	37[7]	25[5]	39[7]	19[5]	24[7]
Czechoslovakia	12,916	15,420	38	14	37	46	25	40
GDR	18,057	16,700	24[2]	10[7]	45[2]	50[7]	31[2]	40[7]
Hungary	9,042	10,690	53	23	26	40	21	37
Poland	23,959	36,570	57[2]	31	23[2]	37	20[2]	32
Romania	15,791	22,550	67[5]	29	15[5]	44	28[5]	27
Yugoslavia	15,679[1]	22,860	67[4]	29[7]	15[4]	35[7]	18[4]	36[7]

Country	Percentage of Population in Towns		Crude Birth Rates per Thousand of Population		GNP per Capita in US Dollars in 1980
	Late 1940s	1982	Late 1940s	1982	
Albania	N.A.	38	38.5[3]	27.8	840[6]
Bulgaria	25	66	25.6	14.0[8]	4150
Czechoslovakia	49	64	22.5	15.2	5820
GDR	68	77	13.0[9]	14.4	7180
Hungary	36	55	18.1	12.5	4180
Poland	31	58	29.3	19.4	3900
Romania	23	51	23.8	15.3	2340
Yugoslavia	16	44	28.2	16.7	2620

1 1947   2 1950   3 1951   4 1953   5 1960   6 1979   7 1980
8 1981   9 Without East Berlin
10 Agriculture includes fishing and forestry, Industry includes construction

Sources: U.N., Demographic Yearbook 1948, Tables 1, 8, 14; 1957, Tables 3, 6; 1983, Tables 5, 6, 9; U.N., Statistical Yearbook 1956, Table 6; 1982, Table 21; World Bank, World Development Report 1982, Table 1; 1984, Tables 21, 22.

the largest divided by the rank of the settlement in question. Thus, the second settlement is expected to have a population which is half that of the largest, the third settlement one that is a third, and so on. The rule is not an explanation of why settlements should be of these relative sizes, but, when settlement size and rank are both logarithmically transformed, it produces a straight-line relationship between them of the type shown in Figure 12.1. However, this is not the only relationship which is possible, and three others are shown in the first graph in the figure. For instance, in a planned economy, with a clear hierarchy of urban functions and an associated set of settlements, a stepped pattern might be expected to occur. Alternatively, in a highly-centralised economy most economic activity and population might be concentrated in the capital, which might then be a 'primate' city; or, conversely, in a federal state, in which several autonomous governments were each located in different cities, these cities might all be of similar size.

These theoretical rank-size patterns may be compared with those for each of the countries, which are shown in Figure 12.1. That of East Germany, for instance, was very close to the straight-line relationship in both 1946 and 1984, those of Hungary and Romania show evidence of primacy, and those of Poland and Yugoslavia of strong regional centres. In general, however, it would appear that there has been some weakening of primacy in all those countries in which it was in evidence – Bulgaria, Czechoslovakia, Hungary and Romania – since the war, thus indicating some success in the building up of other towns and cities, and the resistance of the tendency for economic activity and population to be drawn to capital cities. But these changes should not be taken to indicate that the chief lineaments of the spatial arrangement of the economies have been radically altered. Despite all the attempts to build up new centres of alternative employment in rural areas and to broaden the attraction of small towns, those lineaments have proved to be remarkably stable, being altered only in degree rather than in kind. The major industrial areas and cities have continued to attract large shares of the available investment; have remained the dominant foci of economic and social activities; and have continued to grow economically and in population. In particular, their position has been strengthened by improvements in the transport network, for these

Table 12.2: The Deconcentration of the Urban Population in Eastern Europe

| Country | Population of Largest Town as a Percentage of Total Urban Population | | Population of Largest Towns | | | Dates | |
	(1)	(2)	No. of towns	As a Percentage of Total Urban Population (1)	(2)	(1)	(2)
Albania	16	22	4	53	43	1938	1979
Bulgaria	21	19	10	49	47	1946	1984
Czechoslovakia	15	12	16	37	36	1950	1984
GDR	10	9	18	33	35	1946	1984
Hungary	39	35	12	60	59	1960	1984
Poland	8	7	39	56	50	1950	1982
Romania	28	17	24	64	54	1948	1984
Yugoslavia	13	8	24	60	39	1954	1979

Note: The number of towns used is proportional to the size of the national population at the second date.

Sources: Statistical Yearbooks of the various countries; U.N., Demographic Yearbook, various years.

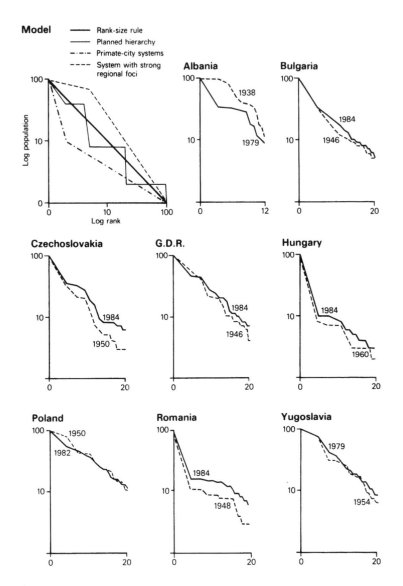

Figure 12.1 The Changing Rank-Size Relationship of Towns in Eastern Europe since the Second World War

332

have tended to upgrade or duplicate the most heavily used routes in all the countries, rather than to create major new foci within their space economies.

Furthermore, economic development has created some new types of problem region. Many rural areas are now characterised by an ageing population, if not a falling one; have proved to be unattractive as places of work for doctors, teachers and other young professionals; still lag behind the towns in basic amenities; and, in areas of falling population, are losing such services as they have. Many of the major industrial settlements now suffer from severe air pollution, housing shortages and growing traffic congestion. And, thirdly, in rural areas around the major cities and in scenic regions in all parts of Eastern Europe, except Albania, second homes have sprung up and much existing housing has been converted to recreational use, often in an unplanned and illegal manner.

It should also be noted that the transport networks, which link raw material sources to places of manufacture and markets, and places of residence to those of work, pose problems in most, if not all, of the countries. Huge increases have been required in the provision of transport services as a result of the development which has taken place, but investment in the transport sector has not been adequate, and, for this reason, the overall growth of the economies has been slowed (Ambler et al.1985, pp.xii-xviii).

Thus, great achievements have occurred in the planned economies of Eastern Europe - though it must be acknowledged that equally great progress has been made during the same period in several countries elsewhere which have not adopted this system of management - but some of the inherited problems have not yet been solved, and new ones have been created. Why should this be? For an answer we must turn to the second approach of this chapter and examine the role of planning within the wider context of decision-making about the spatial pattern of investment in the Eastern European countries since the war.

THE CONTRIBUTION OF PLANNING

Any assessment of the contribution of planning to the development of Eastern Europe since 1945 must acknowledge that it has been subject to a number of powerful constraints and that its 'ability to deliver' has been limited. Few of the plans which have been officially approved have been implemented in the exact form in which they were originally set out, and there have been several spectacular abandonments by governments of Five Year Plans which have proved to be unrealistic. There has also been a long-term trend for growth rates within plans to fall, despite the obvious wish of planners and governments to achieve the fastest possible increase in living standards. Some reasons for these problems have been suggested by Kornai (1980) in his "macrodynamic model of the socialist economy", but there has been no comparable model describing the spatial development of the centrally-planned economy which might offer a framework within which the role and achievements of regional, urban and environmental planning could be assessed. However, such a model is clearly necessary for, as was noted in Chapter 2, official plans tend to contain a wide variety of aims, all of which may be desirable, but many of which involve competition for limited resources and may even be contradictory. It must be assumed that the real decisions about the purpose and location of investments by communist governments are made behind the scenes in debates between pressure groups. Furthermore, it is clear that the economies of Eastern Europe are subject to external constraints and shocks as a result of their links with the USSR and their integration into the world market, and that these also affect the ability of planners to achieve their aims.

One of the chief debates which has occurred since the war within the government machines of Eastern Europe has been between those in favour of economic growth, on the one hand, and the regional, local and environmental planners, who have been more concerned with the pattern and effect of that growth, on the other. Several of the country chapters have drawn attention to the primacy which was given to growth and investment, and in particular, to the growth of the so-called 'productive' sectors of the economies in the late 1940s and 1950s, and to the scant and simplistic attention which was paid to territorial planning, as evidenced by the espousal of the idea of the 'even industrialisation' of countries. Since that time, regional, urban and, later, environmental planning have acquired greater status, but it would still appear from the scale of long-distance commuting, the shortage and small average size of urban dwellings, and the very severe pollution of air and water in many parts of Eastern Europe that the growth lobby is more powerful than that of the spatial and environmental planners.

One expression of this power has been in the continuing concentration of investment in the major industrial and urban centres. Kowalski (1984) has argued, in the case of Poland, that the political and spatial organisation of society are deeply intertwined, and that this leads almost inevitably to the concentration of investment in the regions which are already most developed. He notes that the status of those in the national communist parties depends upon the strength of their local base, and that it is the First Secretaries of the regional communist parties in the 'strong', that is, the industrial, regions who are usually the members of the central committees of the national parties, the nomenklatura, which make the major investment decisions, while those from 'weaker', agricultural regions are not. He also argues that, in the centrally-planned economy, in which so much attention is given to the fulfillment and over-fulfillment of output targets, leaders of industry have an incentive to maximise output, and will do so at the places at which increases may most easily and cheaply be achieved. These places are often the existing centres of production, and therefore industrial officials have both the reason and the means to override, if necessary, authorities in rural areas who might wish investment to be diverted to their regions. Thus, the wishes of officials from 'strong' regions and of industrial officials for further growth often coincide and favour the concentration of all types of investment, including that for 'Research and Development' and 'New Technology' in the existing industrial conurbations and major cities; and Sweeney (1984) has offered evidence which, in his view, illustrates how similar tendencies in the USSR are leading to a spatial pattern of economic activity in that country which is more in keeping with those of western, capitalist economies than the earlier hopes for a more even distribution of development.

The activity of planners is also constrained by the strategic needs of the country, both economic and military. In the case of Eastern Europe, these appear to have been determined to a large extent by the Soviet Union, often working through COMECON. These needs seem to have dictated the proportion of investment which must be placed in the basic, heavy industries, and have thereby influenced the location of economic activity, tying much of it to coalfields, and they have also resulted in the specialisation agreements between the members of COMECON which were outlined in Chapter 11. However, the influence of the USSR upon the general structure of the economies of Eastern Europe may have been even more pervasive. For instance, East Germany and the Czech Lands were already industrialised before 1939, and there is no reason to believe that their economies would not have progressed as those of West Germany and Austria have done since the war to a stage at which services are now their chief source of employment, and modern, light, consumer industries are a much more important part of the manufacturing sector than before. But this has not happened. Indeed, structural change has been rather slow. Developments in the USSR, however, have been more rapid, and have now raised the structure of that country's economy to something similar to those in the most developed of the Eastern European countries. Compton has drawn attention in Chapter 7 to the fact that employment in manufacturing in Hungary is now stagnant, and that that country is entering a post-industrial stage, but it is not clear what this will mean for economies of the Soviet type, and in particular what types of future economic development the USSR will encourage.

The behaviour of the public and of the surviving private-enterprise element within the economies of Eastern Europe may also deflect the spatial development of these economies from the paths which the planners might wish. For instance, several of the country chapters have made reference to the difficulties which planners have encountered in their attempts to entice people to, and hold them in, some rural areas, and to control the development of second homes; and Węcławowicz (1981, p.179) has claimed that there is evidence in the cities of Poland to suggest that

> "in spite of the existence of limiting factors imposed by the political system, the action of the classical ecological processes characteristic of capitalist cities...still persists".

In particular, he suggests that the occupations and level of education of urban residents are closely connected with their location within the Polish city and with the quality of housing and environment which they enjoy. Moreover, it must not be forgotten that the public, through its support of private trade in both the officially-approved

outlets and the black market, encourages activities
which are sometimes beyond the reach of the
planners, and which probably give rise to a spatial
pattern of production and distribution which also
has more in common with that of free-market than
planned economies. Indeed, the
officially-recognised private sector - operating
largely in agriculture, personal services and
retailing - which exists especially in Poland and
Yugoslavia, but also in the GDR and Hungary (Aslund
1984), is driven on by the desire for profit; and,
although the scale of such businesses is strictly
limited, it is clear that there are very
considerable opportunities for profit, and for the
re-investment of that profit, in the private sector
in some of the countries. For example, Kardelj
estimated in 1971 that 'additional incomes' from
moonlighting accounted for more than two-fifths of
all personal income in Yugoslavia (Singleton and
Carter 1982, p.206). Such activities inevitably
alter the pattern of the space economy, giving
greater employment opportunities in some places than
in others, and enlarging the range of goods and
services which are available in some areas, thus
making them more attractive to the public in
general. Many privately-owned businesses have grown
up in and around the larger cities and conurbations
in Hungary, Poland and Yugoslavia, for it is in
these places that there is a ready market for
specialist agricultural products, shops and personal
services, and this concentration of activity can
only serve to maintain, and perhaps enlarge,
existing regional differences within these
countries. Of course, individual behaviour and
private capital are not dominant factors in the
development of the space economies of Eastern
Europe, and in some countries, such as Albania and
Romania, they hardly operate at all, but they are
another influence on the development of that economy
with which planners are obliged to grapple.

Thus, there have been many circumstances which
have constrained the power of spatial and
environmental planners in Eastern Europe during the
post-war years, and to these must be added the
possibility of 'economic reform'. One of the
fundamental questions in all the reform discussions
has concerned who should decide how the surpluses
which are created by enterprises in public ownership
should be used. Those advocating reform have
usually argued that greater freedom should be given
to the management, or even the workers, in such

enterprises as to how much of any surplus should be allocated to investment and how much to wages and bonuses, that is, to consumption by the workforce. However, such changes would remove the power of central planners to determine both the scale and location of at least some investment; and, if such reforms were ever to be coupled with the freeing of prices and the obligation of enterprises to break even or face bankruptcy, the situation would be little different from that in market economies. Not even Yugoslavia had progressed to that point by the mid-1980s, and most of the countries of Eastern Europe had only allowed, at most, minor relaxations of centralised command-type control over the use of production surpluses. It is ironic, in view of the debate between those in favour of growth and the regional, land-use and environmental planners, that in the matter of economic reform the interests of the planners would appear to coincide with those of 'hard-line', even Stalinist, centralisers. However, in spite of all the discussions about reform since the first Yugoslav experiments in the 1950s, it has not progressed to the extent where it has significantly reduced the power of the planners, and responsibility for any failure on their part to solve the problems of Eastern Europe must lie rather with the other constraints which have been outlined above.

Looking back over the post-war period, it is not at all clear that the changes which have occurred in the space economy can be credited to regional, urban and environmental planning. In particular, it should be noted that some of the most important investments, such as the steel mills at Košice in Czechoslovakia and at Nowa Huta in Poland, were decided upon in the late 1940s and early 1950s, when territorial planning was given least attention and had a very weak official, institutional status within the government machinery of both the USSR and Eastern Europe. Moreover, it must be acknowledged that, as the opportunities for extensive growth have dwindled during the post-war period (Zwass 1984), attention has turned increasingly to the more productive use of existing labour and fixed capital. But, in economies in which few enterprises are ever closed or buildings demolished, this can only mean the consolidation of the present spatial patterns of activity. The scope for major new shifts in the map of the economy is now more limited than at any time since the war, and in a situation of falling rates of growth and increasing economic problems in several of the countries it seems unlikely that more resources will be diverted to the achievement of such 'non-productive', planners' goals as large-scale urban and environmental improvements. It is ironic that, at the moment when spatial planning has reached its most established position within the government machines of Eastern Europe and has produced its most detailed and complex plans, such as those for the settlement networks in Hungary and Romania, its real opportunities for affecting the pattern of the space economy may be at their most limited.

REFERENCES

Ambler, J., Shaw, D.J.B. and Symons, L. (1985), Soviet and East European Transport Problems, Croom Helm, London.

Åslund, A. (1984), Private Enterprise in Eastern Europe, Macmillan, London.

Kornai, J. (1980), Economics of Shortage, North Holland, Amsterdam.

Kowalski, J.S. (1984), Polarization Processes in Space in Centrally Planned Economies - an attempt at explanation, Unpublished typescript, Institut für Wirtschaftpolitik und Wirtschaftsforschung, Universitat Karlsruhe.

Rostow, W.W. (1960), The Stages of Economic Growth: A Non-Communist Manifesto, Cambridge University Press.

Singleton, F. and Carter, B. (1982), The Economy of Yugoslavia, Croom Helm, London.

Sweeney, J. (1984), Regional patterns of urban growth in the USSR, Geography, 69, 128-135.

Węcławowicz, G. (1981), Towards a theory of intra-urban structures of Polish cities, Geographia Polonica, 44, 179-200.

Zwass, A. (1984), The Economies of Eastern Europe in a Time of Change, Macmillan, London.

Index

Printed and bound by CPI Group (UK) Ltd, Croydon, CR0 4YY

Index